ZAVOD VEZAL
An imprint of The Vezal Institute
Kersnikova 6, 1241 Kamnik
Slovenia
www.vezal.si

First published in United States in 2017 by The Vezal Institute

Translation: **Laura Cuder Turk**
Editor: **Noah Charney**
Illustrator: **Izak Mrgole**
Photo credits: **Ilona Mrgole**
Cover design: **Izak Mrgole, Matic Štupar**
Design: **Vojko Plevel, Inscribo d.o.o.**

Printed in the United States of America

CIP - Kataložni zapis o publikaciji
Narodna in univerzitetna knjižnica, Ljubljana

37.018.1(035)
159.922.8(035)

MRGOLE, Leonida
    Connect with your teenager : a guide to everyday parenting / Leonida Mrgole & Albert Mrgole ; [drawings by Izak Mrgole ; translation Laura Cuder Turk]. - Kamnik : Institute Vezal, 2017

ISBN 978-961-94198-0-9
1. Mrgole, Albert
289595136

Leonida Mrgole & Albert Mrgole

Connect
with your
Teenager

A Guide to Everyday Parenting

Vezal Institute

We dedicate this book to our children.

Without you, Izak, Medeja, Ilona, Ezav,
this book would have been considerably different
or it wouldn't have existed at all.

Thank you for all the experiences.
The wonderful ones, as well as the difficult ones.
We've all had the opportunity to learn from them.
And especially thank you for all the new opportunities.
You've always given us another chance.
Even when we failed several times.

Foreword

It was a warm August in 2011. The breeze from the lake was beginning to quiet as we were wrapping up our two-day ICEEFT (International Centre for Excellence in Emotionally Focused Therapy) trainers' retreat at the Johnson-Douglas cottage in Saint-Germain, Quebec, Canada. Prior to a quick kayak paddle before dinner, or joining the annual trainers' swim to Blueberry Island, last on the retreat agenda was a discussion of new and emerging areas. John (Sue's stalwart partner and co-compass for ICEEFT) placed a pin on the map, designating Slovenia as one of those areas. Miles from Canada, word of the power and efficacy of EFT (recognized as meeting the gold standard set out by bodies such as the American Psychological Association for psychotherapy research) had spread to this small European country. Albert and Leonida Mrgole had already embraced the theoretical foundations and practical applications of this approach in their work with individuals, couples and families, and were making plans to organize various EFT trainings (along with several other countries on every continent of the globe). Now six years later, they have brought multiple EFT trainings (five, to date) to Slovenia and have continued to provide psychotherapy services, as well as their own trainings and groups with parents and educators, and it is clear that the couples they bring for the live demonstrations have benefited from their clinical skill and intuition. And, against this backdrop, they are now publishing their second book!

Like EFT, Connect with Your Teenager *has an attachment focus. It is a valuable guide to understanding adolescent development, and how we as parents can effectively provide and maintain a "secure base" from which teens can flourish and launch into adulthood with positive views of themselves and a capacity to trust and rely on others during times of need, and resiliently face the various demands of their lives ahead. Having worked with many hundreds of couples and families since the inception of EFT in the 1980s, we clearly recognize the key role of parenting in preparing adolescents for healthy relationships, and the importance of contributions such as that of* Connect with Your Teenager *by Albert and Leonida. Using stories, combined with wisdom, science, and their own insights as parents and clinicians, Albert and Leonida provide readers with various accounts, some evoking tears, others laughter, and all a sense of understanding that parenting teens comes with challenges, and also great rewards, and particularly when parents are able to maintain a sense of balance during periods of storm, and an* open heart during their teens' moments of vulnerability. With the same warmth and generosity they have shown each time they have hosted EFT training events, Albert and Leonida give generously of themselves and their experiences in these stories such that, at times, one is left with the feeling of being in their kitchen as they speak of the tales of parenthood, Leonida with her animated and vivacious voice and demeanor, and Albert with a big laugh combined with bouncing shoulders and a twinkle in his eye.

In addition to their years of experience, it is these qualities that emanate from the pages of their book, Connect with Your Teenager, and that remind us all that parenting can be humbling at times, and at other times a vacillating source of joy and frustration, but always deeply meaningful. Although there is some variability in the protagonists in the stories throughout the book, the consistent message is that parents are not necessarily meant to be the heroes in the family, but it is their responsibility to provide a stable and secure base both for each other, and for their children, and particularly during adolescence, a key developmental period. We congratulate you both, Albert and Leonida, for yet another great accomplishment in your journey together, and for what will undoubtedly be a far-reaching contribution for parents in the small and beautiful country of Slovenia, and abroad!

With love and best wishes for continued success,
Sue Johnson *and* Leanne Campbell

Dr. **Susan Johnson**, Ed.D., is the best-selling author, clinical psychologist, distinguished research professor, dynamic speaker, and recognized innovator who has changed the field of couple therapy. She is director of the *International Center for Excellence in Emotionally Focused Therapy* and distinguished research professor at *Alliant University* in San Diego, California, as well as professor of clinical psychology at the *University of Ottawa*, Canada. She trains counselors in EFT worldwide and is recognized as one of the most prominent researchers and presenters in the couple therapy field.

Dr. **Leanne Campbell** is a registered Psychologist, ICEEFT Certified EFT Therapist, Supervisor, and Trainer. She is co-founder and co-director of the *Vancouver Island Centre for EFT*, and *Campbell & Fairweather Psychology Group* in Nanaimo, B.C.

Contents

Acknowledgments

In the end comes the moment you've been waiting for. The moment when you thank people, and make yourself and others aware that, without them, this book wouldn't exist. Fear of forgetting someone also creeps in. All people are important, when doing something like writing a parenting guide. Each of them contributes a piece of his or her experience.

So we thank all those we have ever done anything with. We drew stories, experiences, and knowledge, and learned from them.

Following the Slovenian edition, which was reprinted three times in the first three years and became a best-seller in a few months, we spent a lot of time looking for a team to work with. Then everything went very quickly. Thank you to Laura Cuder Turk, for your stress-free translation process, healthy curiosity, and thank you for never taking anything for granted. We must say that we haven't met such a disciplined, thorough, and hard-working person as you for a long time. We know you were sent by some power in the universe, and we are endlessly grateful for that.

And there is another person sent by some power. Not just to us, but to Slovenia. It looks like he didn't come because of us alone, but he made our lives better, and brought a lot of safety and trust into our lives as writers. Noah Charney, an American, our editor who is a rock in the stormy sea of publishing, our adviser. All our doubts and fears disappeared after talking to you, Noah. You taught us how quickly a person can be happy. You connected us, and called us a "team." I have known all along that we are a winning team. It feels great to embark on such a large project, knowing you are not alone. Thank you.

Our parents are the most important people in our lives. They taught us what a child needs. Sometimes by knowing, sometimes by not knowing. We eagerly learned from all the experiences. This is the way we all learned.

Grandma, you have a special place: all your questions, encouragement, love for reading, your childhood stories—this special role that gives us strength and awareness that guides is so useful. The book was mostly written in Bohinj, the most beautiful place in Slovenia, where you can work in peace.

Dear sis Ana Nuša, you are a special part, a hidden gem, a savior, a stimulator, a reminder, a beacon, and someone who always tries to be where we need you to be. Whenever we didn't know the answer to a question or needed an external view, and sometimes just comfort, you were the first... Irena, sister, you are always there, with your silent support, and I know that, by being this way, you make many things in life easier for me. Barbara, thank you for all "speedy" translations and your moral support, when we were on the verge of giving up.

It's nice to have a family who is always there like a warm lap. Thank you.

Thank you for all the love, support, and faith in us. It is a great encouragement for us to keep going.

We are grateful to our four children. Izak, Medeja, Ilona, and Ezav, you are our greatest teachers and pacemakers. Without you, our knowledge would be much poorer, and our hearts would be empty. You are the four stars that kept pushing us, and encouraged us to make changes and seek answers. We love you to the moon and back.

Friends Mojca, Sanda, Tomi, Alja, Roman, Neža, Vojko... There are so many of you, and I don't want to leave anyone out. Without you, everything would have been much harder.

Ros Draper, a friend, a mother, professional support, our mirror. Ros, without you, our lives would be dull, and we would wander around, lost. Thank you for being you, and for having a big heart.

Leanne Campbell, our teacher (*Emotionally Focused Therapy*) and supervisor, the main person encourager of our endeavors. Thank you for your good spirit, emotional warmth, empathic response, and your knowledge.

Vojko Plevel, thank you for knowing how to make a book look beautiful, and for not sleeping much.

Thank you to the Municipality of Kamnik, and to the mayor, for your trust and moral support.

Thank you to all parents who confided their stories in us, and came for help.

And, last but not least, thank you to all children of the world, who encourage us to write books which strengthen connections, making the world a more beautiful place.

Thank you for reading this book. It means that you care.

Warming Up—What This Book Can Do For You

We come from Slovenia, a small country in Europe, on the sunny side of the Alps, bordering Austria to the north, Italy to the west, Croatia to the south and other Balkan countries, and Hungary to the east. In terms of distance, this means 500 km from Munich, 300 km from Venice, 300 km from Vienna, 100 km from Zagreb, 500 km from Budapest, and the same distance from Sarajevo and Belgrade. For at least 25 years we, as a former socialist country, have been part of modern flow of global events.

But we have been part of a story common to all people in the world for much longer—the story of attachment and the role of parents in the raising their children, helping them become balanced, responsible, happy adults.

We have been involved in this universal story on two sides: through our experience with parenting our four children, and through our professional psychotherapeutic work. And until recently, we never thought of writing a book.

For the past 15 years, we have been running workshops for parents and partners. The participants tell us all the time that our methods significantly differ from others, that our manner of understanding is completely new, and that our solutions to complicated situations are elegant in their simplicity and efficacy. Following their encouragement and requests, we published the first edition of this book in Slovenian, in November 2013. In the book, we gathered practical experiences as real-life case studies for parents, each case study illustrating one of the points from our workshops—practical information that is easy for anyone to relate to and apply at home. Within six months, the response from readers exceeded our expectations. People mentioned unexpected personality changes in their once-grumpy teens, based on solutions obtained from our book, and our colleagues from abroad encouraged us to have our book translated into English.

Within one year, the first Slovenian edition sold out, so we began preparing for the second edition, which included corrections, and a few supplemented and updated bits. The third printing of the book entered the market in 2016. It has been a runaway best-seller, and one that has helped many. We are humbled and grateful for having been able to lend a hand to so many families.

And so, we decided to write a brand new book on the basis of the book that had been successful in Slovenia, this book. In it, we have kept all the basic ingredients, but have adapted it for all parents all over the world.

A Few Good Reasons Why We Wrote This Book

The original Slovenian title of the book, which might be roughly translated as *Out of Touch Teens and In-Touch Parents* (the original Slovene sounds a bit catchier) is slangy, and a hallmark of the era in which our children are growing up.

Out of Touch Teens refers also to teens who are disconnected from a relationship with their parents. These are teens committed, outwardly, to rebellion, withdrawal from relationships, and opposing to values. But inside, they are in severe distress, and long to connect. It might not always seem like it, but teens *need* their parents. Parents who remain connected allow teens to be independent, and tolerate mistakes. Teens need grown-up parents—in-touch parents, parents who are able to "switch on" a connection. We want to emphasize that parents are often disconnected, too. In-touch parents are simply parents who make the effort, or who know how to reconnect to their teen to their parent-child, loving, supporting relationship, or who know how to help themselves understand their teen. Even better, they are those who know how to fix the cracks in their connection, who make the concerted, caring effort.

The whole book is about connection, bonding, connectedness and cooperation. It is about harnessing specific responses of parents which will allow our growing children to safely develop into independent adults.

We parents are always there, but sometimes we all struggle with how to focus, what to be aware of, how to support, encourage, and teach. There may be situations in which our teen lets us know, through his[1] behavior, words and actions that he's had enough of us, that we're pathetic, and that he's going to move out the first chance he gets. Parents who take all these statements seriously risk contributing to the emergence of a long-running and painful fissure in their relationship.

---

[1]For the sake of brevity, we will refer to teens as "he," but please understand that we mean "he" or "she."

But the reality is different. Our teen needs us, he needs us very much, just not in the same way he used to when he was younger. He needs us to trust him, to silently watch him, to allow him to explore, make mistakes, to observe his first love... During this period, we are our children's silent keepers. We are always where they expect us to be, we are firm, unwavering, consistent and reliable. Teens need parents who are grown-up and emotionally stable. This is a book that teaches us, parents, to look inwards, not outwards. This means that we stop paying attention to what our teens look like or don't look like, instead focusing on things they respond to or don't respond to, when we, as parents, lead our children through the way we act or what we say. So the reality is that teens who express that they don't want us, who reject us, need us badly. We parents must convey the message that we are always there, that we know how to focus and keep our focus on awareness, how to support, encourage, and teach.

When we work with parents of growing children, we recognize distress related to the issues of actions in practice. Parents may read all kinds of parenting books and forums, but can lack inspiration in specific situations, to act efficiently—to learn to react in a helpful way when emotions can be high.

Our intention in writing this book was to help in a very practical way, with proven actions that have assisted our clients and ourselves. Since we have personal experience of four stories of our own teens, coupled with the experience of more than fifteen years of working with parents in distress, we have our own goldmine of examples upon which to draw. As psychotherapists, we track the development of our profession, from systemic theory, applications of attachment theory, Emotionally Focused Therapy, contributions of neuroscience to parenting and mutual relationships, numerous techniques from other fields, and novelties which intensively supplement contemporary knowledge of our experiences, thoughts and feelings (mental states[2]) and mutual interactions. Our work is an integration of expert scholarship and experience, coupled with simple, frequently unusual and innovative practical answers to parental questions, with a focus on how parents might best respond to the often confusing, sometimes exasperating behavior to our teens. In preparing our techniques, we extensively tested them in the situations in our own house, and then at numerous coaching sessions and individual

---

[2]The concept is known as mentalization. Cf. Fonagy et al.; Cooper et al.

consultations for parents, over the past 15 years. These techniques are tried and true, both personally and professionally.

An important reason for writing this book was the enthusiasm of the participants in our coaching sessions who afterwards regularly asked us where they could get in writing all the practical examples and useful solutions we reeled off, as we solved dilemmas and difficult cases for our audience. When we thought about all these stories, we first drew up a table of contents, which was quickly filled with specific examples from our experience.

We wrote the book to offer hope in cases of dilemmas that sometimes seem unsolvable. We also wrote it for everyone who would like to look at a situation from a different angle, to see that there can only be shadow when there is light. And for everyone who would like to prepare, in their mind, for the time when there is a teen in the house.

However, one of the most important reasons for writing this book was our desire to make people in families feel wonderful. Not only children, but parents, as well. Every parent who reads this book is, by definition, a *good* parent, because no matter what their situation is, they are trying, making a concerted, positive effort. But we all sometimes feel that we could be doing better, and this book should help to shake off the guilt and weight of feeling like less-than-ideal parents, to see ourselves and our children from a new perspective. This is also a stone in the mosaic of our desire for all people on this planet to have quality relationships in the future.

How To Use This Book

This book may be used in several ways. When writing, we were guided by the principle that parents should be able to use this book in practice.

If you are setting out to read this book to find instructions on how to change your children to gain a better quality of life together, you will be disappointed. Our focus in the book is on the awareness of your role as parents. When thinking about changes, they should be oriented towards the notion of how we could change ourselves as parents, not how we stay the same and force our children to change. Our relationships with teens are a blend of all previous periods of development and, many times, it seems as if the unresolved histories from all previous periods have accumulated exponentially. This book is especially about how to survive, as parents, alongside growing children, and how to preserve the connection and quality relationships: with children, with your partner, and within your family.

Despite the book being designed to be used in, and oriented towards, practice, it contains an internal logic permeating all the stories and connecting various sections. Some of this logic is explained in Part One, but not repeated in each section. We are well aware of the fact that situations may be understood in many ways, and that we alone control the manner of understanding.

The book contains heaps of questions. All of them are aimed at personal reflection and the processes that can follow. For this purpose, the book may be used as a reference for notes that you may, at the same time, keep in a special notebook, keeping track of how our techniques and ideas can be best applied to your particular situation.

We believe that reading this book will enable you to step onto the path where you can observe and choose your behaviors and responses in a way that brings better integration.

You may also share your experience while reading the book on a special website, or on our Facebook page (you can find the links on *page 348* at the end of the book under the title *"Where can you find us?"*).

Who is the Book Intended for?

The definition of "teens" is rather broad. Puberty or adolescence[3] can come to children 11 to 25 years old, or even more. Most of our stories feature young people we refer to as teens.

Parents, teachers and guardians of young people face a myriad of questions, beginning with: *"Oh, boy, what's up with this puberty?"* We wrote the

---

[3]On the difference between puberty and adolescence in: Siegel (2013).

book thinking about, and remembering, all the people we've met at our consultations, who had struggled with how to deal with problems with their teens. There were several reasons for this:

- ▸ they weren't equipped with appropriate experience;
- ▸ they grew up in different times or cultural situations and aren't sure how to adjust (most of us did);
- ▸ they stopped participating actively and thoughtfully in parenting, because they were excluded from, or encountered disagreements in, their partnership;
- ▸ they gave up because they felt powerless;
- ▸ they had no support from their partners;
- ▸ they felt clueless about what to do, because they had already used up all their ideas.

This book can also be useful for:

- ▸ single parents;
- ▸ teachers who haven't necessarily had experience with their own teens;
- ▸ parents of younger children (who will soon enough become teens), helping prepare us in advance.

Combining Personal and Professional Experience with Scholarship (Minus the Jargon)

This book is based primarily on personal experience. Therefore, we avoid theoretical jargon and quotations from other literature. Although we can't deny or ignore the rich knowledge we have gained through our education, the primary purpose of this book is not to demonstrate our knowledge, but its usefulness in practice.

We know that every family or community has its own rules and dynamics, so there can be *no universal recipes or examples as to what is right and what isn't*. On the other hand, we aren't so very special that we wouldn't be able to compare ourselves with others. But this book's examples and good solutions were not written for you to replay the stories, but rather to broaden your horizons, encourage your creativity, boost your self-confidence, to give you

19

hope, and to remind you that *you* are the parents. Improving a relationship with your teen is entirely up to *you.*

The important things in the stories are messages and questions they ask. Maybe you will feel, when reading certain stories that we were writing about you? This is not a coincidence. It means that you have found the right story for you.

The titles of our workshops, upon which this text is based, are *"Effective Communication with Teenagers," "Challenges of Parenting," "Setting Effective Boundaries"* and *"The Green Key—Addiction Prevention."* Parents have been telling us all the time that they need specific ideas about how to behave in all kinds of unpredictable situations. Stories are the best way to convey ideas and help them to hit home.

Why the Stories?

There is an internal logic on the basis of which each story emerges and unfolds. Thus, it is not decisive that different cultural environments at different times affect the content of the stories about growing up—we may be Slovenian and you may not be, but people are people. There are universal principles of development, universal needs for attachment and bonding, universal principles of brain development, universal principles of social needs, research of novelties, plasticity... And a universal need for responsive parents.

Every relationship has its own story and principles. At the same time, we have become lost in the age of globalization, because there is no one from whom we could draw life wisdom, because we don't socialize and talk about personal matters the way we once did. We feel that narrating life stories is sensible, because every story has a plot and an ending, because the stories originate from the real world of the past few years, from the world we share. The stories contain distress, dilemmas, rumination, strategies, solution methods, endings, unexpected responses. There are true stories which broaden our horizons when we find ourselves in similar circumstances. The stories, and everything written in addition to them, are intended to promote creativity in everyday complicated situations and issues, in our relationships with our relatives.

The stories give us courage to get to the bottom of our issues, because they let us know that there is nothing wrong with us, and that we are not the only ones in the world in such a situation.

The stories give us hope that problems can be solved, that there is always a solution. The stories tell us about other parents who have done something, perhaps initially wrong but eventually right—who have solved something, who have plucked up the courage, and such stories give us a lot of hope when we feel lost.

The stories also convey an important message: You are not alone in this world. There are plenty of us who deal with similar hardships, and who can emerge with similar joys.

What Can You Gain by Reading this Book?

Especially important are issues encountered by the people in the stories and methods people use to help themselves make changes. This is the secret and the wisdom of living with teens.

When we have a teen at home, or maybe two or even more, there are a lot of firsts for us, and we aren't prepared for most of them. The role of this book in such moments is to pull us out of the state of powerlessness, when we wonder *"what do I do?"* or *"I'll throw him out"* without success.

The book is written on several levels. One level is the level of explanations, comments and professional background. The second level is related to the stories and their dynamics. It's a narration which touches on our life experience, including all emotional dimensions. And then there is another level, the level of personal processes taking place during reading. To leave our spontaneous behavior behind us, we need changes at the emotional level.

This book will give you the willpower and a reason to begin tackling your "problems," as well as the power to be patient. Our teens are always smart. Don't forget that, in this period, they are the only smart beings in the house—at least, that's what they think. They have answers to everything, and lots of words, power and energy. Parents usually fall silent, powerless, because we struggle to find the right words, in the heat of the moment. This book is a genuine warehouse of pacifying "ammunition," in the form of words and ways how to use these words in a non-conflictive, but assertive, manner.

The stories interlace, each topic is related to many others, making reading an adventure of contemplation and an invitation to view everyday situations from a new perspective.

This book has three parts and an addendum. The sequence of the chapters is logical in meeting the needs of parents, and it follows the logic of learning and acquiring skills. To begin with, we need to be aware of our own dispositions and forces which participate in our parenting actions. We also need to be familiar with the developmental needs of children, and know how to properly respond to them as parents. And only after all this, are there topics which worry us. So for you to be able to effectively use this book, it is important to follow the chapters as they come. Of course, within parts two and three, it is possible to randomly choose the order of case studies, depending on their relevance in your specific situation. The book is written in a way that enables you to read it according to your needs at any given moment. Nevertheless, we wanted to arrange the case studies in a way that has its own internal logic.

At the beginning of *Part One*, we write about awareness in our role as parents. Tools we can use to enter our relationships with growing children are presented in this part. Without such awareness, we are at risk of being "swept away" by intensive emotional forces and spontaneous behaviors, which often occur during this period of relationships in our families.

In *Part Two*, we discuss topics relevant to the development of growing children. This part includes many skills which are fundamental to preserving the connection and have an important preventive role.

Topics which usually make parents seek professional help will be discussed in a separate book. We decided on such an arrangement for a reason. Our counseling and therapeutic work involves topics marked by parents as problems normally related to the content in this book.

The internal structure and the division of certain chapters are specific, which provides parents with an extra tool to change their current spontaneous and ineffective approaches to parenting.

At the beginning of every chapter, under each case, there is a story summarizing the way parents perceive and articulate a certain problem, difficulty or issue. The endings of most stories are satisfactory, while some aren't. The stories present parents' emotions and actions which haven't yielded the responses they had desired.

Since such topics always intermingle in real life, each story is followed by a description of other related topics in the book. This is followed by a section entitled *"Within the Scope of Awareness,"* which could also be called: *"What Must We Be Aware Of?"* This refers to the concept of mindfulness. What is its essence? The essence is the awareness which arises when we intentionally direct our attention at something at that moment, when we surpass our own spontaneous judgments, when we are present "here and now," focused on the unfolding of the situation. It is the ability to be aware of our own mental states, and to do the same when it comes to other people.[4] This section is designed to broaden horizons and offer help to parents in viewing our everyday stories from another angle. It is intended to help you exit the vicious circle of beliefs and emotions, which are the result of rapid and spontaneous (and unproductive) responses.[5] The most precious thing to come out of our own experience is that, in cases when we feel completely lost and powerless, we can connect with other experiences and have access to other ways of understanding issues. Seeing that other people solved their problems in another way (and survived) gives us support, so that we too can put our story into a new framework.

At the end of every chapter, there is a section entitled *"Tips and Solutions"* that have stood the test of time, where readers can find tips about how to act in specific situations in practice. These are ideas that can help you make decisions about your own parenting actions. We would like you to accept the following message with a special sense of responsibility:

The solutions presented have worked in the specific stories described, but there is no guarantee that they function universally. Every family and every relationship have their own best practice: this is a practice you perceive as sensible, which corresponds to your way of life and, most importantly, you can imagine it being put into practice. In every relationship in which we participate we, as adults, bear the responsibility for the behaviors we choose. We may get plenty of advice from

---

[4] Cf. Kabat-Zinn, 2005; Siegel & Hartzell, 2004; Siegel, 2011; Siegel & Bryson, 2011; Siegel, 2013.
[5] Kahneman, 2012.

more or less important experts or authorities, but the choice of our actions is al-ways our responsibility.

Therefore, we advocate the principle that knowledge and the experi-ence of others may help us in our own creativity, in seeking possible paths, but the choice of, and the decision for, our actions must emerge from our inner balance, harmony and the soundness of the feeling that this is right and good for us.

At the end of the book, there are two tools to help you find the content you need in a specific situation: a *table of stories and subtitles* (see page 331), and a *subject index* (see page 336).

About Us and Our Work

November 1984.
We met for the first time. Leonida was 19, Albert was 22. Then came walks, talks, missing one another. Every time we said goodbye "felt like for-ever," when we spoke on the phone, we drew lots to see who would hang up first. Because these separations were unbearable, we got married after just ten months. So that we could be together all the time. People said that it was just a crush, that it would pass, that we should wait. We didn't believe it. It was completely different with us, it would last forever, our whole lives, we were special... We deeply believed that.

They were right, as always. The period of infatuation passed, and dis-agreements arose. We resolved them with conversations. We held on to the ritual of our evening time together, which saved us. After three years, our first son, Izak, was born. Medeja came along after another two years, fol-lowed by Ilona after three years, and Ezav after another two. Life became more strenuous, we didn't have as much time just for the two of us. The role of parents overtook the role of partners. We were slowly growing apart, and disagreements (also about parenting) were building a high, strong wall be-tween us. No one had ever told us that we had to keep our priorities straight, and that the relationship between partners was the most important for living safely within a family.

24

There was something left over in our relationship from before. That strong connection, love and desire to be together. We both wanted to understand that. We began researching the magic of relationships, we began educating ourselves.

How do we function, how do we understand, how do we communicate? What happens when a person does something with the best intentions, but the other person understands it as an attack, an accusation? The unfathomable desire to preserve our family was larger than any conflict, disagreement or painful experience.

Our awareness that it is the need for bonding and for attachment, the need for safe attachment that keeps us together or drives us apart was a gigantic discovery for us. Such need is obvious in all relationships, but expressed in various ways. When they are little, our children have an absolute need to be safely attached to us. This attachment changes as they grow, and children need us to let them go... This is often hard on us, parents, and requires us to change our responses, which doesn't mean that we are no longer attached to each other.

We need to let our children go and only remain their "safe haven." All we are then left with (if we are successful) is the relationship with our partner. We have learned that we need to tend to it, nurture it, research our needs, and adjust to various periods that come in our relationship.

We daydream again about what we are going to do when our kids leave the nest. We have to say that it is very exciting, and we are looking forward to a new period.

Leonida is a reflex therapist, while Albert, after graduating in psychology, obtained a PhD in sociology, and kept working with marginal youth in a residential care institution. He developed a program for rescuing school dropouts, which received a European innovation award, and has been working is psychotherapy since 2003. At first, he completed his studies in systemic family therapy. Then Lea and Albert continued their education in the imago techniques of the clinical therapy, and work as co-therapists. Since 2013, we have been organizing training in Emotionally Focused Therapy, which is also the modality in which we work.

Along with our individual work with couples and parents, we have also developed several of our own forms of working with groups of up to 14 participants, such as workshops for partners (entitled *"Blue Key: Effective*

Partnership" and *"Patterns, Stronger than Genes"*) and for parents (*"Successful Communication with Teenagers," "Fearless Parenting," "Setting the Boundaries"*). We have introduced a special form of working with groups into our local community, the charming medieval city of Kamnik, Slovenia, where we have been regularly running monthly meetings since 2009, entitled *"Refreshment Room—Relationship-Strengthening Sessions,"* which are attended by around 350 people every year. In recent years, we have also organized workshops for teachers and school staff (*"Prevention of Peer Violence"*), and for social workers (*"Help for Parents of Distressed Children"*). On average, we organize one such lecture at elementary and high schools per week for parents. We often appear in the media, as guests in various call-in shows, and shows discussing parenting, families and partners. In 2005, we established the **Vezal Institute**, located in Kamnik. Our endeavours with this institute are focused on the art of relationships. We provide psychotherapeutic service and counselling for individuals, couples, parents and families, run workshops for parents, couples and working teams, offer lectures, conduct research, develop new services and publish.

Leonida received an award at a national competition for the best erotic story in 2009, and Albert is the author of two books and numerous articles.

Albert is the president of the national coordination of the *"child helpline,"* and a visiting lecturer at the *Sigmund Freud University for Psychotherapeutic Science* in Ljubljana.

What people like most when we work together is our spontaneity and openness. People say that we are a really unusual combination, but that we complement each other in a way that is convincing and fills them with a great sense of security. These are also our basic principles: we pass on what we have tried ourselves, while providing security for people throughout the process.

Puberty or Somethin'...

We were sitting in the kitchen, talking. Me and my thirteen-year-old son. It was a usual conversation. About school, of course. Lately, school has become the essence of our lives. No breath, in or out, has gone by without a school-related feeling passing through my body. It's been frustrating. I've been wondering all the time why the kid's work this year hasn't been as it had been before, why doesn't he think the way he did last year, why won't he believe a word I say... A million whys, all related to him. I haven't had the feeling that responsibility could lie anywhere else.

I was cooking, while he was sitting at the table. The tension in our conversation was rising. I began closing the drawers a little more noisily. I wanted to calm down, but anger forced its way out of my every move, my every word.

Suddenly, there was a loud bang. My son got up, pushed the table away so that a glass tipped over, glared at me, and said: "You're pathetic, you're really pathetic, Mom!!! How did you, of all people, come to be my mom?!"

Then he left the kitchen, holding his head up high, and the space between us was clearly marked out with a loud bang of the door.

The helplessness I felt at that moment was completely unknown to me. Tears flooded my face. They were tears of despair (Where did I go wrong in his parenting?), *tears of sadness* (Where is my precious little boy?), *tears of rage* (No one's going to treat me like this, tell me I'm pathetic, when I've been doing my best my whole life for these kids! I'll go after him and clearly let him know about this!).

I was alone, and the only question running through my head was: "What now?"

A desire to ignore began waking in me. I thought to myself that I wouldn't speak to him again, that I would show him that I couldn't care less about him, that I would really become a pathetic mom.

When I calmed down, I asked myself what it felt like being in his shoes. What is happening to him? Is there any way I can understand this outburst?

I followed him into his room, determined to set clear boundaries to his behavior. Meaning that we don't humiliate each other and break things in our house...

I knocked, and when I heard his invitation, I went in.

The image I saw shifted me to a completely new world.

He was lying on his bed, tear-stained, the expression on his face oozed despair. I was just standing there, and the words I had prepared got stuck somewhere between my heart and my brain.

He slowly raised his gaze, and asked: "Mom, does this last long?"

"What?" *I answered with a question.*

"I don't know, this thing you call puberty..."

That's when I learned that this was a period when we parents don't have it tough, but that it is much tougher on our teens. I learned that teens need parents who are grown-up and stable. Parents who will never be moved from the point of reliability, even by the cruelest of acts.

I sat down on the bed next to him, and hugged him.

"I don't know how long it will last, son, but I promise you we'll go through this together," *I said.*

...and the journey began, despite no one wanting to buy the ticket...

PART I
Foundations of the Parent Role:
How Awareness and Responsiveness leads to Connections

When our child is born, we are given a new role, the role of parents. How do we accept this role? Do we take it on consciously?

We are always in a relationship with our children, in which we are the most important person for them. In this relationship, we shape the quality of the children's experience with our responses. Are we aware of this?

Perhaps we act automatically and spontaneously in our role as parents until setbacks occur in our relationship with a child. If not earlier, such setbacks emerge when there's a teen in the house.

A teen in the house is a change we are generally not ready for. What are we usually surprised by?

Changes in the child's behavior.

New image.

New friends.

New vocabulary.

Experimenting in all areas.

They squash our values.

What was logical until yesterday is not logical today.

The rules they observed yesterday are no longer suitable today.

We're pathetic.

They don't hear what we tell them anymore, they disregard us.

Poor results at school.

Everything is pointless.

We hear more and more often: *"I don't feel like doing anything."*

They're tired all the time.

Parents send us, time and time again, questions related to the respect of authority, the consideration of rules and boundaries, submission to certain rules and manners of behavior in children, even children younger than ten. When puberty kicks in, such questions get even worse.

These questions include:

- ▸ Why does my child disregard me and doesn't listen to me?
- ▸ Why can't I achieve anything with my child anymore?
- ▸ What should I do for the child to respect at least the minimum standards of tidiness at home?
- ▸ Can't they do one thing without arguments?
- ▸ How can I understand that the more I provide for them, the less they respect me?
- ▸ Why one and the same pattern is repeated all over again?
- ▸ Why does my child throw me off balance and make my emotions escalate more and more often?
- ▸ Why do I feel so powerless in parenting?
- ▸ Why do my partner and I agree on parenting less and less?
- ▸ Why things that have worked so far no longer work?
- ▸ Why do I feel that I have failed as a parent?

And the key question is: *Who can help me change my child?*

Relationships between relatives are based today on completely different foundations than in the past. Especially children are no longer afraid of adults. And parents are lost because authority in our role is not something self-evident.

We understand the role of a significant other as too important and resort to ineffective beliefs with which we can't solve anything:

- ▸ We look for the reasons for our mistakes in the past and this is now reflected in our child's behavior.
- ▸ We find the reasons or guilt as to why we aren't satisfied with our child's behavior in our partners.
- ▸ We see the reasons for our teen's behavior in the history of our relationship with our partner, especially in disagreements on parenting.
- ▸ We feel empty, lost, powerless, afraid, panicky.

In such difficult situations and internal dilemmas, we usually choose behavior that only complicates the situation even further. What happens in relationships?

At first, we lose the connection, followed by the loss of authority, parental power, we get caught up in repetitive dances in which our power gradually accumulates in the hands of our teens. Down the line, this leads to behaviors of teens that worry us.

All of the described above happens when we as parents respond to teens spontaneously. So it is reasonable to make a change in our spontaneity. Only if you drop the idea that the child has to change first, and that us, parents, don't have to change anything, you will be on the road to follow the stories below in which we will show you:

- ▸ What is the essence of our parental power?
- ▸ How to act to preserve the connection with our child?
- ▸ How to re-establish the connection if we have lost it?
- ▸ How to overcome our own parenting patterns that stand in the way of us making the connection?
- ▸ How to change our beliefs that do not lead to connectedness?
- ▸ What does it mean to truly understand?
- ▸ What are developmental needs and what is a healthy response to them?
- ▸ What does it mean to set boundaries, rules and authority?
- ▸ What does it mean to learn how to be responsible and independent?
- ▸ What does it mean to be in tune with all other needs and peace at the house?

You can discover all this through true stories from everyday life and domestic situations, where you will get specific solutions to difficulties and an inspiration of good hope.

1 What is the Circle of Safe Responsiveness?

There are a few basic principles that apply to relationships between parents and children and are related to the shaping of the child's mental and physical development, the development of the child's personality, personality traits, capacities and potentials.

The concept of safe responsiveness of parents is the foundation for shaping the child's most important life experiences and must be present since birth. Attachment, which is the most important basis for our influence on children, also shapes within this concept. Safe responsiveness enables us to participate in the shaping of interpersonal integration which then facilitates the shaping of meaningfulness of all events that take place within such interaction.[6]

It is impossible in relationships not to respond. With every response, parents shape their child's experience. What we all want is for our children to grow up healthy and to shape experiences with their own responses, which will get them through all life situations, and to be equipped for independent and successful life.

How do parents shape the value of the child's experience with our responses?

And what is a safe response that facilitates healthy development of our children?

Safe responsiveness of parents is composed of three functions combined in the manner of responsiveness:

First step:
We provide our children with a safe base and a safe launching pad.

Second step:
We enable our children to be the owners of their own experiences.

Third step:
With his experience, we give our children the response that enables them to experience that we are their safe haven.

---

[6]Cf. Bowlby, 1969, 1973, 1988.

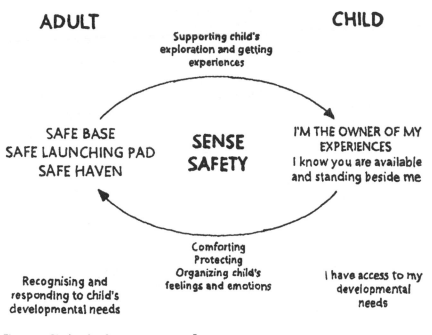

Figure 1: *Circle of safe responsiveness*[7]

How do parents provide a safe base?

A safe base means that family members are connected, that we feel mutual belonging and attachment, that we are there for each other and can trust each other, that parents respond to our children's developmental needs, that we notice what is happening to our child, while respecting his autonomy, and respond in a way that encourages our child's own value (self-esteem). A safe base is an experience we are aware of and feel it as permanent (felt experience).

---

[7] *"This brings me to a central feature of my concept of parenting - the provision by both parents of a secure base from which a child or an adolescent can make sorties into the outside world and to which he can return knowing for sure that he will be welcomed when he gets there, nourished physically and emotionally, comforted if distressed, reassured if frightened. In essence this role is one of being available, ready to respond when called upon to encourage and perhaps assist, but to intervene actively only when clearly necessary."* (Bowlby, 1988: 11)

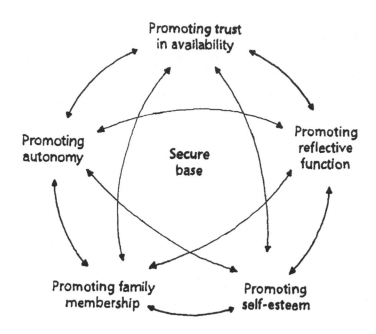

Figure 2: *Secure base*[8]

Let's take a look at an example: How did we teach our child to ride a bike?

A safe base means that we see our child and experience him as competent, mature, equipped enough to embark on his experience of independence. We see that when he rides a bike with training wheels and expresses his desire to ride it without any aids. Or we assess that he is old enough and convince him that it is worth a try.

A safe launching pad means that we trust our child's abilities. That we encourage him. When we feel safe thinking that it is the right time to learn a new skill, that he can do it, our child will feel safe enough to take a risk and dive into his experience of independence.

Through the process, we stand by him, hold him and encourage him. Our presence conveys the message: *I'm here for you, everything will be okay*. Here, a child's new experience with balance kicks in. Some children need more time, our presence and patience to feel safe in a new position. A safe response from parents means that we understand the child's distress and are there for him.

---

[8]Summarized from Schofield & Beek (2005).

Then comes a moment when we let the child ride off. He is left alone with his experience which may end in two ways.

He begins riding safely. Or falls.

What is a safe response for the child in this case?

In the first case: *"Well done, you can do it. Great, you've learned to ride the bike without help. You can do it."*

If the child falls, we comfort and encourage him: *"I know you'll get it right sometime."*

And keep repeating this throughout the learning process until he makes it. And ensure him safety all the time.

Let's take a look at responses with which we as parents get stuck and our child doesn't have a safe experience.

If we are terrified, insecure inside, we won't accompany our child with the message that it is safe to embark on an independent experience. If we are afraid that the child will hurt himself, we will accompany him with fear. Perhaps we think that he is still too young. What if he falls and there is blood? What if hurts himself? We may be convinced that he is too clumsy and will never learn how to ride a bike. Such thoughts aren't a safe launching pad for a child. Such thoughts prevent him from developing his inner strength, self-esteem and self-confidence in his abilities.

Instead of fear, we may forbid the child to embark on an independent experience.

It may happen that the father is convinced that his child is old enough to have this experience, while the mother opposes.

All these situations do not provide children with a safe launching pad.

If a child has an experience which we as parents assess as being unsuccessful, we risk that our response won't give the child a safe haven.

After the child falls, instead of consoling or encouraging him, we may say:
"I knew you couldn't do it.

I told you that you were going to fall.

Can you see now that you can't do it?

You could try harder, like Luke next door, he can ride a bike by himself.

You'll never learn.

You see, we won't be able to go cycling together."

We may oppose to the child gaining the experience, but the child starts learning by himself. And when he falls, we say:

"Now you've done it. I told you so. Will you remember this for next time and do what I tell you to do?"

The responses described do not provide the child with a safe haven. What does the child learn?

Our response shapes the child's experience which is the basic unit of what we know. We should keep in mind the following: it is not the words that count in what we learn and especially how we learn, it is the experience. If our response isn't safe, the child doesn't develop self-esteem, he becomes insecure, he stops before new challenges and hurdles, he checks all the time what is right and what isn't, he doesn't have the courage to take risks in new situations, he isn't bold and brave to overcome hurdles, he doesn't have the courage to explore, he isn't curious, he doesn't have the courage to perform in public, he doesn't have the courage to express himself, and similar. All these are skills and mental functions that we need in order to develop healthily and be successful in life.

Let's mention another kind of response that isn't safe: we leave the child alone in an experience that is too difficult for him.

The child is scared and in distress, but doesn't have a safe haven where he could find comfort or encouragement.

Let's summarize various ways of responding in parenting which form different experiences and thus the child's attitude to life situations. Let's take a look at another example: How do we teach a child to tie his own shoes?

We may pick the time when our child starts school and teach the child how to tie his shoes in a playful way. First, we make a knot. The child repeats the steps after us, we encourage him, we get in tune with his learning process, his emotions, we are happy, the child feels the excitement and curiosity, we help him with his moves, we encourage each successful attempt and stand by him when he fails, and instill hope in him to motivate him to continue learning. This is a learning experience which includes connection, bonding, even physical closeness, thorough play, with the possibility to learn through trial and error, where errors are a constituent of progress, where errors are allowed. This way, the child learns, with your support, a skill that helps him develop a sense of independence and self-esteem.

Our second option is to tie the shoes for the child. If we choose this option, we deny the child the experience of learning and deprive him of all of the aforementioned experiences and skills. Such a response may also arise from our belief that the child isn't mature enough, perhaps we believe that he is too slow when we are in a rush, we know that we will do it faster. Or we are convinced that it will be too difficult for the child if he has to tie his shoes by himself and so we save him the anguish. That's when we usually buy shoes with Velcro closures and avoid all complications with tying.

What does this example tell us? As we have already mentioned, we deprive the child of the possibility to learn, and to acquire skills and pertaining mental functions. This brings us to the parenting style of intrusiveness described in other sections of the book. The child is not aware that he can do it, and will go numb in new learning situations and wait for someone else to do the task for him.

The third option is to leave the child in the situation that is too difficult for him without our help. We accompany him saying: If you can't tie your own shoes, nothing will ever become of you. I had to help myself too, no one else helped me.
This way, the child experiences that learning is something that he can't do, that the hurdle is too high, and that he has no support to help him jump over it. The experience that stays in his mind is emotionally marked with fear and distress: Hurdles are something unbearable for me, I can't do this, I'll never overcome it.

This is a description of the safe responsiveness model with possibilities for parents to diverge to methods that aren't safe, where the content isn't important, but the underlying principle is.

Tips and Solutions

We often complain that our teens don't tell us anything anymore, that "everything's fine", that we don't know them anymore, we don't know how their mind works, we don't know their concerns...

---

(1) What Would You Do if You were Me?

I'm sitting in the kitchen with my teen, we're having lunch. The kitchen is filled with tense silence. I'd like to ask him about school, but don't want to, because I know he'll just leave the table and won't eat his lunch.

I watch him eat, pick out peas and vegetables from his risotto because he doesn't like them, and push them to the edge of the plate.

I'm a nervous wreck, I have a feeling that he's making fun of the food, me and my efforts. I'm about to start crying with rage, I'm squeezing the fork really tight so that he doesn't notice. Because such moments of us sitting together are nearly gone. Although, for quite a while, there hasn't been a connection between us like there should be between a mother and a son.

Then he says: "Greg (my best friend) hasn't spoken to me for two weeks. When I call him he promises that he'll come but then doesn't."

He speaks very slowly, I raise my gaze, surprised, and my initial spontaneous impulse would be:

"I don't care about Greg, I want to know when you're going to get your maths and chemistry grades up, and when you're going to start behaving NORMALLY!" *(a response that ignores the basic need of a teen—the need for friends).*

As I'm overwhelmed by these horrible feelings, my phone starts ringing.

It seems like a great lifesaver before I hit the roof. I say to him: "We can talk about this later." *I answer the phone, a girlfriend is on the other end. Somewhere in the middle of our conversation, I begin feeling like I didn't do the right thing. By pushing him away, denying his feelings, showing him openly that I didn't care. When I ended the conversation, I followed him into his room and asked him if we could continue talking.*

He looked at me, probably just as furiously as I did before, and snarled: "It doesn't matter what's happening to me, you just keep talking to your friend. You don't have time for me anyway. And you don't even know who

I am. What could I possibly discuss with you?!? School? My failure? Oh, fuck, that would make you happy!"

I was just standing there. I though I was going to suffocate. I understood where he was coming from. My response could indeed be explained in such a way. I plucked up the courage and said:

"What I have just done and probably did several times before is not right. I'd like to be interested in you and everything that's going on with you, but, as you can see, I'm not really good at this. So I need you to give me more chances to accept all these changes. I know it's tough on you, but I need to learn a whole bunch of new stuff. I'll be waiting for you in the kitchen for the next half hour. I hope you can calm down and come there so we can pick up where we left off or rather where I left off. Friends matter. To you and to me."

He came after 29 minutes. We talked for quite a long time, but very cautiously. I tried to respond with understanding and empathy, and what surprised me the most was that, in the end, he said to me: "What would you do if you were me?"

2 Safe Belonging and Bond/Rapport

People need safe emotional connectedness with important relatives to survive. This is the basis for us to even respond, to seek help, to lean on others, to see sense in overcoming hurdles, to be empathic, to be interested in what goes on in other people, to be human.

The awareness that parents care for their teens is one of the most important experiences teens need for their life. That is awareness with by far the strongest preventive power. If teens are aware of emotional attachment, belonging and connection, they will, in spite of tumultuous episodes, remain in the circle of our rules, values and life principles. A teen develops such awareness on the basis of sincere messages that his parents really do care for him, that they are interested in him, that he matters to them, that they accept him, that they worry about him, that he is present in their thoughts, that they notice changes in him.

Living in the world of safe belonging is the fundamental condition for us to be able to share and communicate openly with others.

Part of a safe living environment is also the security of important relationships. If the relationship between partners is at risk during the child's puberty, the child may call for help with his "problematic behavior". In issues related to relationships between partners, the impulse of children is that they have to solve something (thus taking on a burden that is not theirs to carry). In this case, it is more effective for us to focus on solving the relationship with our partner as this will in turn put a stop to problematic behavior.

---

(2) Let Him go to His Father

At first, we met at school; with the parents and a fourteen-year-old boy with long hair. The mother said carefully that he was being treated as a child with behavior problems. In one year, the boy went from a smart and hard-working student who practiced karate and went to music school to a completely different student: he dropped all of his interests, shut himself into his own world, he's dreaming about going to America, and is not even remotely interested in work and school. He has Fs, doesn't participate in class, provokes teachers and argues with them.

His stepfather was explicitly impatient with the boy, got mad about him not carrying out his duties, humiliated him...

At this meeting, I saw a strong dynamics of power struggles in the family. The stepfather talked about how he and Ryan had been living together since Ryan was five, how they got along the whole time, and the mother described this relationship as very gentle.

The actual situation reflected the boy's introversion, his gaze strictly directed to the floor, silence on his face, and the boy's firm determination not to move from his position, to remain shut as a shell, and completely unwilling to cooperate.

At the first meeting, the tension between the stepfather and the boy grew, the mother was completely powerless and divided between her loyalty to her husband and their three-year-old, and to Ryan, her first child. The stepfather increased the pressure with ideas that the boy should move out, live with his biological father.

I saw the blend of factors that were not connective by nature. I perceived the situation as rather hopeless.

Then the mother came again, just she and Ryan. I expected an open conversation, as the barrier I so resolutely denoted at our first conversation to be the source of problems was absent. But what happened was quite the contrary. The mother came because she wanted to talk about the boy's goals for the future. A change was lurking, namely a transfer to another school brought on by disciplinary measures. Many questions arose. What changes will have to be introduced for old stories not to be repeated over and over again? What will happen to the boy after he completes elementary school, where does he plan to enroll? What gives him joy in life?

Ryan didn't want to cooperate to give his mother at least some peace of mind. Every time we came close to the idea for him to think about his future, about the situations where he'll have to assume some responsibility, he fell silent, played victim, and removed himself from the possibility to even speak.

This way he accumulated enormous power on his side and made great despair accumulate on the other side, as he gave the impression that there was no way anyone could get close to him.

After some reflecting, some things in this story didn't add up. Ryan's favorite thing to do was to play with his younger half-brother. So the presumptions on hatred or jealousy or the significance of ties that are not biological are not true. In brief, biological or non-biological father—among the factors of his behavior, this one isn't' important. The whole story and the teen's distress were related to the dilemma of belonging and safe attachment.

Within the Scope of Awareness

Teens can't be made, or influenced from the outside, to cooperate with us. They will cooperate when they see sense in it. Situations when we see obvious negative behavior and hatred between relatives often refer to the experience of attachment at risk. When teens don't feel connected, their life loses its meaning, they stop trying, and drop their interests and pleasures into which they invested their time and energy. They slack off at school, give up their interests, close themselves in their own world, spend time on empty activities, preferably on their computers.

Teens are quickly left feeling like they are losing connection and security.

To change their teen's behavior, parents, in their powerlessness, send messages (verbal, non-verbal, through actions) which may be understood as if they wanted to get rid of their teen, send him somewhere, put him in a residential care institution. These can also be messages of non-acceptance (*What did I do to anyone to be punished with you? / When will this ordeal end?*)

Even more often, teens themselves say that they will leave home, that they can't bear us anymore, that they will find another environment. In their hectic responses, they drive us away from the area of closeness, they won't let us into their room, they won't allow any physical contact anymore.

These are all strategies that destroy connections and connectedness, which we reinforce by responding to them and diminishing their power with non-responsiveness or ignoring and disconnection.

Many times, parents respond to changes with rejection, disappointment, criticism, even withdrawal and isolation. This way, we convey messages to our children which they understand as that we don't accept them, that there is something wrong with them, that they are bad and unworthy of bonding with us.

All these messages are messages that put the feeling of safe belonging with our relatives at risk.

Responses from parents with a connective note convey the message: *"I won't leave you, I'll be there for you, no matter how hard you try to achieve the opposite."*

In many cases, disharmony occurs in the relationship between partners due to developmental changes, shaking the fundamental value of the whole family system.

Adolescence is the time when children search for their identity. Related to this time are fantasies about who my real parents are, which are closely connected with the fantasy: no one likes me. In this relation, we may expect several more or less surprising ways to check the idea of abandonment and belonging[9]. The need to check how much and in what way my parents care about me is common to all messages and manners of communication.

Parents who are able to remain in the role of adults provide security and stability. Remaining in safe connection with the parents is the child's fundamental need. Without it, the child's independence won't be successful. Research shows that the experience of safe attachment is directly related to healthy development in many areas: emotional flexibility, social functioning and cognitive abilities.[10] Safe attachment builds resilience when tackling distress during development. On the other hand, research confirms that children who are not safely attached show emotional rigidity, problems in social relationships with others, poor concentration, problems understanding mental event in others, greater risk when managing social situations[11]. Unsuitable experience with attachment lead to greater vulnerability of children. The most unfavorable among experiences with attachment when safety is at risk is disorganized/disoriented, confused attachment which contributes to the shaping of behavior of growing children and requires clinical treatment (schizoid episodes, psychopathological results, violent behavior).

Therefore, it is the responsibility of parents to put care for connection and safe connectedness to the top of their parenting values. Also important is the awareness that this is the responsibility of adults, not teens. Many situations may occur when parents, due to their child's behavior, end up in

---

[9]This is especially intensive in cases of children who don't live with their biological parents.
[10]Cf. Mikulincer & Shaver, 2007.
[11]Cf. Siegel (2001: 77).

counseling offices, from school counselors to social work centers, and various forms of assistance within the health or judicial sectors. When undergoing such experiences, parents often feel that they are bad parents, that they are incompetent, that they have made a mistake somewhere along the line. Even if they explicitly hear that, parents and guardians are the only ones that can provide their children with an experience of primary attachment. This carries much more power than the idea of using external professional help to change the child's behavior.

When in puberty, children of separated parents express with their behavior the need to bond with each of their parents. The need to bond sounds like a threat or blackmail: "I'll go to my father's house." Whereas, in fact, this means that the child is lost in his sense of security and bonding. On the one hand, friends become very important persons to our teens, the family annoys them, the parents are pathetic... on the other hand, they feel that their parents are the only ones who can ensure their safety and bonding. Teens become confused in the grip of the two worlds, so parents need to be extra present in this awareness through messages like "I'm here for you." This sometimes looks as if trust should be built anew, although we don't know what we did to ruin it. Adolescence itself is marked with distrust, checks, control... All this speaks about the importance of the role of both parents during this period. The father and the mother. Which means that couples even though separated as partners still remain parents. We can say from experience that separated couples who are responsibly aware of their role of parents may offer their children safer growing-up and more self-confident gaining of independence. Couples who manipulate separation from their partners usually lose their connection with the child, increasing the possibility for the child to get lost in an unhealthy environment. When a new partner or even the mother says that the teen should go to his father's house, the teen hears that as being unwanted, that it isn't okay, that they got tired of him, he explains to himself that he is redundant and that they don't love him... Like an animal we take to the shelter when we don't have time for it or can't cope with its character. At that moment, a dam of destructive emotions opens up, which we recognize in teens' obnoxious, hostile, aggressive behavior. The child usually flies into such a rage that his parents are afraid of him. But, in fact, underlying all this is the powerlessness to build the connection which his life depends on.

Tips and Solutions

We invited Ryan's family from the story at the beginning for a dialog, since they had been quite firmly moored into their destructive beliefs and behaviors. During the discussion, they could say what was important for them in their family, state their opinion on how they thought other family members saw them in the family and how they would like to be seen by other family members. Dialog acts in a connective way, especially in terms of building emotional closeness.

Ryan could express his doubts about whether his stepfather liked him at all, while the stepfather met Ryan in his emotional world. Perhaps this was the most important meeting. On the other hand, the mother experienced her importance in Ryan's emotional world. When parents manage to see the foundations of emotional belonging, the bond is strengthened to the point where all other matters become marginal. It sounds simple, but for some parents, this represents an insurmountable hurdle.

Parents who didn't have the experience of safe attachment in their primary families have a lot of problems remaining stable during shocks from their teens. They can't hold on to the awareness that the connection with the child is the greatest value.

We already know behaviors which make us withdraw from the relationship from the dynamics of relationships with partners. These may be activities that seem "urgent" and noble (doing household chores, parenting, work or other obligations), but their real function is to avoid connection and closeness. We also call this exit from a relationship. Exits are catastrophic choices of behavior: threats with a divorce or suicide, extramarital affairs, consumption of intoxicating substances or other addictions, escapes into a disease.

In a similar way, we are tempted to use exits in our relationships with teens, which teens initiate. We can hear their statements that hurt, shock and anger us: *"Get out of my life. / You mustn't enter my room ever again. / I don't want to see you near me. / I'll leave home. / You're not my family."*

(3) Provoking Teen

 Lucy was the last child in the family, her two older brothers had already moved out. She lived with her parents in a new house, and she had her own room. She invented a very interesting way to test the security of attachment in her family communicated to her parents as dissatisfaction with all material things. At the same time, she expressed her need for autonomy in a very provocative way which her parents managed to support her without any problems. She said that her room was too luxurious for her, that she would give away everything redundant to others and move to the basement. Her parents felt bad because they interpreted this as their daughter being ungrateful and spoiled, but were completely power-less. However, at the same, they were telling her all the time that they loved her just the way she was. When the basic dilemma in the teen's head wouldn't subside, she used one last maneuver. She announced to her mother that she wanted to go to a residential care institution. Her mother had enough of this game and she used the mirror technique. "Be my guest, but you'll have to call and arrange your accommodation by yourself because this isn't mine and dad's idea." *Lucy really called an institution and spoke to a social worker who asked her some set questions:* "Is your family socially disadvantaged, are your parents getting a divorce, do they beat you or abuse you in any other way, do they care for you, do they neglect you..." *Lucy realized that, in terms of safe belonging, she doesn't meet the "conditions" to be placed in the institution, and this was a new way in which she understood the value that had been self-evident in her awareness until then.*

Even though we use statements to threat our teens that we will send them somewhere, this opens up opportunities for exit in our heads. Thus we are on our way to the exit really happening.

The first step towards preserving safe connectedness is the awareness that we won't choose exits from relationships and that we won't respond to exits offered by teens in a way which strengthens the power of exit. This requires soundness of our belief and feeling that we wish to remain connected with the child. That we want this to be the value for lifetime, beyond the period of puberty.

From this perspective, problems and disasters that we see at the moment seem less fateful and less final.

If we manage to devote ourselves to the significance our connectedness with the child as a person bears for us, if we can recognize, and be aware of, the human qualities of our child, this will be a strong enough principle.

The question how I see my connection to the child in five or ten years can help us more specifically. Do I wish to be a grandparent whom my child will trust to look after my grandchildren? Do I see that we will be in contact, that we will meet, that the child will come visit me and will take care of me when I'm old on the basis of our connection? Also on the basis of the power of our connection that overcame hurdles when my child was growing up.

In circumstances related to diminished economic safety, the awareness that we have each other, that we care about each other, that we wish to remain connected in the long term and are consciously devoted to that is the support that helps us survive difficult situations.

In this sense, the final scene from the movie Thirteen[12] where the mother changes her responses to her daughter's rejections and tirelessly persists in keeping the connection with her daughter at all costs bears an important message. It is the message carrying the power to heal wounds with attachment.

It is difficult to see cases where parents give up on the option to be connected. In such cases, other skills and missed opportunities in many other areas are at work, which parents missed or overlooked, largely because they weren't equipped and aware enough.

So what is key to preserving safe attachment with a growing child?

1. **Compatibility and cooperation.** Safe attachment is built though cooperative and constant communication in which two people are in rapport. Compatibility in communication is reflected in eye contact, tone of voice, face expressions and body movements, and in the time and intensity of responses. Growing children still need us to have the same connection with them as when they were younger. Sharing signals of compatible cooperation means meeting on the level of primary emotional needs.

---

[12]Thirteen, an American movie from 2003. Directed by **Catherine Hardwicke**, the scenario was partly written by **Niki Reed**, a leading actress, based on her own story when growing up.

2. **Responding with reflectiveness and empathy.**[13] Through mirroring, we let our teen know that we heard him, that we get the meaning of his messages, that we understand and allow his emotions. By doing so, we give him value. Empathic and reflective responses pave the way for teens to get permission to have their own mental processes, but at the same time, remain open and willing to accept and understand the sense in the mental processes of other people.

3. **Restoring interrupted connection.** When children are growing up, the time overwhelmed with resentment, pride, power, defense and other reasons that tell us to persist in the *"let him see what he has done to me"* position, an important function of parents is to provide and take the initiative to "fix" the damaged contact points. We can neither expect nor demand this from children! By fixing, we open up the opportunity to change the story in new frames, for new opportunities, a new path, where we don't want to repeat the patterns that led us to lose the connection. This is an important message for skills of living in a relationship, which allow predictability and safety in the long term.

4. **Harmonious stories.** Adults' past, present and future stories should be harmonious, meaning that we are able to talk about our past stories as about an experience that helps us live our current life. This conveys the message to growing children that experience, which may now seem a distress or a hurdle, will be part of our soundness in the future.

5. **Emotional communication.** Emotions are the main part of our experience of sense in life, and are in the center of our awareness of attachment. Allowing emotions to be part of communication makes us available to each other when we share the most important matters.[14]

---

[13]Example *see page 123* in the book.
[14]Cf. Siegel & Hartzell (2004); Siegel (2014); Johnson (2004, 2008, 2013).

3 Parents as a Safe Base

For teens, puberty is a period of insecurity and search for their own path to adulthood. During this period, they gain important life experience through trial-and-error learning. The experience of firm support from parents can help them on this road. This means that parents, through all extreme deviations, are able to preserve the stability in their role of adults, the soundness of the rules and principles they live by, as well as personal soundness and stability. Someone in the family just has to be the adult.

As children enter their teens, parents enter mature middle age. This is the time when parents carry a lot of stressful events on their shoulders. On the one hand, teens' parents enter the period that end in the final goodbye, and on the other hand, teens face bidding farewell to their youth and issues about the meaning of the life they live. In many cases, parents see an opportunity to prolong their own youthful power by identifying with their teens, but unwittingly, slip into regression.

Being in a satisfactory relationship with teens also means being connected with livelihood and greater zest for life, which brings pleasure to all of us.

---

(4) Mom wants to be My Peer

Dear Lea and Albert!

You came to our school, and the workshop we attended was very educational and interesting. I have a big problem. You said we can write to you so I plucked up the courage.

I have a dad, a mom and a sister who is five years younger. My dad is not at home most of the time. He works and travels a lot. When he comes, he brings us great stuff, phones, clothes, and perfumes...all three of us pretend to be happy about it, but in fact, it feels like someone is visiting. I can't even tell him anything about me. My sister is still very childish, and my mom...

I'm kinda embarrassed to write about this. A while ago, I said in a joke that I'd like to have a tattoo because I was interested in what she would say. But she didn't say anything. I think tattoos are beautiful, but I don't know if it hurts and what it feels like. I wanted to make her talk to me. But mom wouldn't budge. So I quit. After a few days, she called me to my girlfriend's house and said that she'd like to show me something, and to come home.

When I came home, she showed me, on her breast, a brand new tattoo, red and blue, with a dragon, huuuuge, still red with fresh wounds... My mom is 42.

She watched me if I'd jump for joy. Instead, I ran out, away. My problem is that my mom behaves worse than my girlfriends. She walks around in clothes that are too tight, she pierced her left ear six times last year, she wears mini-skirts, and now she has a tattoo over her entire breast. I'm ashamed, but she thinks she's a cool mom.

My dad doesn't even notice stuff like this. I don't know where he lives. I'm lonely in my family. My sister's too young, and I don't want to influence her with my bad thoughts.

My classmate's mom makes great food for her many times when she comes from school, looks for stuff she's interested in on the Internet with her, talks to her about sex, sometimes she gets mad... I'd like to have a mom like this. Please tell me is there anything wrong with me?

Within the Scope of Awareness

Teens' parents or friends?

Many parents feverishly mull over the dilemma whether to treat our teens as parents or as friends. This brings a lot of insecurity and confusion into their parenting behavior. On the one hand, we read about having to play the role of adults and be especially parents. On the other hand, we wish to be on the same wavelength and on good terms with our children.

The dilemma, misleading in its core, arose on the basis of beliefs and experience which marked modern parents when they (we) were growing children. Especially if we received authoritarian and non-understanding parenting, we vowed to ourselves that we would never inflict a similar experience on our children.

Other kinds of experience could also be involved, for example a separation of a young mother whose child replaces her partner and she decides to be a friend to her child.

Relationships that emerge from an unclear boundary between the role of an adult and the role of a child cause problems during puberty in terms of respecting rules, boundaries and authority, and learning how to satisfy other needs in a safe way.

We have chosen the story from the introduction to this title as an illustration what it is like in the world of children, how much they need their parents who are stable and balanced in the role of adults. And that parents who slip into developmental regression and believe that they can experience puberty again are a burden to their teens and shame their teens in front of their peers.

The title "cool dad" or "cool mom" are earned with behaviors which are understanding to the needs and the world of teens, while remaining adults who carry the safety and reliability of the world for their teens.

Creating the experience of a safe foundation is part of our mission and personal growth while our children are growing up.

For a growing child, soundness is, first and foremost, the awareness of soundness of important people the child lives with. This is especially the relationship between partners or relationships in a larger system, but can also be inner personal soundness.

During this period, children test our soundness, which is often tiring and draws strength right out of us. What children actually need is the soundness of our messages that we really do care about them.

4 How to make and Preserve The Connection with Our Child?

People cannot survive without mutual connection and attachment.

When they turn thirteen, our compliant and obedient children suddenly turn into something that is difficult for us to accept, and the connection is silently and unnoticeably lost. Not the child-parent connection, but vice versa.

When the connection is lost, communication shrinks to everyday technical topics, and with teens, school is the most convenient filler. Without the connection, there is no bonding, no trust, we no longer ask the right questions, we feel excluded and used by our children. In the next step, this puts us in the middle of conflicts, power struggles and rebellion, where we lose our authority, teens cross the line and demolish the established rules, while we feel powerless and lost.

Therefore, preserving the connection is the royal path to peaceful coexistence, cooperation and impact on our children's behavior. We all agree with this, but the question remains—how?

This is perhaps also the most sensitive area controlled by subtle and most frequently unconscious dynamics of our mental apparatus, linked with our experience of early connections.

As a legion of complications occur in practice in this area, let's take a look at a true story that includes many open questions.

---

(5) How to Connect

 The atmosphere at home is becoming unbearable. There's no joy any more. We have two teens. The connection with the older one is virtually non-existent. The communication between my wife and me is just about the essentials, what we'll buy, who'll pay the bills, ...

The younger one is slowly following in the footsteps of the older one. I don't know if it's slowly or there will be a time when the younger one is worse than the older one.

Actually, I don't know any more what is wrong with whom. With all of us, probably. I prefer to be at work. I feel good there. I have a coworker, we trust each other, and I can talk to her. This eases the stress at least a little bit.

But at home, there are two sweaty teens, and a depressive wife. At least, it seems that way.

Let me describe to you what out late lunch looks like when we all show up at home. We sit at the table, my wife waits on us as if we were in a hotel. No one (except sometimes me) even thinks about taking part. My wife used to ask us to do something, but the answers were something along the lines of: "C'mon, Mom, you're standing as it is, can't you do this too!" or "Oh, c'mon, I was at school and I'm shattered..."

None of us responded or we even raised a kind smile. So the disease of non-participation spread among us like the plague. Now we eat in silence. There's no use talking about school, since, after a few moments, everyone screams, nor about household chores, since everyone just promises, but nothing ever happens, nor about the computer, as we are old imbeciles who don't have a clue about technology, nor about the dog that only I walk and already smells of carcass...

So we are silent, gulp down food with no gratitude, the kids compete who'll finish first to get the best seat in front of the TV or the computer. My wife and I remain at the table, in silence ... and then I start looking forward to going to work. I have no idea what she looks forward to.

I feel no attachment, no love. I'm terrified, I'm afraid that I'll attach elsewhere. But everything hits rock bottom sometime.

A phone call. It's school. My son hasn't been to school for two weeks. His grades are disastrous. Where is he ... they're asking. Everything seems like a voice from a distance. I can't breathe, tears are rolling down my cheeks. I call my wife. She doesn't answer. I have no idea what she's doing. Is she even at work? Who do I live with? I know nothing about anyone...

I'm shaking all over. I call my son. His answer to my question about his whereabouts is: "What is it? Now you're gonna nag? For ages, you haven't wondered who I was, what makes me happy, where I was ... And now you're bitchin'? C'mon, man, take a hike!" He hangs up.

Powerlessness, despair, shame... I'm highly educated, I work in the public sector, and I messed up my son. Maybe even both of them. And my marriage.

I went home, turned on my son's computer, looked through his emails, messages, Facebook, photos ... In the end, I felt sick to my stomach. Sick from the contents of his computer. Pornography, violence, weed ... These were three shocking types of information I hadn't known about until that moment.

I called a golf buddy who has a son the same age as mine. He helped me find a way to learn about the whereabouts of my son. He told me that he knew how hard it was, that they also encountered problems when the kids were growing up, that they sought help, and that now everything was fine. I felt relieved when I realized that he didn't think that I was an irresponsible loser of a father.

I stopped by the drugstore. I bought a THC test, as my son would just deny everything, and went to pick up my wife from work. Everyone watched, be-mused. In the middle of a meeting, I walked in and said: "You need to come with me even if you lose your job or our kid will lose his life!"

The golf body advised me to calm down. I took my wife to lunch first, and we cooperated again like we hadn't in a long time. We agreed that we needed help, so the first thing we did was make an appointment with a counselor. Then we found our son. When I saw him, I felt like crying. "No, son, I won't let you screw up," I told myself.

My wife and I started discussing things, stood together and introduced changes, beginning with the simplest things, like: remove the plate from the table. We practiced persistence and consistency. We knew that it was us who had to learn first.

There were wars, tears, my Apple was thrown from the third floor ... many things happened. Today, we are reconnected and we cooperate.

What message did I want to convey? It's never too late, and the worst thing to do is give up, but many times, the burden is just too heavy for us to carry alone.

Within the Scope of Awareness

If our patterns don't include the experience of connection between our parents and us, as growing children, from our primary family, and we engage in repetitive disconnecting behaviors, we will struggle to find a way to change alone, as we are not equipped with the experience of any specific behaviors. In such instances, we need a person we can rely on, at first, a partner; or it might be sensible to find the core of the issue with professional help.

We remain connected if we nurture and preserve mutual responsiveness in communication. If we know how to take interest in things a teen responds to. If we apply methods through which relationships are built. To help you, there are a few starting points related to the issue:

How well do you know your child? (This question may also be used when thinking about your partner.)

▶ Do you know what their favorite chocolate is?

▶ Do you know what their favorite food is?

▶ Do you know what their favorite drink is?

▶ Do you know what their favorite dessert is?

▶ Do you know what their favorite band is?

▶ Do you know what their favorite actress/actor is?

▶ Do you know the name of your child's best friend, where they go to school, where they live, who their parents are? Do you possibly have their phone number?

▶ Do you know what your child's favorite clothes are?

▶ Do you know what message your child's style conveys to the outside world? (We aren't talking about what you, as parents, think or see ... We're talking about what **your child** wishes to convey.)

▶ Do you perhaps know who your child's role model is, and how come that they picked this person?

▶ Can you talk to your teen about their ideas, goals, and thoughts ... By really listening to them, allowing them to see things through their own eyes?

▶ Do you and your teen have common rituals?

▶ Do you know of a problem your teen might have?

▶ Do you know what your teen's view of the world is like, how they accept difference?

▶ Do you know what really enthralls your child?

▶ Do you know what his/her longings are?

▶ Do you know what your teen dreams about?

All these questions are the right questions that will enable you to connect with your child. Why? When you know the answers to these questions, your teen will feel that you are interested in them, and that they are very

Table 1: *The choice of behavior to connect or disconnect in a relationship is ours.*

Seven deadly habits	Seven caring habits
Criticizing	Supporting
Blaming	Encouraging
Complaining	Listening
Nagging	Accepting
Threatening	Trusting
Punishing	Respecting
Bribing, rewarding to control	Negotiating differences

important to you. In such a state, their behavior will be considerably more acceptable. Of course, there are many more such questions

Responsiveness and conscious presence are among the most effective behaviors to achieve the connection in a relationship—and this applies to all relationships. Responsiveness ensures feedback and conveys the message to our children that they matter to us. Conscious presence means that we are aware of our role and impacts in a relationship, that this is present in our awareness when we act and are active, that in specific interactions, our actions stem from this awareness, and that this is not a mere general principle we advocate with words, but which is missing from our actions.

Through responsiveness, we choose the path we will enhance in a relationship. Being aware of the fact that we choose our behaviors may decisively affect our relationships with growing children. **William Glasser**[15] drew up a list of seven behaviors that destroy and seven behaviors that build relationships. These are behaviors that we may choose at any given moment if we are aware of them, and if connection is part of our list of values. Many times, we face dilemmas when we are completely lost and overwhelmed with feelings, and when the only behaviors that come to mind pertain to the abuse of power and the destruction of relationships. Table 1 describes connecting and disconnecting behaviors. The mere inner reflection on the behaviors we choose when we are angry or overwhelmed with emotions will help us not to choose destructive behaviors.

[15]Cf. Glasser (2010a).

5 Principles of the Parenting Circle of Responsiveness

Let's take a closer look at what response is. What is the meaning of a response? And what are the principles underlying our responses?

Knowing the principles of mutual responses is important for us to understand relationships, to be aware what is happening in relationships, and finally, to change relationships. This doesn't only apply to parenting, but to all relationships.

We have already mentioned that our responses shape our child's experience. What does that actually mean?

In the first chapter, we explained what is the circle of safe responsiveness.

Now let's take a look at what is circular causality, one of the most important principles underlying our understanding of mutual relationships.

Imagine a picture of a dog chasing a rabbit. Who is to blame? What is the reason for what we see in the picture?

If you ask the rabbit, it will say: I'm an animal whose inherent survival traces mean that I save my life by fleeing away from everyone who could be dangerous and especially from everyone who is bigger than me.

If you ask the dog, it will say: I'm an animal with a hunting instinct whose survival traces say that I have to hunt if I want to survive. When I see something running away, I need to chase it.

And there is the circle: the rabbit influences with its fleeing the behavior of the dog which is chasing it. And the dog with its chase influences the behavior of the rabbit to flee.

It is a metaphor for systemic approach.[16] Some also call it the big picture, context and dynamics.

In short, to understand what is going on, we first need to see the big picture in which the relationship between two actors is part of a system and systemic principles. There isn't just one person to be blamed or just one person responsible. Every person carries his own share, and the behavior of one person influences the behavior of another person, and in the

---

[16]Cf. Dallos & Draper (2015), Jones (2000).

circle of infinity, the behavior of the other person in turn influences the behavior of the first person.

When we spin in the circle of infinity within the circle of mutual influence, we quickly find ourselves in a battle, which, in our case, is a life-and-death battle.

Remember that mutual relationships take place in a circle, in circular dynamics.

The dynamics of mutual relationships doesn't work according to the cause and effect principle. Instead, we mutually influence each other with our behaviors in every relationship, thus co-creating the outcome of our interactions. This is really important! Each participant contributes his share to each situation. Therefore, we can't act like: this doesn't concern me or this has nothing to do with me.

The circle of mutual effects may also be seen as a dance[17]. In this dance, dancers are in a mutual relationship, the steps and energy of one of them influence the response of the other one. And the steps and energy of the other one will in turn influence the actions of the first one. You know from experience that dances can be pleasant or unpleasant. We can dance in harmony or stumble all the time. We can enjoy the dance, complement each other, be finely tuned, create a common above-average experience, or step on each other's toes, and think about how to put an end to this misery as soon as possible and never to repeat this experience again.

Also in relationships, there are dances that lead to connection, contact, mutual harmony and understanding. We could call them integration dances. And then there are dances that don't connect. Dancing a dance of connection with our teens is undoubtedly a difficult task. Disconnecting dances are usually easier for us, but it is important to learn how to get out of them, which we will show in the rest of this book.

Another important principle is feedback. Feedback in relationships means that we can strengthen or expand a certain behavior with certain responses. This is called a positive feedback. With other responses, we alleviate, reduce or even abolish a certain behavior. This is called a negative feedback.

---

[17]Cf. Johnson, 2008.

(6) Positive Feedback And Reinforcing The Behavior We Don't Want

A daughter came home every day with information that, in the first year of high school, teachers bluntly humiliated her classmates, that they were biased, and that they lacked a sense of respect. Her parents responded by listening and commenting that it was really bad.

The daughter brought new stories every day, which were increasingly intensive, emotionally exciting and difficult.

With their responses, the parents wanted to show their daughter that they understood her and tried to console her.

But what was really going on? Their responses reinforced the feeling of powerlessness when trying to change something which was beyond their influence. What happened was a surprise for all of them: the daughter got a stomach disease which was an obvious psychosomatic reaction.

The parents realized that their manner of communication reinforced the forces which contributed to the disease. They decided to only respond to their daughter's information about the pleasant things that happen at school. She recovered and turned her attention to other, more encouraging and optimistic topics at school.

So what are the elements of circular communication?

One element is the awareness of the influence of positive and negative feedback. Positive feedback refers to the principle of operation, to a systemic principle that applies to all mutual relationships, and not to the content. So it isn't about that we want or wish for something positive to happen, and it will happen. It is (also) about how we act. That we are aware of our share and how we direct the interaction with our share. We know that we can wish for something very positive to happen, for example prosperity, financial welfare, but at the same time, we are afraid of that and we act out of fear, which hinders our ability to express and spread behaviors which can provide prosperity and welfare.

Another principle applies to the principle of responsiveness, which is:

(7) If it Doesn't Work, Change it

I was annoyed during the winter if the door to the hallway was constantly open. I tried commenting, persuading, begging, ordering, with decisive and raised tone of voice, with comparisons, threats, humor. The more I tried to make my kids close the door through my speech, the more the door was open. So I had to give up and face the bitter realization that my behavior was reinforcing the response I didn't like (although my internal intention was to change the response). When I realized that, I had to make a decision to change my behavior. But how? Just the question and my awareness of the action of feedback were enough. Next time the door was open I said to myself: "If it doesn't work, it needs to be changed." Searching for a more appropriate response, I remained silent, and when I didn't say anything the next time, I noticed that the door was closed. It seemed like the door began closing automatically.

We would like to emphasize another thing related to parenting situations, which applies to parents, teachers, coaches, youth workers and all persons with parental influence on children and adolescents. Most responsibility for circular action in relationships between children and adults lies on adults. In short, adults are in their role which requires the awareness of this role, boundaries, stability, firm support, safe responsiveness, of their share of patterns and past experience, emotions and all other elements from which we choose our behavior.

If we combine all principles of responsiveness, we can imagine just how decisive and important our impact on our children is. And we can be aware that our responses really shape the quality of our child's experience in relationships.

The principles of circular causality and feedback work like a grinder. The grinder will grind what we put into it, which will be the result.

If we think that our child is clever, that he will make it, that he can make it, we will direct our energy and shape the behavior which will support such beliefs. In our relationships with our children, we will respond in a way that will support the development of independence and self-esteem. We will respond in accordance with what we have mentioned as elements of a safe response.

Let's think about our beliefs about our children when they were up to ten years old. How did we see them?

How did we believe in them?

How were we happy for all their achievements and progress?

Then came puberty and teens.

Did we start complaining in ourselves about our teen:

that he is lazy, that he is apathetic, that he has no interests, that he doesn't like to do any work, that he doesn't listen, that he disregards us, that he doesn't do his schoolwork, that he doesn't care about anything, that he doesn't tidy up his room, that he doesn't do what he is told, that he always wants to have things his way, that he is being a smart ass, that nothing will ever become of him (if he goes on like this), that he isn't clever, that he doesn't finish anything, that he is a regular lazybones, that he doesn't appreciate what we invested in him...?

Let's think about the principles of responsiveness and be aware of the fact: *what we think of a child will become of the child.*

As parents, we have several options as to how we see our teen and which content we bring into the feedback principle:

1. Do we see our teen as a child who announced the transition to a new period of development with his behavior?
2. Do we see ourselves as adults whose job is to hold the world full of changes which sometimes seem very dramatic?
3. Do we see our child as a failure of our past parenting, and experience him as a rebel and an enemy?
4. Do we see ourselves as unsuccessful parents who give in to powerlessness and despair?

We have learned from experience that the thoughts we have when we enter mutual relationships are much more decisive that the actions that follow. Thoughts create beliefs and forge the frame for response on the other side. Many times, we don't check our beliefs, which then paves the way to the world of complications and eternal misunderstandings.

The thoughts than don't connect us destroy mutual connections. We will discuss the reasons why connection is so essential in several sections of this book. But for now, the important thing is the awareness that we don't choose behaviors that destroy our connection with our growing child.

Perhaps you recognized voices in disconnecting statements with which you had been brought up. There are plenty of such voices within ourselves. They are patterns we are equipped with and are the heritage of our growing up. This opens the subject that not only our conscious beliefs are hidden in our responses, but many other elements we are not aware of.

The realization of the feedback principle requires us to make ourselves aware of it. If we are to remember that we choose the response and that if we don't consciously bring destructive contents into the response, we are on the road to not reinforce behaviors we have problems coping with.

This doesn't mean that we should just let go of situations we try to manage but are ineffective (for example certain urgent matters and obligations). It isn't about withdrawal and capitulation, but the presentation of our active role of adults and a change in strategy with which we will attain our goal in a different (especially less stressful and more constructive) way. Below, especially in **Part 2**, there are many concrete options how we can attain it.

6 What are Parental Dances in which We Lose the Connection and our Parental Power?

The awareness that relationships happen according to circular causality and not according to the cause and effect principle opens up new opportunities for neutral observation and control of forces that affect the dynamics of our mutual relationships.

What does that mean specifically?

First of all, this is the awareness that each side involved in a relationship has its effect that determines how the relationship will progress. So it isn't about someone being guilty (meaning: you're weird, you're mental, there's something wrong with you) or that someone should change (he should be checked out by a psychiatrist because he wasn't brought up right, because you brought him up...). No, the cause in a relationship is not on one of both sides, a relationship is something we create together. Which means that we *co-create* the relationship. In relationships between adults and children, the responsibility (and duty) to be aware of all those principles and especially influences lies with adults, as we have mentioned in previous chapters. Most often, the issue is in parenting, in the fact that adults aren't aware of their influence. We already emphasized that when we wrote about various types of responsiveness.

We would like to present another model which—if we understand, and are aware of, it— can make parenting situations easier for us.

It is the model of parental dances.

What do we mean by parental dances?

If you think about everyday situations in mutual relationships, not only in parenting, you'll surely see that certain behaviors are repeated time and time again.

For example: I tell her things all the time, but the more I tell her, the less she hears me.

Or: Every time he has to do his homework or every time I tell him to do something for me, he starts arguing—and this can take all afternoon. I try to get it across to him why he has to do it, but he won't hear me and talks back instead. And this doesn't stop...

Or: I told him nicely that he can use the computer only after he has done everything for school. But no. I come home, and see immediately that he's on the computer, and then I have to threaten him with punishment to get him away from there. And it's the same every single day. Like a broken record.

Have you recognized yourself? Does this happen to you in your everyday life? What is happening in these stories?

It seems as if both sides kept repeating one and the same dance moves. As if the behavior of both sides was programed in the same way. As if they were dancing according to a learned program. When I do something, something will happen on the other side which is predictable and expected. Always according to the same model, only the content changes. We know that from our feelings when we get home and think: It's going to be same as every day... Described here is the dynamics of repeated interactions, where the behavior of one person affects the behavior of the other person, and the behavior of the other person in turn affects the behavior of the first person. That's a dance.

We know from other sources how we can influence the outcome of certain situations with our beliefs.

It is the same in parenting situations.

Of course, when dances evolve the way that suits us, when we dance a dance of connection, mutual understanding and cooperation, we can only wish they would never stop. In such cases, our proven principle is: if it works, don't change it!

However, we also know dances in which we aren't connected with our child, in which we lose our power and authority, dances in which we lose the connection and parental influence. There are dances with which we achieve the exact opposite of what we would like to achieve—dances with a destructive effect.

So it is sensible to know these dances, to be aware of our share in such dances. Of course, we would like to know how we can get out of the dances that aren't functional and change them to achieve a more functional out-come.

First, let's take a look at the most typical dances into which we are drawn by our growing or even young children. They can be our established mutual behaviors which run along tracks known in advance—which we don't even realize. We usually deal with issues and our internal thoughts (for example why won't he listen to me, why do we always have to argue, when will he begin studying, how can I make her tidy up her room, must our Sunday lunch really be spoiled every time)—but don't see the pattern or the big picture of the relationship in which we actively participate.

Now let's take a look at parental dances[18] through typical behaviors re-peated by both sides. A dance begins with mild forms, and gradually pro-gresses towards harsher and rougher ones.

Dance 1: "I'm Afraid of the Child"

Parents are afraid of their children or of conflicts.

On the other side, children have a growing sense of power, they disregard boundaries and rules, they disregard the authority, they seem convinced that no one can touch them.

Dance 2: Inconsistency and Indecisiveness

Plenty of words from parents, but none of them come true. Children per-ceive them as inconsistent and indecisive.

Such behavior of parents enables children to evade their duties (some children achieve it with blackmail; when younger children, for example, don't want to go to bed, they provoke behaviors when their parents give in, for ex-ample they throw up, get a fever, have cramps in their stomach...). But teens just do it their own way.

---

[18]With the metaphor "parental dances," we are describing the circular influence pattern that develops when parents and children interact. That metaphor was already used by Salvador Minuchin as "family dances," and also by Susan Johnson with "dances in partnership." In our next book, we plan to focus on the outline of parental dances, which will be systematically arranged on the basis of parenting examples from childhood to adulthood, and shown as a search for connection and solutions in the form of safe attachment.

Dance 3: *"Please Do What I Tell You"*

Nice parents who ask and plead nicely, beg, and repeat their pleading.

What happens in the child? Disregard, of course. The child doesn't hear and doesn't do what we ask him to do.

(Do you realize that this also applies to relationships between partners and relationships at work?)

Dance 4 (a very popular dance, who doesn't know it): Arguing

Parents believe that they can convince their children with words, they explain and justify.

On the other hand, children rebel using the same weapon: by arguing. The dance looks like this: the more the parents argue, the more the child argues (in the end, children always win, while parents feel powerless and despaired).

Dance 5: Pursuing

Parents try to use pursuing to get to the truth, to information about their teen, they ransack the teen's room, browse their mobiles, enter the teen's room uninvited...

Such behavior leads to evasion, concealment and secrets in teens.

Dance 6: Intrusiveness, Control

Parents who are intrusive usually don't even realize it. Intrusive behaviors are behaviors which don't allow teens to have their autonomy and independence, in which they need space to explore, test, acquire their own experience. Intrusiveness is expressed as: *"When will you start studying? Have you made a study plan for your next exam? How many equations will you do today? How many calories have you eaten? Look at the way your shoes are tied. Are you wearing skateboard pads?"*

Teens who perceive their parents as intrusive will rebel to, withdraw from, hide from such parents. If the parents' intrusiveness is related to close control, teens tend to develop hidden rebellion, sabotage and other physical symptoms which usually really worry us.

Dance 7: Prohibiting

We may know this dance from when we were growing up.

If our parents (or other adults) prohibited us something, we developed rebellious behavior. In teens, prohibition leads to an even greater desire to achieve the prohibited.

Dance 8: Deadly Habits

When parents are aware of their parental powerlessness and ineffectiveness, they switch from a friendly to a less friendly mode. This results in behaviors whose common denominator is that they destroy connections. We have already mentioned 7 deadly habits according to Glasser[19] (criticizing, blaming, complaining, nagging, humiliating, comparing, threatening, bribing, punishing). Think about how much some of the aforementioned behaviors are part of our everyday spontaneous responses in relationships with our teens.

And what happens when parents or adults (especially teachers) use such behaviors? Withdrawal from the connection, attitude of rejection, perhaps even unplugging from the relationship. In a word: disconnection.

Dance 9 (this is an area of emotionally more intensive activity from the very beginning): **Power Struggle**

When parents face their teens with the idea of using power, along the lines of: now you'll see, I'll show you, we declare war on the teen. Teens usually translate the use of power into an invitation to power struggle, which they misunderstand as a fight to the end, meaning that they'll show us that they won't relent in their power. The more parents (and other adults) try to manipulate or control teens' behavior by using power, the more teens will rebel using even more power, also above all boundaries.

Dance 10: Ignoring

When parents run out of power, they usually give up. That's when we hear that they don't care about the child anymore. It is even more worrying when parents show their children with their behavior that they don't care

---

[19]Example *see page 58*, Cf. **Glasser**, 2002, 2010a, 2010b.

about them anymore by ignoring them, excluding them from the relationship and attachment.

This results in great distress and anxiety in teens which they usually don't show because of their pride. Instead, they develop behaviors with which they hide their vulnerability.

Dance 11: Chaos

When parents' behaviors are chaotic, meaning that life one day is one way and completely different the next day, or when one set of rules is used one time and no rules the next, or when for example the father is sober one time and drunk the next, or when the mother is psychically stable one time and completely off balance the next, children don't get safe responses and develop a chaotic experience. In such cases, children don't have the fundamental sense of security, and in the future, they spread chaotic patterns in those areas where they themselves endured a chaotic experience.

Dance 12: Abuse

This dance is the most horrible of all, and we must not let it happen. When adults abuse children, children get stuck at the level of development when the abuse took place. For children, abuse represents a trauma, preventing them from developing healthily and undermining their fundamental sense of security.

Table 2: *Endless alternation of parental dances*

Adult behavior (Important Others)	Teenage behavior
Fear of conflicts, fear of teens	Expansion of power, violations of boundaries, disregard for authority
Indecisiveness, inconsistency	Evasion of duties (by blackmail, the child won't go to bed, he throws up...)
Pleading, begging nicely	Ignoring
Arguing	Endless arguing
Pursuing	Evasion, concealment, secrets
Intrusiveness, control	Rebellion by disregarding, violating rules, hidden rebellion (eating disorders)
Open prohibition	Open rebellion
Choice of deadly habits (criticizing, blaming, complaining, nagging, humiliating, comparing, threatening, bribing, punishing)	Withdrawal from the connection, attitude of rejection
Power struggle, abuse of power (punishment)	Demonstration of unyielding power (escalation of rebelliousness)
Ignoring, disqualification	Silence, absence of emotions, anxiety
Chaos (mixed messages)	Chaos
Abuse	Setback

7 How do We get out of Ineffective Parental Dances?

Now that we have seen which parental dances we are involved in, and understand slightly better how we lose connection and the basis for parenting in them, that we carry our share in preserving these dances, the next questions are how to get out of the dances that aren't effective and how to reestablish the connection through which we can exert our parental influence?

We will discuss every dance separately, along with a specific story.

1 Fear of Conflicts with a Child

The first dance revolves around parents being afraid of their child's (or teen's) rebellion and of a potential conflict. When we are afraid in the role of parents or authority, we bring our reinforced powerlessness into feedback. How can we set boundaries if we act out of fear that our teen won't respect the boundaries? How can we maintain our authority if we are afraid that the teen might hurt us? Whenever we bring fear into a relationship, we also bring information that increases the chances for the fear to come true. Parents express that they are afraid of their children, which brings the sense of insecurity into the parenting system, and teens don't feel safe. We will write more about this in the chapter on authority in **Part 2**.

Let's say that our intention is for the child to take out the trash from the kitchen to the dumpster in the street.

How does the dance evolve?

PARENTS		**CHILD**
Fear of conflicts, fear of teens, loss of the power of authority. They don't even want to meddle with subjects where their teen could rebel or oppose to them.		The child acts like a king towards his parents, who doesn't know any boundaries, doesn't respect the authority, power accumulates in the hands of the child.

73

Behaviors and beliefs we see in our parents.

"I won't even say anything so that we don't have another argument."

"I'd better not say anything, he won't take it out anyway." "I'd rather do this by myself so there isn't any fuss."

Let's take a look at what is going on with parents' feeling.

Parents or adults fear that our child would be hurt, of causing him pain, that our child would suffer, perhaps even fear of getting into a conflict with the child. Over the years, this could turn into fear of the teen. With such behavior, parents won't be able to assert their authority or stand by the consequences unfavorable, but deserved, for the child, they won't be consistent and firm.

Such behavior allows the child not to respect authority, to exercise his power, to believe that no one can touch him.

Two similar dances belong to this category.

On the one hand, parents are indecisive or inconsistent.

On the other hand, children are evasive and they disregard us.

PARENTS		CHILD
Indecisiveness, inconsistency		Evasion, the child disregards us, the child is convinced that we have no authority

"Could someone take out the trash?"

And, of course, inconsistency: We announce to the child that there will be consequences, but there never are.

Or when parents, with their requests, begging, nice begging, believe that their child will hear them.

But the child consistently ignores them.

PARENTS		**CHILD**
Pleading, begging nicely		Ignoring

"Please, take out the trash, you'll do that, won't you, please..."

Crucial in all dances in which we participate but aren't effective is for us to get out of them.

But how do we do that?

At first, we need to be aware of the basis for fear or restraint due to which we can't play the role of authority which requires and achieves this task to be carried out. This may be a deep emotion related to an internal promise to, or contract with, ourselves. We get visits from divorced parents who have a sense of guilt towards their children. Also from parents who protected their child due to his illness or a similar reason, even fear of losing the child. Then there are parents carrying other kinds of guilt, namely that they don't spend enough time with their child, that they aren't good parents, and similar.

It is sometimes enough to be aware of inner obstacles, but many times, parents need additional professional help.

This requires a change in the belief that if the child expresses dissatisfaction, that doesn't make us bad parents. And also a change in the belief that authority, boundaries and rules provide children with a sense of security.

The awareness of the goal may also help us along the way: in our case, that is *"Take out the trash."*.

Perhaps we are convinced that children will do what we tell them, but when that doesn't happen, we don't have the power to act, to make something happen. This is bad news: parenting means for parents that we need to step out of our own comfort zone. That a consequence must happen, that we must react.

Because when something happens after the child has ignored us, the child will understand that we are serious.

What can happen, what can we do differently? What can we do without abusing power?

The simplest way is to look the child in the eye and say: *"Tell me what I told you to do, tell me what you heard!"*

When the child says: *"To take out the trash."*, this will make him aware of our instruction.

When we give instructions to the child, we must be in direct contact with the child. We don't do this from a distance.

Another way is to take the child's hand and gently, but decisively, lead him to the trash can and repeat: *"Trash."*

Caution: few words, no moralizing or preaching, no threats and other deliberations. Short and simple: *"Trash."*

At this point, we should explain what authority-based parenting is.

When we say: *"Take out the trash."*, we will say this with authority if we visualize the child actually taking out the trash. And only when our inner image of it actually happening is sound, our message to the child will be based on that image and the thing will happen.

This is very important, and we will probably repeat it on other occasions.

2 Arguing

What does the arguing dance look like?

PARENTS		**CHILD**
Arguing		Endless arguing

"Take out the trash."

"Why always me, you always find me of all people?"

"Take out the damn trash, do you always have to argue with me?"

"That's not fair, I took the trash out yesterday, today it should be someone else's turn."

"Well, you know, we're all busy and are running errands."

"Yeah, I know, you like others better and you torture me, I'm your slave, I'll report you to social services..."

"Look, it isn't true what you're sayin', we love you all the same."

"Yeah, yeah, keep talking. Yesterday, you promised me that we'd go buy a new phone for me, but you always break your promises."

"Wait a minute, do you remember us have an agreement that when you don't talk back for a week, we might go..."

"Yeah, yeah, you and your maybes, you're always makin' excuses. I know. You don't have any money and you're lying to me. You promise me stuff just to use me."

"Oh, man, whoever gave me this child. Beat it before I give you a harsher punishment. I'd better take out the trash myself..."

The example above is a fine example of a common way how our teens trick us. The mother wasn't aware of the focus on her goal which is clear: Take out the trash! In her answer, the teen offered a new area and a new subject, which the mother, due to the lack of focus on her own goal, accepted and every time slipped a step further into the mechanism of manipulative evasion. This happens outside of conscious intentions, it is merely a strategy skillfully used by teens to evade their obligations (and, let's face it, adults are no stranger to this strategy either).

Repeating the aforementioned experiences reinforces the learning of the behavioral pattern of withdrawal, lack of persistence, loss of focus, diverging, avoiding sense, short-term focus, disregarding agreements, ignoring each other, exclusion...

Is it possible not to get involved in arguments and still attain our goal?

"Take out the trash."

"Why always me? You find me every day, you always dump this trash on me..."

"Because you're my favorite."

"... But I have to study."

"Take out the trash and you can start studying immediately."

"But..."

"Trash!"

What, in this case, is important in parents' response?

Focus, focus, focus.

Perhaps also the awareness that we refuse to argue.

Answering the child's question: *"Why me?"* with *"Because you're my Favorite,"* will stop the child from asking this again.

Another thing is that we must be in contact with our goal. Our goal is for him to take out the trash.

So the focus on this goal and as few words as possible.

Naturally, you are going to say what if the teen turns around and walks out? And doesn't take out the trash.

Keep your focus. Because teens will need something urgently in an hour or two at the most. If nothing else, they will be hungry.

Just move that peanut butter jar you store on the first shelf in the cupboard one shelf higher and a bit further to the back.

When the child returns and looks for food: *"Are we out of peanut butter?"*, you will wait for him with the answer: *"Of course, we aren't, but first, take out the trash..."*

Let's repeat: FOCUS with which we wait for the child at the first opportunity he needs something from us.

This requires us to decide what is more important: to keep the focus on the child taking out the trash or to let go of our belief that the trash can must be empty right this minute.

3 Parents' Intrusiveness

Let's take a look at what happens in a dance with intrusive parents.

PARENTS		CHILD
Intrusiveness		Hidden rebellion

At four o'clock, a mother says: *"Take out the trash by five."*

"Yes, Mom, I will."

Mother in five minutes: *"Haven't you taken out the trash yet? Look, if you don't take it out now, you'll have to stop studying..."*

"Yeah, Mom, I'll do it by five."

Mother: *"You're always doing stuff your way. I'm telling you now is the best time to do it, later you can forget and you'll be punished again..."*

"Mom, can you let me, for once in your life, do something my way? I said by five, now it's—I've still got 45 minutes left—don't you trust me?"

Mother: *"Yes, of course I trust you, I just want what's best for you. It's better for you to get things done now and not to worry about them later."*

"If you don't stop right this minute, I won't take it out at all."

Parents are intrusive when we don't allow our teen to have his own space of individuality and autonomy.

However, you don't want to mix that with letting up on boundaries and rules. That doesn't mean that the teen gets to decide and that he doesn't have to do anything.

It is about that he has to, but we can be flexible about the way he does it.

Intrusiveness means that we know what is best for our teen.

"Look at the way you're wearing your pants. And put your shirt right, look at the way it's hanging."

"How can you go to school with your hair looking like that..."

"How many calories have you eaten today?"

"Don't drink that, it's not healthy..."

"When will you start studying? Will you do maths first? You have half an hour for maths exercise, then you'll read a book for your home reading after practice."

"You can't present your seminar paper like that. In the introduction, you should..."

Intrusiveness is often associated with pursuing, while the other side evades, hides and keeps secrets.

It must be emphasized: Teens need their privacy and secrets.

PARENTS		CHILD
Pursuing		Evasion, concealment, secrets

Supervision is another kind of parents' behavior from this family of dances. Rebellion may be expected in this relation.

One of the commonest strategies of circular effects is a dance between pursuing and avoiding.

We probably know this dance best from the dynamics of relationships between partners. On one side, there is the strategy of avoidance in conflict situations, and on the other, the strategy of pursuing. This creates a wonderfully complementary combination: the more the first person avoids, the more the second one pursues; the intensity of pursuing increases the intensity of avoiding; and the intensity of avoiding increases the intensity of pursuing. We are trapped in a vicious circle from where there is no escape without making a change.

This way, we co-create numerous situations that affect the atmosphere of our domestic life.

The more we are angry about obligations that haven't been carried out (pursuer), the more obligations are not carried out (distancer). The more we encourage independence, the more independent the child is. The more we forbid, the more the child rebels. The more we approach with humor, the softer the child's responses. The more aggressive we are, the more aggression we encourage in the response of our teen.

The most frequent example of pursuing is urging children to do schoolwork. We repeat the same story every day. We remind, encourage, fuss, urge, try using fair means or foul every day... But the response from the other side is always the same—opposition which only reinforces with time. This is a telling example how our behavior maintains ineffective feedback.

Our responses also define the response from the other side. Certain behaviors reinforce the response, while others reduce it. It is worth asking ourselves which behaviors reinforce certain behaviors of our children, especially behaviors we don't approve or that worry us.

Remember the previously mentioned example: **if it doesn't work, change it.** (see page 63)

This example nicely shows that our share is outside of what we believe to be good and effective. Seeing your own influence in the creation of relationships is the most difficult, so we need to put in a little extra effort and some help. Persisting in firm beliefs can prevent opportunities for us to learn. In the example above, the exit from an established dance is in the mere fact that the father no longer contributed his share. Silence was a change, an absence of the former response which had previously spun the loop of the teen's disregard of orders. Silence was a new choice which created a new interaction with a more favorable result.

PARENTS		CHILD
		Rebellion
Supervision		by disregarding
		and violating rules

With teens, we usually believe that our feedback will achieve supervision or a change in certain beliefs or behaviors. While, usually, the effect is the exact opposite of our notions or expectations.

What is supervision?

Tidying the teen's room, ransacking all his drawers, pockets and other hidden spots...

Searching their phones, rummaging their computers.

Yes, we are worried about something and we check that in secret.

Parents play a lot of movies in our heads, and we have a lot on our mind. If we don't check them honestly and openly, we will have the opportunity to receive an answer. If we pursue like detectives, we will trigger a game of cops and robbers, if we supervise, we will trigger rebellion.

This group of parents' behaviors also includes us supervising the obligations of our teen, not waiting for the teen to tell us about his achievements by himself, digging them out from other confidential sources instead.

What kind of dynamics drives intrusiveness? What underlies such parents' behaviors?

Of course, we worry about our children.

Perhaps we don't trust them.

We may carry a pattern from our primary families that we need to pursue, we don't trust, we always need to check and have everything under control. That things must always be our way. That we don't tolerate difference. That we are very stiff within.

All these can be the bases for us choosing the behaviors of intrusiveness, pursuing and supervision.

How can we get out of this?

"Matthew, I'm worried about what you do when you are on your computer. I know, it's none of my business, but I'm worried that you watch those porn sites. Can you put my mind at ease?"

"I know I'm a hysterical mom, but I just play movies in my head that... Do something to calm me down."

Remember how important privacy was when we were teens.

We can remind ourselves (and come to terms with the fact) that our trust directs the child towards not wasting it.

Supervision may be replaced with observation with a clear conscience. If we carefully observe our child, we quickly learn to recognize when he is in distress, overburdened or hiding something. To do that, we don't have to go through his stuff, read his diary and texts. From our practical experience, we have learned that our children don't actually mean to hide things from us. They always leave traces. Especially when they are in distress or do something really dangerous. They want us to notice but don't dare say. While parents often turn a blind eye to this and not notice anything. We don't notice because we are afraid, because we think that our child doesn't do that... The child is scared, we are scared, and no one does anything on purpose to hurt someone. We act in good faith because we want the best for our child, and the child doesn't want to hurt us either.

4 Prohibition

A dance of open prohibition and open rebellion is a dance in which the generation of parents who are today parents of teens and the generation before them probably grew up in. So we know from experience that prohibition just calls for a teen to violate it.

Forbidden fruit is the sweetest. It was for us and it is the same for our children. Sometimes we wonder if we even have the power to prohibit something. Namely, for teens, the period of growing up is a period of pure freedom. Despite us not feeling that way. Before that, we have parents who raise and direct us, after that, we have a partner with whom we mature together. But teens are years of pure freedom. We don't let anyone tell us what to do, limit us or be smarter than us. During this period, parents are almost powerless.

We just watch the fruits of our past labor, and wish for our child to let us be his support and role model. We can prohibit many a thing, but how do we supervise it? Will we watch our child's every step? Impossible.

PARENTS		CHILD
Open prohibition		Open rebellion

"I prohibit you to hang out with your friends."
"You can't go to that party."
"You mustn't wear that piercing."

How do we crawl from this model of parenting? Let's take a look at a story from behind closed doors.

(8) Inexcusable Absence From School

 A son missed a lot of school during his first year at high school. To the crowd he belonged to, skipping school was part of their school activities. The father came up with the idea to stop his son's behavior with authority which, in fact, meant resorting to the use of power, supported by belief along the lines of: "You're gonna listen to me in this house. I'll show you who's boss. By hook or by crook." These were, of course, statements to teach kids something, used on the father when growing up which hadn't brought any connection with teens in family history.

The more the father was losing his temper about inexcusable absences, the more their number grew. After two months, the number of inexcusable absences came close to the extreme consequence—expulsion from school. The father didn't know about the feedback principle, and only reinforced his son's behavior with his responses. However, in his powerlessness, he was seeking reasons for that in the fact that the mother's parenting was too permissive, which also led to clashes between partners. The situation in the family was becoming intolerable, and the parents increasingly lost.

One day, the mother went off the deep end.

She informed her son: "This is getting us nowhere. Dad and I have been trying to steer you to the right path, but you're showing us that all the power is in your hands and there's nothing we can do about it. We've decided to let you have the power. From now on, you get to decide what you're going to do with this power and where you're going to direct it. You can use it to prevent yourself from going to school and getting an education, and destroy the relationships in our family. But you can do something more constructive with it. Go and think about this, and then let us know what you've decided."

The son went to his room, and after a while, he came back with a message that he had decided to use the power in a more useful way.

He sat down with his parents and agreed on new rules.

"We understand your need to leave school sometimes, that sometimes you're not ready. We won't supervise your absences anymore, that's your business. You can miss five lessons of your choice every month, but you tell us about it in advance, and let us know what you're going to do at that time and how you're going to catch up with the subjects you miss."

Prohibition is very closed to power struggle. When the parents left the power struggle and the son had the opportunity to manage his power, the vicious circle of the previous dance was broken. The son's absences were acceptable and in accordance with school rules.

What was the principle underlying the response?
The formula to say "NO" which we utter so quickly.
Instead, we should try using *permission with a condition*.

This way, we can step out of many battles:
"Yes, you can have a computer in your room when I see you doing schoolwork by yourself without anyone telling you to do it until a certain time."
"You can have a dog when I see you walking an empty leash every morning for two weeks."
"You can buy yourself ... when you amass half of the amount, Mom and I will give you the other half."

These are ways to introduce rules and order, but we will discuss this in more detail in **Part 2**.

Trust or distrust? We believe that these two words hold the key to success when trying to get out of the dances of pursuing, supervision and prohibition. We build trust from the moment our child is born. We don't only mean our trust in our child, bur largely, whether we succeeded in showing our child that he can trust us through parenting, actions, resolution of child's distress when he was young. Always, even when he "blows it"? Even when he doesn't set an example? We managed to wait for him to get his own experience, albeit unpleasant, and resolve problems or unpleasant events by talking to him. If our teen trusts us and we trust him, all opportunities for rebellion will be taken away from him.

5 Destructive Dances

Next is a dance in which steps are filled with more intensive emotions and become rougher. Since this is one of the worst and commonest destructive manners in our relationships with teens, we will devote a special section to it. In situations where parents aren't satisfied with the child's achievement, we spontaneously choose behaviors that are destructive for every relationship and connection. These are: criticizing, blaming, complaining, nagging, humiliating, comparing, threatening, bribing, punishing. Children who receive such behaviors withdraw from the connection and the relationship, and have a negative attitude towards their parents. Perhaps this is the key point which represents a turn in our mutual relationships at the beginning of teens, which we must understand and which enables us not to lose the connection and to sail through this period more peacefully and safely.

PARENTS		CHILD
Choice of deadly habits (criticizing, blaming, complaining, nagging, humiliating, comparing, threatening, bribing, punishing)		Withdrawal from the connection, attitude of rejection

Just think of all the situations related to school and the results of our children at school, in which our intensive disappointment steals the ownership of their achievements.

What does that look like?

Throughout the Christmas break, I was pushing and asking him, by hook and by crook, when he would study for his test paper they were to take after the break, when he would write the essay, when he would correct his seminar paper... Of course, he didn't do any of this.

Then they write the test—at first, the teacher didn't give them back yet—then she forgot—then she didn't remember writing the test at all—they never wrote the test—and, needless to say, one day we are faced with the reality of her result.

What happens in us? We are overwhelmed with anger, and when we are angry, we say many things:

"Well, there's the payment for your laziness."

"This way, nothing will ever become of you."

"When I was at school, I didn't dare do anything like this."

"Now you'll remember, you won't see the computer for a month, not even from a distance."

"Everyone can study and get a positive grade, only you have to always be among the worst."

"And after all this, I should say that I'm proud of you..."

"I don't know who you take after, there are no such losers in my family."

"When are you going to understand that you go to school for you?"

"Another one like this, and you'll see what will happen. I think you'll remember it for the rest of your life."

"I understand youth, but this way, you show complete irresponsibility to life."

What do we do? In our intensive emotions of anger, rage, disappointment, etc., we use a whole catalog of destructive behaviors. And with such intensive feeling, we steal the child's ownership of his achievement.

First, let's take a look at the essentials of our emotions. Anger always hides something else.

We are completely without power to influence the school-related work habits of our child. We want what is best for him (success at school), but he doesn't listen. I fear for his future. Perhaps, even deeper: I realize that we don't have a connection, that my child disregards me, he doesn't listen to me, he doesn't believe me... These are softer emotions.

The second layer in us is related with the fact that we choose our behavior. It is about the awareness and the decision on whether we wish to choose behaviors that destroy the connection. One option to step out of this devilish dance is not to choose criticism, threats and other behavior that drive our child away from us. To be in touch with our emotions and first process them within ourselves. Then we ask ourselves how to return the ownership of the achievement to the child.

If, before every word or action we intend to use, we ask ourselves if that is connecting or not, and make a conscious decision not to use destructive manners, we make a huge step forward.

In **Part 2**, we will show you ways how to teach children responsibility, how, in such cases, leave the ownership of the achievement to children.

How to praise?

A lot is being said that we don't praise enough and often enough. Our opinion is that we praise all over, but, in fact, *don't realize* what we praise. We utter praise because we have heard that it is good for our child. By the way— we often bring our children up the way we have heard to be right, and we don't ask ourselves often enough what is good for our child. We also don't ask ourselves often enough what we want to see and experience when our child is 30 years old, showing us (among other things) the fruits of our labor.

There are different kinds of praise. Most commonly used are way to go, well done, good job, good for you... uttered in a usual monotonous voice. That is when our child knows that praise doesn't come from the heart.

Think about how we react when our child messes up, when he gets a bad grade. We yell, threaten, scare him, and express our powerlessness in impossible ways. We act like we messed up, not our child. We should behave as adults, whereas, in fact, we are children. Have you ever thought of jumping to the ceiling when our child succeeds with the same intensity?

What we want to say is that our child is not a robot or a collector of 'good job'. Our child needs encouragement. Especially when he messes up really badly and we can't mumble 'good job'.

Such praise means that we observe the child, we know how much work he put in the result, and we help him overcome hurdles. (A school subject the child doesn't like may also be a hurdle.)

A practical example of praise which encourages:

"Oh, you've tidied up the kitchen! I'm very glad. I can see you're happy about it too."

"You got a D? That's probably tough for you. I'm sorry that you'll spend another week studying. How will you fix this?"

"Great job! I love seeing you so happy."

"You've washed the car? That's great. Can I ask you to clean the car windows separately?" (When something isn't done according to our standards and we would normally lose it about the job not being done properly.)

"You've put in a lot of effort to achieve this result. You can be very proud of yourself."

When we simply mirror the child's emotions after he has done something, we show him that we understand him and we know what it feels like being in his shoes. For every person, including adults, this is a great encouragement to do even better next time. Except if you can't imagine that your child is happy with bad results or that he 'achieves' them on purpose.

When he achieves a bad result, the child is in distress and, many times doesn't know what to do. When, in addition to all this, we tell him that he is lazybones, a loser or an incompetent person, we close all paths for him. We take away his faith in the sensibility of tackling the task again.

When we tell him that it is really bad that he didn't make it and that he will have to put in more strength, energy and time. But we know that he will make it, it is worth another try. That is when the child will tackle the task with the energy of 'they believe in me, I have to make it'. He will do his best and conclude with the feeling 'I really can do this'.

Three ways how to avoid criticism

Teens give us endless opportunities to point out their mistakes to them. In some families, this is the prevailing manner of communication. What are our personal experiences with accepting criticism?

When we hear that we did something wrong, does this personally affect us? Do we interpret criticism like there is something wrong with us?

When we have to tell our teen that he didn't put away the tools, that she left her make-up kit lying around in the bathroom, that she left a plate on the table, that, despite our agreement, the dishes have still not been put in the dishwasher, that she hasn't walked the dog for the past three days, etc., we can choose either the connecting or the destructive manner. We are quite well trained in manners which don't connect. How to express criticism in a connective manner?

The first principle says that, before conveying criticism, we should find something which builds the awareness of the quality of the whole personality, perhaps even with a humorous note.

"I'm on my way home. I know how terrified you are of the dishwasher, but I also know that you know how to cheer me up immensely and that the dishes will be in the dishwasher by seven."

"I know that you started fixing your bike enthusiastically and how skillful you are with tools. So I also know that you can fix it."

"You've done a really good job with your seminar paper. What is missing is the observation of the rule on stating literature you got at school."

"I know how meticulous you are and how thorough you can be. Those dirty clothes which have been trying to find a way out of your travel bag are waiting for you to take them to the laundry."

The second principle says that criticism may be replaced with a description of what we want more or less of. Sentences beginning with:

"How can you be so cruel (rude, humiliating) to your younger brother?"

"What really annoys me about you is..."

"I truly can't stand..."

result in destructive criticism.

89

More connecting cues:

"I'd like you to be gentler (more tactful, patient) with your younger brother."

The 'more/less' principle is used to show a specific constructive solution. We don't emphasize (and thus reinforce) unacceptable matters, but we put issues alongside them which lead to desired behavior of the other side.

The third principle is related to our attitude when we evaluate a certain achievement. Do we see 87 per cent of correct answers in a test as:

How much did you miss 100 per cent by? (Why couldn't you try harder? How many people were better than you?) The top-down view (from the position of a perfect assessor) which places the provider of feedback 'above' the owner of the result, and the provider of feedback sees the owner as someone who doesn't correspond.

Or do we see the achievement as a bottom-up creation? *"You've reached 87 per cent. Do you know where did you go wrong—it will come in handy next time."* The bottom-up view, that is from the level where an achievement is built, creates trust in the possibility to correct mistakes.

Many people claim that the first example is a path to preserving a high criterion, to setting the norm of high quality for children. In the first example, the holder of the result hears 'I'm not (wasn't) good enough, it's never enough'. This is criticism which suppresses the will to make progress.

When we organized workshops on the preservation of connection for eight-graders, we collected their answers in which they clearly described the behaviors with which their parents lose the connection and the behaviors with which they preserve it.

At a workshop, we heard an educational story of a boy who managed to persuade his parents to trust him and not ask him every day how was school for one term.

"I was more successful at school, but, guess what we talked about at home all this time."

"???"

"Nothin'."

Table 3: *Connection with parents as seen by children*

Deadly habits	**Caring habits**
You ignore us	- You are interested in us and our world - You take us seriously
Impatience	- You try to understand us better - You put yourselves into our shoes more often
You are intrusive with your ideas	- You let us make our own choices
Distrust	- You trust us more - You allow us to learn from our own experience
Exaggeration (with words *'always'* and *'never'*)	- Think about what it was like when you were our age
You give absurd punishments	- Think about the consequences that will teach us responsibility
Humiliation (swearing, etc.)	- You don't insult us when we make mistakes - You don't laugh at us if our opinion differs from yours
You don't accept the role of adults	- Don't allow puberty get you into its grip - We need adult parents
You don't allow us to learn from experience	- You trust us enough to let us learn from life and stand by us during the process
Unawareness and disregard of our needs	- You respect our time and don't compare it to yours - More privacy - More independence - You hear what we really want - You listen until we are finished
You don't respect our age	- You trust us with difficult tasks and responsibilities you understand our needs to have fun, for new stuff, friends and exploration
You compare us to older people and you have double standards	- You don't compares us to anyone you show consideration to our difference you are tolerant to our trials and searches
You bring work problems home	- You take more time to be with us
Insincerity and secrets	- Put yourselves into our shoes

6 Punishment and Abuse of Power

When we resort to the use of power, we trigger a dance which will proceed in endless power struggles of who will get the upper hand. In relation to teens, it is worth remembering that our notions of the use of power will always be understood as an invitation to power struggle in which they will be the last to relent. So whenever we think *"Now I'll show you."*, we need to know that this struggle won't end well.

It often happens that parents only seek help when their relationship with their child is severely damaged or when the connection is only conditional. Before that, they try to solve the issue themselves, and usually end up entangled in a cluster of four classical approaches: punishment, prohibition, distrust and supervision. The messages conveyed with such behaviors are very important for our growing children.

For them, punishment is humiliation, and deprivation of the sense of autonomy and independence. Of course, this doesn't mean that we have to let our teen enjoy and live his life without limits. However, it is wise to make agreements with him before a conflict arises and our desperation kicks in. We ask ourselves: *"Now what?"*, and then, powerless, grab hold of the first tool we can think of—*punishment*. Then we prohibit him from going out for a week, meeting a friend or something even worse. Punishment imposed in the heat of the moment usually doesn't work out because the teen will rebel in way which parents won't be able to bear. Such conflicts normally develop into a game of 'who will get the upper hand'. It is better for us, parents, if we manage to be a step in front of our teen, if we anticipate behaviors and desires of our teen. (We just need to remember ourselves when we were growing up.) And if we talk to them about them before a real problem or desire emerges. This will be a relaxed conversation when our teen will find out about our expectations, desires and fears, and, most importantly, he will hear our point of view. We will also be able to explain how come that certain things are unacceptable for us and we don't allow them. This doesn't mean that our child will indeed stick to this; it means that he has a connection with us, that it will always matter to him how we feel, that his experiments will have a limit, that he will make his own opinions about the surroundings, pleasures, relationships, etc., which will be supported by our opinions because he will perceive as sensible and sound.

PARENTS	CHILD
Power struggle, abuse of power (punishment)	Demonstration of unyielding power (escalation of rebelliousness). The child withdraws from, or leaves, the relationship

(9) Before the Judge

We got notice of a report from a judge that our fifteen-year-old son had been in possession of prohibited substances.

It was the same when we got a notice that our child had been punished for an offense at school, or in a traffic accident, or had been sanctioned in any other way as a consequence of his disregard for rules and laws.

Usually, intense feelings of anger wake first. And of shame—what will other people say? I can't even tell this to my closest relatives. They will think that we are raising delinquents.

We can take time to talk to ourselves and think. To talk to our partner, a trusted friend, perhaps with a counselor. First, we need to balance our emotions and feelings, and connect with the awareness of our parental role.[20]

The important thing is that we are aware of the fact that our child is the owner of this experience. That the consequence he faced because he had broken the rules was his own consequence to bear.

Therefore, our response is important. Remember the role of a safe haven. Our child needs to feel that he still belongs to us, that we still care about him. The experience is indeed a very unpleasant one. For the child, too.

So outbursts of moralizing, threats of additional punishments, vowing for things to be different from then on, and that we will show him...won't work.

It is also true that our brain works quickly, and that we would like to find a quick solution, we would like to achieve a rapid, definitive result.

However, it is sensible to first calm ourselves down, and wait for the child become aware of the consequences. We can ask him how he felt about this judicial notice. What does he think will happen when he stands before the judge?

---

[20]Cf. Part 1 of the book, especially chapter 9 and 10 on the regulation of intensive emotions.

We can rest assured that the drama of our internal processes is completely clear to our child, without us reporting about it to him.

To become aware of this, we can help the child by asking: "Probably, the judge will want to know the answers to the following questions: Are you under sufficient supervision at home? Do you live in an orderly family? Are we attentive enough as parents? Do we have rules you respect? Do we control your behavior? Can you respect our rules? Do we have problems in parenting?"

At this point, it isn't at all sensible to impose punishments (or consequences) on him—for example, "you're grounded, you won't hang out with these losers anymore, you don't have access to the computer, you have a curfew..."[21]

It is more sensible to ask the child what he thinks our reply to judge's questions will be. We need to get his answers to the questions.

What was the reason for him overstepping the boundary?

And we need to assess what the real reason was. Was it experimenting and naivety? Was it rebellious behavior? Was it the influence of his company, peers? Was the child unable to observe the boundaries because he wanted to be comforted immediately? Should we be worried about the child's behavior?

If it was about experimenting, we can wait until the court date, and observe the child during this time, to gauge whether his behavior has changed.

If we are worried that our child has problems with respecting boundaries, we must act immediately. What can our action, consequence, healthy response be, in this case?

"I can see that we haven't taught you how to respect boundaries. So this is what will happen from now on (less money available/more control from us/we will test you for THC at the end of each month; if it is positive, there will be consequences/less time for hanging out with your friends, etc.)"

The same happens with all other measures taken along the lines of: I'll show you... This results in losing the connection and provoking revenge through fights and endless resentments which may never untangle.

This topic is further discussed in the rest of **Part 2**.

---

[21]Cf. Chapter 1 in Part 1 of the book.

7 Ignoring

Underlying the behaviors of teens which worry us (intoxicating substance abuse, living on the edge, criminal behaviors, apathy, loss of sense, membership in violent groups, acting contrary to social values, and similar) is most often the experience of unplugging from the attachment to parents or other significant attachment figures. Parents who have tried and failed in all of the described dances tend to resort to their last option: *"I don't care about you, I don't care what you do, your distress no longer affects me..."* Children experience ignoring also if parents get a divorce, when their father (or mother) moves out, no longer calls, isn't interested in the child, doesn't send greeting cards...

When teens feel that they have been excluded from their relationships with significant others, when they don't feel that they have a safe base and a safe haven, they find themselves in a state of disintegration in which they lose their sense of security and their limbic system activates. That is when teens act as if they were thrown off balance, they breach the boundaries endlessly or freeze. The feeling that parents don't care about them is often behind sudden and dramatic changes in the behavior of teens. On the surface, we will notice in teens expressions of rejection and repetitions that they don't care. But in fact, behind such expressions is the distress of abandonment and the loss of a safe attachment.

PARENTS		CHILD
Ignoring, disqualification		Silence, absence of emotions, anxiety

(10) Mother without a Connection with her Daughter

 A mother and her 14-year-old daughter who was completing her elementary education came in for counseling. The mother complained that her daughter completely disregarded her, that she slacked off at school, that she didn't care about household chores, that she hung out with inappropriate people, that she didn't respect the rules about her outings and came home whenever she felt like it, that she

consumed alcohol and smoked weed. The mother tried to make a connection with her, but her daughter won't let her anywhere near her, so she is completely desperate. Her older son is a completely different story, and the mother gives him as an example, but nothing rubs off.

The mother has been living alone with her daughter and son. Her ex husband, the daughter's father, committed suicide a while ago, and before that, he had been treated for schizophrenia. The mother now lives with her new partner.

As I watch my daughter, I see complete absence, I see her completely unplugged from the connection with me. Her mom's words leave her completely indifferent. Her reply to the question about how she hears her mom's words is that she doesn't feel anything and she doesn't care.

As I watch this girl who has reduced her teenage life to hanging our with her peers, I feel deep loneliness and a great deal of sadness somewhere below the surface. As I say this, tears appear on the girl's face. Are these tears saying: "Mom, I miss you so very much."? She nods silently.

I was observing her mother who was watching her daughter's emotional episode, risking asking her how she heard her daughter's call for her mother.

The mother answered that it was hard for her to believe her daughter, that she had lied to, and betrayed, her so many times that she no longer believed in her sincerity.

I had to ask the mother what was holding her back for her not to be able to connect with her daughter's sincere emotional expressions of the need to connect and bond. After a while, we established that her daughter reminded her of her ex partner, her daughter's father, from whom she had protected herself with a wall and inaccessibility. As we articulated the essence of the mother's emotional experience, the dam loosened and the mother cried out her distress, hugged her daughter, and then they cried together for a long time (with my support from the background).

After this experience, we met again and the mother told me about a complete change in her daughter's behavior. Now they are connected, the daughter appreciates her, and there are no complications about the respect of boundaries and rules. The daughter told me that her mother was now much warmer, nice and understanding.

8 Chaos and Abuse

Parents who live in the state of mental chaos cannot provide their children with a safe base. Chaotic parents create an environment for their children in which the children never know what is in store for them. This means a complete absence of a solid structure, absence of emotional stability, absence of rules and order, absence of expected behaviors, boundaries, agreements. Chaotic responses to the child's need reduce his sense of security, and often contribute to behavioral and emotional problems of growing children.

PARENTS		**CHILD**
Chaos (mixed messages)		Chaos

Parents who respond in a chaotic way as a repetitive behavioral pattern need professional help to work on themselves.

PARENTS		**CHILD**
Abuse		Setback

Parents who abuse also need professional help to develop empathy with their child and consequently, change their inappropriate behaviors.

8 How Can We Understand Our Parenting Baggage?

Behaviors which build, preserve or destroy connections in relationships are chosen from among our own experiences and patterns whose spontaneity is related to the mental traces of the period when we were growing up. These may be conscious, but more often, they are unconscious decision-making processes. We know about situations with which we are at peace, and there are situations in which our internal stability completely fails us. We suppose this book is (also) being read by parents who have experienced imbalance in parenting situations, which causes distress or provokes fears and insecurities. This was also the perspective from which we started writing.

Examples which throw us off balance and mortify us may be related to the stories about our "past debts".

Our growing children and their needs push the buttons to which our topics are attached. In relation to these topics, we have received various messages from our parents or guardians, which are also part of our parental behavior; we may have acquired the latter as default patterns or as beliefs and internal promises we have created ourselves (most often aimed at us not repeating the behavior of our parents which we experienced as inappropriate and painful).

Experience is shaped in our own stories with attachment figures. Such experience left in us emotional traces which were the basis for our pattern (model) of attachment[22] that arose outside of our awareness:

- did our parents (or guardians) respond to our needs so that their response gave us safety (and we got the message that we and our needs are okay);
- did our parents respond by ignoring and denying (and we got the message that our needs don't have the right to exist, are inappropriate, and

---

[22]For more in-depth understanding, a more extensive demonstration is available in Bowlby (1969, 1973, 1988), Dallos (2007), Hughes (2009; 2012), Johnson (2004; 2013), Mikulincer (2007), Siegel (2013), Siegel et al. (2004).

we had to satisfy them in parallel or fantasy worlds—which made us conformable and subordinating);
▸ did our parents force their needs on us and forbid ours (and so we had to fight for ours, making us open or hidden rebels);
▸ did our parents, when responding to a certain topic, act chaotically, and we developed a chaotic attitude to the said topic.

Most parents didn't respond to important areas of our development in the same manner. In some areas, they responded in a way that gave us safety, in others, they responded by ignoring, prohibiting or forcing. Perhaps even with chaos. It is not our intention to bring the generation of our parents to account for their past actions the effect of which we see in ourselves now. Our experience is that attempts to clear things up with our parents usually cause more pain, and unjustifiably bring on guilt and mutual misunderstandings. We must also be aware of the fact that most parents do their best to raise their children, and that we had (sometimes) experienced their parenting completely differently as they would have wanted. And now we are experiencing the same thing as parents. The purpose is not to change past stories, but future stories. If we find out for ourselves that certain parental behaviors didn't function for us, we have the opportunity not to repeat the pattern we learned on our children. The power to make a change is in our hands. Therefore, we see more sense in clearing up topics which are the heritage of our own experience when growing up. It is a lot more reasonable to be aware of these influences from the aspect of an adult and with the responsibility to convey parenting messages to the next generations.

When, with our growing children, we assess our stability in the role of adults, there are a few questions that may help us:
▸ Did we learn first hand the responses to the key needs of the period of growing up: did we get the permission to develop emotions and sexuality, to explore and acquire our own experience, to experiment, to develop autonomy and independence, to learn how to be responsible, to transit from the fantasy world to the real one from our parents?
▸ What are the emotional traces of our experience of connection with our parents? Were we allowed to express the impulses of growing up or were such impulses criticized, rejected, or perhaps, there was no room

for them? What was happening to our connection when important topics were involved? What were our conclusions when we survived this? What agreements and promises with ourselves did we make as we left this period behind?

▸ Did we experience our parents responding to our developmental needs as growing children? How did they respond? Were our emotions allowed, or were only certain emotions (socially acceptable) allowed, or were emotions overlooked and denied? What communication patterns about emotions do we carry and how are these patterns present in our communication with our growing children?

These are very important areas where growing children need the responsiveness of their significant others. Responsiveness means providing a reflection without our additions, just like a reflection in the mirror. Are we able to be a safe mirror for our growing children? Only with the response of significant others can we create our own value. Responsiveness is the prerequisite for the rise of healthy self-esteem and important mental functions of the self[23]. Reflectivity is a gesture which gives a growing child permission to accept images without criticism and corrections. We will further discuss the role of reflective (mirror) function in practice in one of the chapters below (see page 121).

Responsiveness must be accompanied with focus on conscious presence. If, when we get home, our mind is still at work or in another relationship, if we are, in parallel, still on the phone or watch TV, if we are focused on cooking or urgent household chores, if we are aware of the stress we are in contact with, it is difficult for us to be consciously present and dedicated to the person we speak to. This applies to relationships between partners and with children[24].

---

[23]This is a wide topic of self psychology and contributions of psychoanalysis developed with concepts of mentalization, mindsight and reflective function. Cf. Fonagy (2004), Siegel (2011; 2013), Siegel & Hartzell (2004), Slade (2005).

[24]The rule of circular causality, in which one person influences the behavior of the other person and the behavior of the latter influences the behavior of the first person, applies to mutual relationships. This way, we can't say that one person is the reason for the behavior (or feelings) of the other person. What emerges from the actions of two persons in a relationship is mutual influence. This is one of the basic rules of systems theory. Cf. Dallos & Draper (2015).

In order for us to be able to play the role of parents who satisfy the needs of teens, we need to be aware of our own experience and inner wisdom regarding the satisfaction of needs. We mustn't mix needs and wants. Needs are related to what teens need in their development to grow up and be independent. They are presented and supported with concrete examples in **Part 2.** The introduction to Part 2 also includes an explanation of the significance of understanding the difference between needs and wants.

So where do opportunities to change and preserve the connection with growing children, and consequently, for their greater responsiveness to values we would like so much to give to them lie?

Influence still comes from adults. How do we contribute to the responsiveness of children with our behaviors? Do our teens withdraw, rebel, do they respond at all?

We have already mentioned four possible types of the experiences of attachment, which are engraved, with deep emotions, in our own growing up through the relationship with our parents. This was the origin of our beliefs and other motives which are the basis for the dynamics of our relationships with our children. On this basis, we also created an intimate image of us as parents. In other words, relationships with our children are balanced by stories we experienced ourselves as children. These stories carry only one truth, and that is the truth of our experience and feeling. We are in contact with, and draw from, this truth when our teens lure us to new experiences and challenges of our everyday relationships with them: consciously to some, but unconsciously to most. If any of our needs weren't satisfied sufficiently or pain is related to satisfying them, our behavior will arise from spontaneous defensive survival methods and strategies we developed.[25] The choice whether we can put ourselves in the conscious role of adults or wander spontaneously into the unfinished stories of our past in which we most certainly cannot be adults depends on the level of our awareness and on how much we have processed, and grown from, stories of our own growing up.

---

[25]Whenever we are thrust off our internal balance, we resort to rigidity or chaos in our spontaneous behavior. Cf. Siegel, 2013.

The first option of our story of development is that we had a safe relationship with our parents. This means that our parents' responses provided a safe support for us, and that they knew how to stand by us as a strong figure a growing child needs. They gave us protection and comfort. We could explore what it meant to be independent in various important areas and learned from the experience of life. This way, along with independence, we learned about responsibility, social rules and boundaries. We learned the most important lesson of all—that we bear the consequences of our actions. Parents were also the mirror of our developing sexual identity, and our emotional support during our searches and fears as we were discovering new and unknown dimensions of our experience. Parents conveyed messages to us that we were accepted and fine just the way we were, and we developed a sense of our own competence, we learned about our inner strength and a sense of effectiveness. We learned a lesson that we were worthy, and what it meant to accept ourselves. In these stories, our parents acted as authority with which stability and determination, if necessary also relentlessness, were associated, while at the same time, they were our emotional connection and a safe haven. Based on this experience, we are fearless and trust in the paths of development in our relationships with our teens. We are aware of our role which is to fearlessly reflect reality, be comfortable in the role of adults, and to preserve the connection and authority of adults. We dare say that this is the role we who are parents wish to play.

The second possible ending may be related to experience of not getting an appropriate response from our parents when exploring and getting new experience. We felt ignored, overlooked, and developed a tendency to be anxious and to avoid. One of such experiences, which is almost a generational pattern, is ignoring sexual development. Our fears upon new physical happening was not supported by a suitable response from most important persons, which would let us know that our development was just fine. That our difference was just fine, and that nothing was wrong if we wondered if we were even normal. Our important stories revolved around topics related to important emotions, and we needed response, recognition, permission and acceptance. If, instead of what we needed, we received messages from parents which we understood as worshiping conformity, we developed behavior that adjusted to the given circumstances. If our parents avoided topics they felt uncomfortable with, if we experienced it as if they had been ashamed of the signs of our growing maturity, it was easiest for us to withdraw into fantasy world and daydreaming. In this world, we moved away from the reality and pain that our uniqueness wasn't accepted, that we obviously weren't important enough to our parents or guardians, that we had no right to exist. Fantasies we developed to survive with such emotions helped us survive, but they didn't equip us to be able to solve our issues in reality. We probably also made intimate vows and concluded important long-term contracts with ourselves, which makes it likely that we will simply repeat the pattern when our growing children provoke us. It is almost impossible being an adult with such an experience without our own story having an end (with external help).

In the third version of our story of growing up, we received messages from parents which we understood as prohibition and rejection of important areas of our emotional and sexual development. Or our parents were intrusive. They didn't allow us to go on a date, party with peers, they didn't allow us to develop our own fashion style, to have our privacy... Emotions and pain related to the experience that our world didn't matter to them made us rebels. On the outside, we protested loudly or silently because our needs were overheard. But deep inside, we experienced pain because we understood that our developmental needs weren't permitted. We also experienced that we didn't matter to our parents or interpreted to ourselves that something was wrong with us or that sex is appalling (a sin) or even forbidden. Instead of safe traces of our experiences, we preserved the traces of confusion and insecurity. We didn't know where to place emotions and feelings. The awareness of the power of rebellion concealed the sensitive and vulnerable areas of our experience. However, deep inside, we probably made a decision that we wouldn't spoil growing up for our children this way. Such stories carry dilemmas of parents when a teen is in the house, in which parents assume the behavior of teens, and it is sometimes difficult to distinguish who is the mother and who the daughter.

The fourth and least favorable option is related to parents' chaotic responses. We developed a disorganized model. If we faced intimidation, violence or neglect because of alcohol, other kinds of addictions or mental illness in the family, because of violence in the relationship between partners, we never knew the response we were going to get. We couldn't count on our needs being met, so we protected them by withdrawing in a world where they couldn't be hurt even further. We also removed the possibility to long for bonding and resorted to the belief that we could do it alone. In a relationship, we often wonder whether we are competent at all to be parents, we often feel that we can't rely on nothing and no one.

Every child's growing up is a set of various types and paths described above, in which our growing children offer us opportunities to grow in our relationship with them. In some areas, we can do it by ourselves, but in many, we can't. We have learned from experience that recurrent complications in everyday life are a sign that we need professional help.

One option is to embark on the path of guided exploration of our patterns and beliefs which are imprinted in our spontaneous behaviors. When we can understand our impulses and responses especially in situations that throw us off balance, we are on the road to act consciously from the position of adults. This means that we can recognize our emotions, that we can easily distinguish the reasons for our problems from the needs of the child, that we can withdraw and think before we react. In everyday language, this means that *we are not* spontaneous. Only then can we effectively use the skills and parenting methods with which we build and raise authority, boundaries, rules, responsibility, work habits, values and everything we wish to pass on to our growing children.

Being aware of responses within ourselves is a good basis for parents and all persons who influence and educate young people.

All behaviors we choose are based on emotions and information arising from emotional value for us. Therefore, we will take a closer look at how we can understand and bear emotions and accompanying events in cases when our children trigger uncontrolled processes in us elsewhere in the book.

9 Awareness of Emotions that guide Us: Emotions Above and Under the Surface

(11) Failure at School

When a teenager comes home and it's written all over his face that he's up to something, and when, after endless beating around the bush, he finally utters that he failed the test we spent the holidays fighting about ... that's when I could explode with anger.

That's when movies about the holidays roll in my head, when I knew at the beginning what it was going to be like. I kept trying to convince him to study, when he was going to study, why he wasn't studying, and why he was postponing so much, and that no good would come out of his lack of work... All this just because I have no authority in this house, because all we do is give in, because we are so very considerate.

I knew that nothing good could come of this. I also know that he has no work habits, and that this is not going to get him anywhere and he is not going to achieve anything. The awareness of anger started to awake in me. Anger with myself for feeling as if I had completely failed as a father and a parent. I feel like a complete failure as a father. And anger because I have no influence, because I'm being completely disregarded. I anticipated clearly what was to come out of this, but I nobody listens to me in this house anyway. How can I not be angry? And I shouldn't even show it.

We know that when we act out of anger our actions do not connect. We also know that such behavior comes from the limbic part of our brain where we lose our internal integration. If we let ourselves be overwhelmed by anger, it will be difficult for us to remain in the role of an adult. Instead, we will get carried away to an area we have problems managing. Bearing emotions is the ability and skill to be aware of them and to be in contact with what is really happening within ourselves. The fact is that there is always something underlying anger.

On the surface, we may be in touch with our emotions related to the disregard for authority and the role of a father, but underneath, there are other layers of emotional events. One of the next layers surely includes

105

powerlessness the father faces. It is easier to conceal powerlessness with nagging, complaining, criticizing and humiliating. Here, we find ourselves choosing behaviors which don't connect as described in Table 1[26]. It is more difficult to be in contact with a sense of powerlessness, especially if we think about what we should be and achieve as responsible parents.

Within the Scope of Awareness

When we are in touch with emotional events within ourselves, we are usually aware of the intensity we attribute to an external trigger. We are aware of the intensive anger and attribute the reason for it to child's inappropriate behavior. So we direct our behavior at this alleged reason. Whereas in fact, it is about the intensity of emotions underlying anger, about the pain because of our own powerlessness, and about the perception of ourselves because of the fact that we are too powerless to influence the behavior of the child—especially because we are convinced that the behavior our child chooses has adverse effects. Perhaps this layer of our feeling is related to our experience and promises through which we have shaped the image of ourselves in our role as parents. This involves something deeper and more intensive, something that is of greater significance for us. The awareness that our feeling has many layers is important to remain connected with emotions within ourselves. In short, the awareness that there are emotions on the surface which we come into contact with first, and that underlying them are other intensive emotions which convey the true meaning of our experience.

To distinguish emotions which are the remnants of the traces of our childhood experience from emotions which we have as adults, we must consciously work on ourselves.

---

(12) She spends the Night Elsewhere after a Party

My thirteen-year-old daughter is asking if she can go to a birthday party to a girlfriend's house—and spend the night there. She must be crazy! Of course, I told her—NO, that she was too young, that I didn't even know her girlfriend, that I didn't know

---

[26]See Table 1 on *page 58.*

where she lived, that I didn't know what they were going to do there. I couldn't have said anything worse. My daughter goes beserk. At first, she slams doors, rants, insults me, threatens to move to her father's house. That there was nothing I could do against that and that she'd run away from home. What can I do? She cornered me. I left her, feeling bad, and cried my eyes out in my own powerlessness.

The mother from the story above was overwhelmed with contradictory emotions in which she got lost. There were fears related to the movies in her head about what was (and wasn't) going to happen at the party, about whether her daughter was equipped and independent enough to go, without supervision, into the world of threats her mother saw. Those were fears that scared even the mother who chased them away from her world by choosing the ineffective 'no'. The daughter chose power struggle and undoubtedly won. The mother collapsed under the feeling of guilt because of the divorce and her own powerlessness, under the feeling of loneliness in parenting and sadness about the fact that she was bringing her daughter up alone. She got lost in questions below she couldn't share with anyone: *"Have I given her enough? Is she independent enough? Will she let other people influence and deceive her? Does she know the boundaries? Will she be able to respect the values I imparted to her?"* These are questions all parents have when their growing child goes out alone for the first time.

And there are also dilemmas: *"Are we doing the right thing not letting him go out? Are we invading his autonomy and individuality, and provoking rebellion? When is the child old enough to spend the night at his friend's house?"*

When we have great fears about the behavior of our teens embarking on the journey of independent experience, when we play the most intensive movies in our head, horrors, thrillers, dramas, that is our sincere feeling to which we as parents are entitled to. And the fairest thing to do is to share that with our children.

Typical fears regarding boys are: that they will drink themselves into oblivion; that they will drive around with drunk friends; that something will happen if he does; that they will get recklessly involved in criminal activity or vandalism under the influence of a group; that they will get involved in physical violence among peers and end up in the ER...

Typical fears regarding girls are: that they will be seduced and abused by an older man; that someone will put something in their drink, take them to a secluded place and rape them; that they will get drunk and pass out; that they will have unprotected sex; that they will be seduced by inappropriate friends, that they will assume their values about contempt for parents and pointlessness of education...

We will put our emotions at ease if we say:

"When I imagine you going alone to..., I see movies in my head that... I know they are my movies and that probably they don't have anything to do with reality, it's just that I'm so old, I've heard all things possible, you can call me conservative, but that just happens to me because I worry about you. What I need from you is to make my fears smaller. Do you have any ideas?[27]"

When emotions emerge in our role of parents, we need to come into contact with them, and also into contact with what those emotions need to calm down. We need to distinguish emotions on the surface (which are related to our image of ourselves as parents) and underlying emotions. Some of them are deep and show our, mostly unconscious, childhood stories and pains, while others refer to our stories of attachment. But when dealing with emotions, we need to recognize if we are afraid. What does fear refer to? Are we ashamed? Of what? If we are angry—what underlies this anger?

How to convey the message if we are worried about our child's behavior?

Do we feel powerless and are afraid of our child's behavior? Where and with whom can we built our inner strength to be able to bear these hectic events?

---

(13) Teen won't go to School

Mary was the mother of a growing fourteen-year-old boy and a daughter who was three years older than him. At first, she attended a workshop on communication with teens because her son was skipping school. After a few years' of struggles to get him to attend classes at a primary school, he was transferred to another school, but the story repeated itself. Her husband didn't participate in her attempts

---

[27] The method of setting boundaries and saying 'no' without provoking rebellion is more thoroughly discussed in Part 2 of this book.

to set clearer boundaries to the boy together. There were more complications, inclusion of other external institutions, even an attempt to place the child in a residential care institution... Endless meetings took place and advice was given by all kinds of experts on education and health, but the boy stayed at home, had bad company which worried his mother, but nothing ever changed. All attempts to coerce the boy to attend classes ended up as an exact opposite. After all hopeless efforts, his mother realized that she had no proper answers to all the dilemmas, and that her parenting attempts put the connection she had left with the boy at risk. She decided that preserving the connection was more important than any other goals. However, she was very lonely in all parenting situations, since her husband simply withdrew and wouldn't participate in any conversations on parenting. He couldn't even respond to her explicit request to help her. Her powerlessness was also reflected on their relationship as partners, and she gradually figured out that her husband didn't give her the support she needed. Mary realized that she was left alone in the parenting process, and found help which encouraged her to face everyday issues by herself. She met a person with whom she could share her fears, dilemmas, seek solutions, tried to understand certain behaviors, and remained strong-minded on her path of preserving the connection with her son. She received as much support as she needed to keep the balance within herself on which basis she could act.

After one year, her son returned to school, accepted the conditions set to him, and fulfilled the missing past obligations, and relationships at home became endurable. Mary accepted the circumstances, and her authority grew which made her son respect her rules and boundaries.

Parents, especially single parents, seek our help many times because they have lost their power and authority. When parents are afraid of the response of their children as they set boundaries, demands and tasks, they need help to gain support for their inner strength. This is not physical strength and most certainly not use of power for violence or physical predominance. It is the inner strength of balance which is related to the awareness of the role of an adult and the power pertaining to it. A functional relationship between partners and the possibility to share parenting dilemmas and issue with relatives or friends are the best support for this.

A few prompts may help us manage and restrain our own emotions, and thus remain in the role of an adult:

1. Describe the facts of the situation which triggered emotional responses. Which behaviors did you notice, who said what, what did they say? It's just that—without our additions (how we understood, how we explain intentions of other people...).
2. How did we respond? How did other people respond? Who did or said something?
3. How did I feel with all this?
4. Do I know these emotions and feelings (an important story from my past)?
5. What did I need in my important story to preserve the connection and trust?
6. Can I understand how my child feels?
7. Can I understand what the child needs to preserve the awareness of connection with, and trust in, me?

10 How to calm Impulsive Emotions? Three Important Steps to Avoid Impulsive Responses

When we face an unsolvable issue, when we lose our common sense, when we're thrown off balance, when we're overwhelmed by emotions of anger and fury (under which, in fact, lies the awareness of complete power-lessness), we need support and a safe space in order for our response not to arise from momentary impulsiveness which we always regret afterwards.

We have all experienced certain information or behaviors of teens throwing us off the track, making us see movies of various genres in our head, from horrors, melodramas to science fiction. Some movies are about us: that we need to maintain our authority, that we don't allow ourselves to do that, that everything exceeded the boundaries, that... And that we must firmly show him (or her) that this is unacceptable, that things are only going to get worse if we don't react now. These also include movies about the injustice in this world, how come that this happened to us of all people. Does that mean that we completely failed as parents? That we aren't competent? That it's best if we don't do parenting anymore and let someone else do it?

All these movies keep us away from being aware of the role and responsibility of adults, which is our only acceptable role.

Other movies are movies about our teens. They include disaster and other scenarios which hide our fears and worries.

And another type of movies are movies about what we are going to do. They may be action stories about us, in which we, as a Batman, James Bond, Superman, Sherlock Holmes and other action heroes, save the world from unsolvable puzzles, deadly threats, beat evil forces, and rescue our children from the impact of the external world, "evil" teachers, "weird" neighbors, inappropriate company...

These mind games that usually take place in the area between the unconscious and the conscious in us trigger large quantities of emotional energy. Typically, this constitutes the conditions for our impulsive and destructive behavior. Apprehension or rage most often show our fundamental powerlessness. We know from the state of our internal emotional balance that when we are upset, we cannot make judgments as adults, and that we first need to calm down and think about our actions.

So we may conclude that when we are upset and thrown off the track, we need the time we are entitled to to connect with ourselves—and that's okay. There's never such a rush that it couldn't wait for our sounder judgment. This may be announced by:

"I can't make a smart decision now because I would do more harm than good. First, I need to calm down and think."

or

"Just a sec, I need to go to the toilet..."

Everyone has their own ways how to find time to think and connect with themselves. It is important to let ourselves feel the way we feel when we can't find effective solutions, when we're angry, desperate, powerless. And it is also important to be aware of that. Such attitude will enable us to find a solution much easier.

This is an important step towards the awareness of our own internal events. What is going on in my body? What do I feel inside right now?

When contemplating and searching for the connection with ourselves and doing our own re-balancing, we may use three sets of questions which will help us see the situation in a different light and open the path to answers we carry within.

STEP 1: **What does my gaze see and how am I aware of my share?**
What are my behaviors and what is the child's response?
How have these behaviors arisen throughout the history of my relationship with my child?
What are my fears?
What am I worried about?
Which emotions and feelings within myself am I connected to?

STEP 2: **How do I understand my own view of the situation within myself and through myself?**

What was my experience with this subject when I was a teen?

What are the patterns related to this subject from the family I grew up in?

What are my needs and longings related to this subject, which have remained unsatisfied?

What are my potential contracts with myself and promises I used to end this subject in my story?

STEP 3: **What can I do differently?**

What really preserves the connection and puts me in the role of an adult?

Which effective behavior may I choose from adult awareness to fix connectedness and trust?

Does my choice of behavior preserve the values that are most important to me in a relationship?

Let's see how we can follow the described steps through a concrete story of a father.

STEP 1: *What does my gaze see?*

---

(14) Difficulties accepting a Teen

 When my son was about to become a teen, I, suddenly and for no real reason, began seeing him in a different light. He used to be my boy I could hug, have fun and play with. Then, I suddenly saw him as something that was no longer my child. I could see that he no longer looked me candidly in the eye, I imagined that he was hiding something from me and lying. All of a sudden, he started getting on my nerves, I became impatient with him. More and more of our conversations revolved around my questions when he would fulfill his school obligations and his household chores. His answers were increasingly blunt and rare. In the end, I played movies in my head that he was a loafer, that he hung out with bad people, that he'd only lie around, that he had no interests in life. I saw him in a more and more negative light, and he was distancing himself from me. Our

communication was reduced to hissing at each other, and my attempts to find a suitable topic to which he would respond were no longer successful. We began avoiding each other, and the situation was only tolerable when my wife was present, who (luckily) had a good connection with him.

The movies in my head were about his failure at school, disastrous scenarios regarding his actions when he was with his friends, inundated with fears that he would get into trouble and nothing would ever become of him.

What does the awareness of one's share mean?

We usually see that someone got us mad, that someone else is the reason for our feelings and emotions, that we get mad because of something outside us. When we experience something is such a way, we are at great risk of projecting part of our internal events onto a person or persons outside us. By doing so, we transfer all responsibility outside us. If the person our experience is being projected onto is our growing child, we'll receive, as a response, decisive rebellion from them.

The father from the story above didn't see his share because he looked outside himself. And because he wasn't connected with himself, he transferred all emotional events within himself onto his view of the teen.

The awareness of our emotions that lead us may help us in this case (as described under the previous heading).

We have an issue if we can't see our behaviors and their effect on our teens objectively. The support of a safe relationship with our partner may be of great assistance in such cases. In our case, the wife presented her perception to her husband:

"When our son gets home from school, I can see you're very impatient. You always used to be kind and welcome him nicely, now you're just looking for something on him to complain about."

STEP 2: **How can I understand my view in myself and though myself?**

---

(15) I'm just like My Dad

One summer day, I was sitting in front of the house with my son. He was thirteen and I was in my forties. I said to myself that this image was identical to the image I'd been experiencing with my father when I was my son's age. A copy no photocopier can

make. I know exactly how he experiences me, I know that he thinks I'm not interested in him, that I don't have a clue what's going on with him, what's going on in his head, what he likes, what fascinates him and what worries him. I feel the alienation between us, and I don't know what to do. Even though I promised myself that I'd be a different father, I couldn't muster either the will or the power to ask my son anything, to say anything. I saw the power of the pattern that was controlling my rational intention.

I understood that I had no communication pattern, and the pattern of behavior between a father and a growing son. I could imagine my son's longings that were the same as mine when I was his age. And I could imagine his disappointment in me.

At this point of the story, we have the most opportunities to work on ourselves. We usually get stuck in issues in which there is an unfinished story in our own development or in which, in our experience when growing up, we didn't get appropriate (safe) responses to our developmental needs.

Observe your answers to the key question: which unfinished stories from when I was growing up and my puberty bring my child's behavior to the surface?

Step 3: **What can I do differently?**

(16) Using Conversation to achieve Connection

To make a change, I had to face the pain of my unfulfilled longing. I managed to do that by having a conversation with my son, in which our emotions met. When I let him go to the party, which I'd rather not do, on the condition that he can go when we sort out our relationship. That's when the pain arising from the break-up with his friends, which we knew nothing about, erupted from my son, he expressed his pain of loneliness, and conveyed, through criticism, that he needed me, that he needed me to be interested in him, that he'd like to know more about me, my work... It was a connection between two helpless boys, through tears, who encountered each other in mutual empathy of the need to bond and belong. That was enough for us to be inseparable allies since then.

When we are lost, and think about which act or parental behavior is the most sensible, we should help ourselves by looking into the future.

Some questions:

What are the child's developmental needs at this moment? What does he need to learn for life? Which skills does he need so he will be able to follow the path of functional development?

What kind of a relationship do I want to have with my child in five or ten years?

11 Parents here and Now: be Aware and Present

Awareness of everything which balances our behavior and mutual relationships gives us an opportunity to raise the quality of our life and health. Awareness is the cultivation of, and contact with, our perceptions, emotions, physical sensations, thoughts, movies in our heads, impulsive ideas... This enables us to be more open to the perception of what is really going on, thus preventing the threat of slipping into our own 'film production' where we get lost in imaginary worlds of our own movies, beliefs and fears.

The first exercise on awareness requires focus on one topic in communication. First, we can check with ourselves how skilled we are in focusing when it comes to everyday chores.

---

(17) Learn how to Focus

Saturday morning. We agree to go shopping together at a certain time. There's some time left until then for us to do some chores. We tell each other about it and go our separate ways. Someone finds a chore and then another chore, he gets carried away, and at the agreed time, he is perhaps enthusiastically doing his sixth, seventh chore. This sounds like: "I'll clean the basement really quickly." Once there, I realize that glass needs to be taken to a landfill. As I put away the glass, I realize that I have no suitable container, so I go look for it in the attic where I get the idea that I'll, quickly and by the way, clean the skis that have been left there since winter. I need to put some oil on them. I search for oil in the room with car accessories. Once there, I stumble upon a car washing kit that hasn't been put away... As I wash the car, my wife, her face red with anger, yells that she's been waiting and looking for me around the house for an hour, that I'm late and that she can't rely on me. Just what I need. She doesn't see my effort, all she can do is criticize, she's always the smartest...

Where did you recognize yourself? Are you in a relationship with a partner where one of you always sets the rules and gets angry because they aren't observed, while the other one avoids and never sticks to what you agreed? This is, actually, a problem of non-presence in situations and the relationship.

We know how the story ends. Conflict, argument, defensive behavior, mutual hurt, withdrawal, distance, persistence in your opinion, a feeling that we don't belong together... We can focus on the consequences, our role as a victim, hurt and pain very firmly. We can persist for a period each person determines in view of their needs.

It is especially important that we as parents are aware of our parenting goal in each situation. This is one of more dynamic areas in communication with teens, which we have already mentioned in our descriptions of parental dances (arguing), especially of keeping the focus and retaining the parenting goal.

Our attitude to be aware and present as parents balances the described dangerous behaviors. Conscious presence is demonstrated in our responsiveness, which will be discussed in more detail in the next chapter. Some general principles apply to mindfulness parenting[28].

1. Our life with a teen in the house can still remain lively and fun.
2. If we remain curious, it will be easier for us to listen to our teen's world which we don't understand at first.
3. Allow the possibility that our teen's behavior has its own internal sense which we might not understand at first. But this is our child and we want our attitude to him to be empathic and compassionate.
4. Be aware of the idea that we wish to remain connected and solve our issues in a peaceful way. Let's not use extreme rigidity or permissiveness. Use strategies which seek solutions to problems through negotiation where everyone can participate and accept his share of responsibility. Identify the problem, brainstorm about solutions, write down who agrees with what, try, evaluate, re-shape if necessary.
5. Always devote time to conversations in which issues have remain unresolved. Wait for intense emotions to calm down, and start a

---

[28]Cf. Duncan et al. (2009), Kabat-Zinn (2005), Siegel & Hartzell (2004).

conversation afterwards. Use a dialog of conscious listening, which is described below.

6. Remain connected with your partner as parents and on the same side, even if we don't agree. Stop fights between partners, since this opens boundaries and demolishes the power of authority. The position of two united partners standing together against a teen gives greater power to the message.

7. Plan in advance and be ready. Certain things are simply not negotiable. Some of them are more and some less important. We are willing to negotiate some of them. When we set boundaries and rules, we must anticipate consequences.

8. Allow ourselves to take time if we don't have an answer readily available with which we are comfortable with. We can always take time: *"I'll think about it."*

9. Overlook issues and other insignificant behaviors which aren't worth complicating things (the manner of speaking that bothers us in our teen, a fad...).

10. Don't punish twice. If our teenager experienced some logical life consequence, or some other authority (teacher, coach, judge) arranged for him or her some defined or prescribed consequences, then ask yourself if we, as parents, need to double it. It could be that our child would understand our supplemental punishment as injustice.

11. Don't let their eye rolling, comments how pathetic you are, and other complaints and contradictions that you don't trust your children get to you. Parenting is our task, and as parents, we need to know where we stand, where and with whom our children are, and especially, when they intend to come home.

12. Don't get upset when your teen storms out the door and slams them. An acquaintance told us a story about how he took the door to his teen daughter's room off its hinges because she was slamming them. *"This is my door. If you intend to keep slamming it, buy you own door."* The door to the teen's room is a more important blockage than the door to the toilet. This measure worked and still does.

We want to add a culturally and temporally determined change to the topic of awareness. The orientation of modern parenting is no longer based on the awe of authority. If generations of parents were brought up by intimidation, even punishment, for centuries, today we come into contact with generations of parents who were brought up differently. This change was first reported by teachers in kindergartens and elementary schools. The generation of children growing up today is a generation that doesn't respond to intimidation, but to cooperation and connectedness. All approaches based on the use of power, punishment, unconditional respect of authority and without personal connection are prone to failure and rebellion. The awareness of this fact will significantly affect the manner of organization in all educational establishments, as well as in mutual relationships in work teams.

12 Empathic Responsiveness and Reflective Function

Responsiveness is one of the most important manners of conveying that we care for each other. It is one of the basic safety nets which enables us to preserve the connection with our teens.

Responsiveness means that we don't ignore, delay, avoid, and run away from, a relationship. Responsiveness means that we are consciously present in a relationship, and respond to all provocations and invitations to communicate coming from our growing children. Many times, these are manners for which we aren't ready and don't recognize them as invitations to communicate—from a shocking change in the child's fashion style and physical appearance, complaints and nagging to being called to account to school or other places and authorities.

More important than fear of a wrong response is to pluck up the courage to respond, even though we later discover that we could have chosen a more effective way. Not responding causes more damage to a connection and bonding than responding in a "wrong" way. Being unresponsive conveys the message: *"I don't care about you."* Responsiveness, on the other hand, is an opportunity to continue communicating. Responding also means taking time to contemplate and letting our teen know that.

There are ways of communication where we let the other person know that we heard him. The technique is known in various therapeutic practices under different names (active listening, imago mirroring, reflective function[29]). We will name it conscious listening[30].

Conscious listening isn't our established communication practice. Therefore, we need to consciously switch ourselves to this mode. Everything written under the previous subtitle should be considered. We need to be in harmony and stable which will enable us to be safely positioned within ourselves. This will provide the safety of the whole communication situation.

We will be able to keep our internal events at a distance, and to fully commit ourselves to the message conveyed to us by our teen. Our only task is

---

[29]Cf. Allen & Fonagy (2006), Fonagy & Target (1997), Grienenberger, et al. (2005), Slade (2005; 2006).

[30]The technique originates in Carl Rogers' "client-focused therapy".

to return the message through mirror response. Reflectivity means that our mind is like a mirror that accepts a message and returns it to the addressee without a trace of our rational processing in the following way: *"I hear what you're saying and I'm trying to figure out the sense it has for you."* This isn't insensitive and heartless parrotlike repetition, but a skill which requires us to be connected and empathic with other people at heart. Consciously, we need to control spontaneous flows of our thoughts. The latter may be influenced by certain typical disruptions with which the rational part prevents the possibility for us to truly hear the person we speak to.

Let's take a look at some of the most frequent disruptions.

Before the person we speak to finishes his thought, we, in our mind, draw a conclusion on what he wanted to say. We compare statements we listen to, and evaluate them in our value system or judge them. We anticipate the course of the dialog and prepare strategies for us to have the last word. We listen only partially and filter information according to what comes in most handy in the given situation. We listen under the influence of the basic prejudice about the other person (for example he doesn't know how to express the point, will we ever hear anything from her that makes sense, always the same empty words...). We only listen with half an ear, while we think about other issues or errands with the other part. We listen to everything as if it happened to us, we take everything personally, we remember our own experiences and compare them. We listen focusing on the advice we need to give to the teen and waiting for the opportunity to do so. We seek, or wait for, points where we can't agree with the person we speak to and steer the conversation in that direction. We are concentrated to have the last word. We reduce the focus of the person we speak to with jokes, comments, changing of the subject. We agree with everything, while in fact we only listen with half an ear and aren't present in the conversation.

At first, reflectivity may be an awkward experience, especially if it is just imagined and not experienced first hand.

Responsible and conscious responsiveness allows reflectivity.

(18) An Example with and without Reflectivity

Conversation in a car

Father: "I hear that there's something new at the bar at the end of the town. To attract more guests, they now have pole dancers. They say they're from Ukraine."

Ava (fifteen years old): "Duh."

Father: "I feel sorry for the girls. I've heard that they're being used and treated really badly."

Ava: "I think that it's just a job like any other, and that people who do this do it for joy."

Father: "How can you think like that?!"

Ava: "I can easily imagine being a pole dancer."

The father starts arguing about selling her body, exploitation and deceptions, and keeps looking, appalled, at his wife who just smiles and silently stares through the window.

Mother: "I heard you; you said that it was a job like any other. Did you mean that?"

Ava: "Yeah, right, Mom. I'm not serious. I'm just teasing dad."

The mother was capable of mirroring without her mental and emotional additions because she was in touch with the curious attitude of mindfulness parenting. The father was caught in his own movies driven by fear of seeing his daughter as a stripper and a pole dancer. Therefore, he wasn't able to keep a neutral distance to what his daughter was saying. The mother delimited responsibilities for the ownership of the message through mirroring. She heard what her daughter said, and immediately evaluated her own message as nonsensical when the daughter explained that she didn't wasn't serious.

In our communication with teens, a lot of messages are aimed towards us as a provocation. Mirroring is an excellent technique to keep us away from mine fields and return the responsibility back to where the provocation emerged.

At the beginning, we presented a simpler example. The next step is the mirroring of topics which take us by surprise or awake in us a strong emotional charge.

Seventeen-year-old: *"Mom, I'll have to resit three exams this year."*
It is difficult to stop the movies and emotions which create a story about how much work we still have to do, how we will go on vacation, where we will find help, if it is because we suspect that he comes into contact with marijuana too often... However, if we allow ourselves to speak through our movies and projections, we won't respond in a way that returns responsibility where it belongs. We need to stop the emotional part in us which probably first asks the question: *"Why did this have to happen?"*
Reflective response: *"I hear you'll have to resit three exams."*
Such response faces the teen with his share of responsibility. Perhaps he was used to higher frequencies from us upon similar news, blamed him for being irresponsible and everything which pertains to that. But at the same time, we thought about how we were going to fix it, that we will be ashamed in front of our relatives, and so we took on more than our share. Perhaps we went astray with words into an area we later regretted (humiliated, offended him), and the teen used this as an opportunity to shift focus. At the end of such a dialog when we use a "classical" manner (without mirroring) which we spontaneously use, we are left alone feeling more powerless than at the beginning.
When a teen receives exactly what he has said instead of what has been expected as described in the paragraph above, he is faced with the horror of the content of his own message and with the fact that he will have to bear the consequences. At this point, emotions involving tears or anger may appear in the child.
Our task is to mirror, and give meaning to, those emotions in the world where they occurred, not only in our world.
"I can see that you're angry and it makes sense. I would probably be too if I imagined that it meant studying during the vacation, only few evenings out, and fear if you'd pass the first time around, since you know that you could've easily passed during the school year."

Example Of Conscious Listening And Responding

Teens are growing persons with whom we don't get to spend much time any more, so we need to be extra organized. Moreover, the time we do spend together is precious, and it isn't right that it is frequently "spiced" with arguments and squabbles.

I am off to work in the afternoon, and I want to know what Tyler is going to do:
"I'll be at work until the evening, what are you plans?"
"I don't know exactly. I'll just hang with my friends, I have to study, and if I have time, I'll spend it on the computer."

Such stories often blow parents' fuse, school is mentioned by the way, and the rest is just killing time. I emphasize that only certain parents see it like this, not all of them. Such parents would argue, complain about school and leave home angry, leaving there a rebel who wouldn't do a thing.

If we listen with awareness, we can proceed:
"I hear you intend to hang with your friends, study and be on the PC. Is that right?"
"Yes, Mom."
I proceed: "Please, put school first and do everything you need to. You need to clean the kitchen by the evening when I come back. Do other stuff as you wish. Okay?"
"Okay, Mom."
Then I get ready to leave. Before I leave the house, I go see Tyler and say to him:
"Bye, have a nice day."
"Bye, Mom."
Me: "Can you please repeat what I told you to do?"
Tyler: "I remember everything."
Me: "Well, let's hear it."
Tyler: "School first (I've already done half of the stuff during this time), then I have time for me,... oh, and I need to clean the kitchen by the evening. Do I remember, Mom? And dad told me yesterday that I had to mow the lawn. Oh, man, there won't be any time left. You're torturing me."

Such a dialog enables us to spontaneously and naturally show that we heard him, that we were interested in his plans. By asking him what we have told him to do, we invite him to repeat what his responsibilities and obligations are. If he repeats, he can't say that we haven't told him what to do, that we are making things up, and the chance of him "forgetting" is much lower.

With reflective function or mirroring in the role of parents, we carry out the most important task: we give the child permission to have a different world, his own individuality and autonomy. Reflective function enables us not to involuntarily absorb or take over the share that isn't ours to have. The mere announcement: *"I hear that you're saying..."* carries a message which announces that we are ready to listen and that we care for our children.

The fear that mirroring means agreeing is unfounded. Especially agreeing with subjects which are unacceptable for us. Usually, the teen, when he hears what he said, corrects himself and eliminates internal contradictions with: *"I didn't mean it like that. / It's not as bad as it sounds. / I can see that it isn't going to work out..."*

Mirroring is only a way to give permission to be different to another person—while we remain the owners of our values and beliefs. The gesture with which we give permission to be different mitigates the urgency of defensive behavior. This way, we avoid the dangerous game of convincing and fighting about "who's right". The teen may be right that school really does suck—and we can hear that. And on the other side, there are we, parents and grown-ups, determined that going to school is a rule in our family we aren't willing to negotiate. And this rule stays the same while we mirror with a clear conscience: *"Yes, I hear you, school sucks."*

But in the end, there is still room for our questions: *"What are you going to do now? How will you fix this? When are you going to sort out this problem?"*

13 Source Of Our Spontaneous Responses: Family Patterns That Affect Parenting

Let's take a look at certain patterns or recurrent experiences in relationships in our primary families with our parents or foster parents along whom we built our internal emotional experiences. This is part of our spontaneous responses when we find ourselves in the role of parents.

The awareness of the patterns which are deeply emotionally imprinted in our spontaneous behavior is the first step towards managing them and making them more suitable, while still effectively using functional patterns.

This chapter consists of questions with which we may explore our stories. By answering these questions, we will more easily understand some of our spontaneous parenting responses.

1 How were our experiences with connections and bonding shaped? Which patterns about bonding did our parents give us?

How did we learn to take care of other people as our parents took care of us? (When we were sick, in distress, where could we go to find protection, advice?)

Who were persons I was most attached to as I was growing up? What was the subject of our attachment to important people?

How loyal were we to our primary family? How (and in which cases) did we protect loyalty to our family?

When did family members show mutual bonding and attachment?

Which manners of preserving the distance to others did we learn?

How did we demonstrate physical closeness? What was (is) our notion of sexuality in terms of sexuality between parents? What was the message about intimacy with which we left our primary family?

2 What patterns did we develop about expressing emotions in our family?

What were the responses (and who delivered them) in the family when I expressed emotions like fear, concern, joy, pride, jealousy, envy, enthusiasm, love, hate, anger, shame, disgust, etc.?

Which emotions did we express most in the period of development in our family?

Were any emotions in any period of development absent?

Were any emotions in any period of development forbidden?

With whom did I share my emotions in a certain period of development more easily?

Were any emotions expressed in the relationship between my parents? Which ones?

What are our experiences with the following emotions: humiliation, inferiority, fear of abandonment, feeling of guilt?

3 Which beliefs about bonding and relationships with relatives were passed on to us from our primary family?

Beliefs are part of our behavior and don't reflect what we say or think.

A belief is the truth in ourselves, even if we say otherwise on the conscious level.

A belief is the sense which only we understand—even if it nonsensical to others.

Examples:
- We mustn't show that we are miserable.
- What grandparents say is always right.
- If we go shopping for something new, we first consult our parents.
- In our family, women are the ones who always fight.
- We never fought in our family (but there was silent treatment for days, weeks...).
- Emotions are for women.
- If someone deserves to be praised, it is better to humiliate him, so that he doesn't get conceited.
- Rich people have amassed their wealth in an unfair manner.
- What will other people think of us?
- You don't talk to friends about money.

Which *values* did we bring from our primary family? Values are part of beliefs.

128

4 How did we solve conflicts in our primary family?

Which conflict solving strategies we used in our family (looking for the guilty party—someone always has to be guilty, shifting guilt outside ourselves, did we enforce the principle of power, did we look for a scapegoat, were conflicts resolved with silent treatment, did we suppress the conflict and sweep in under the rug, did our parents engage in make-up sex, which were the typical behaviors that were signs of reconciliation)? How much did we talk when in conflict situations?

In what way did our parents solve conflict situations?

Which conflict situations are especially imprinted in my memory?

What was the message from my parents' behavior in conflict situations?

How did I feel as a child in conflict situations?

Did I make any agreements with myself?

Could I find the elements of the pattern my parents used to solve conflicts? Which were the underlying beliefs? Which behaviors recurred (every time)?

Did they look for someone to blame?

Did they argue about who was right?

Who used power in conflicts and how did they use it? (the power of word, the power of argument, the power of authority, the power of voice intensity, the power of humiliation, the power of fists...)

Did they compete who was stronger?

What was the behavior of the one who was "right" like? (How did he achieve being "right"?)

What were the results of conflicts?

Did we, children, know what they were about? Did we participate in conflicts and how?

Were we able to express our opinion?

Are we used to express our emotions in conflict situations?

Which questions remained unexplained for us as children when our parents argued?

5 How did we learn about responsibility and accepting the consequences of our actions?

What are our memories of the events when we broke the rules?

What personal experiences (own stories) with this subject I remember?

Are these experiences related to the patterns of my actions in situations when I encounter authority?

In situations when we broke the rules, did we learn how to accept responsibility?

How did we as children understand the consequences of our breaking the rules?

Did we learn anything from breaking the rules?

What are our beliefs about breaking the rules and its consequences?

6 What was my experience with balance in the family?

Which state of relationships determined balance in our family? (Was it when the parents kept each other at a distance? When one of the parents had the last word? When the atmosphere in the family was tense?) Balance in the family is shaped in every relationship both functional and non-functional.

Do parents really always have to agree?

How did our parents and our family system respond to developmental changes (birth of a new family member, beginning of school, onset of puberty)?

---

(19) Example of Balance and Disturbed Balance in the Family

 In a family with a 20-year-long crisis between partners, the children learned that their father never took their mother's side. The mother and the father used to always be on opposite sides. The children learned that if they stirred up a fight between their parents—and they mastered this skill, the parents stopped dealing with parenting and engaged in fights. So the children developed a habit and a belief that they can insult and humiliate their parents without limits. This gave the children the green light to use the computer and avoid schoolwork, and the

tension between their parents suited them to a certain point. Of course, deep inside, they craved mutual understanding, belonging and warmth in the family.

The parents decided to work on their relationship, and after some hard work, they established a connection and mutual belonging. They also agreed that, in front of the children, the father would always take the mother's side.

The mother was preparing lunch which wasn't according to the wishes of one of the children. He started humiliating her, criticizing her work, and in line with the old balance, expected the mother to require the father to say something to the child, but the father would keep silent—and the fight would begin. In line with the old ways, the child would blame the parents for the fight and retreat to his room. Now, however, the father raised his voice and decisively forbade the child to speak to his mother like that.

Instead of the expected relief, the child's fierce reaction set in. For the first time, his father actually set a boundary to him. The child began threatening, blackmailing, he was acting offended, even threatened suicide.

A situation that was unbearable for all and wasn't functional was a state of balance for this family. A change in balance significantly shakes the functioning of the whole system.

14 Accepting Developmental Changes and New Balance

Growing up and starting puberty signify an onset of a new period of development which requires changes in all people we live with. The change is noticed by parents in the teen's behavior, who turns from a compliant and obedient child into something we haven't known before. The rules no longer apply, his behavior is beyond all boundaries, he uses expressions that leave us speechless, he has tantrums not allowed in the family, he has ideas and mindset as if he didn't grow up in our family... That is when parents usually wonder: *"What did we do wrong? Where did we go wrong? What did we miss or overlook?"* In this case, putting burden on yourself is a gesture in the spirit of domestic mentality which, however, doesn't bring any possibilities for the role of parents to be solid.

We are faced with a developmental change which speaks in the language of this change. We need to establish which old balance in the family was disturbed and which new balance must be tuned. Which areas need changes? In what way did the family adjust to new developmental needs? Which topics will need to be redefined?

Growing up is surely something that may be very stressful and a new experience for the "people suffering" this process, something not yet lived and something unknown, which requires adjustment and completely new responses. This isn't only about the adolescent. Each individual faces, anew and in a unique way, a fairly equal set of demands, developmental tasks and new needs. This is especially about parents who have to define new boundaries, rules and responsibilities, which doesn't mean abolishing the old ones, but making adjustments. However, changes that affect families when puberty starts are often the ones to point to the need to introduce rules, boundaries and responsibilities.

To become independent, learn how to take responsibility for your behavior and for the consequences of your actions, face the fact that independence means making an independent choice which always brings some kind of consequences we experience first hand and see in other people...all these are great lessons some people never learn. Then there are biological changes, changes in feeling, a completely new understanding of all mutual relationships, the shaping of own identity, and fight for your autonomy. And more and more. All this is taking place in in the sphere of schoolwork and space, during fights with teachers and classmates, events in during and after classes, with parents ad other authorities somewhere in the background.

The communication of a growing child is no longer childishly naive, direct and open; adolescents usually shut themselves in their silent world, they no longer respond with bright and honest eyes; all the time, we have a feeling that they're hiding something, that they aren't satisfied, that they spite us. Their message is that we stink and they don't have respect for anything that is valuable to us.

This requires a change in communication.

Such a change also personally affects parents, most often unconsciously. Going through the period of growing up with our children brings back our stories of growing up and unfinished stories connected with them. A lot of mothers see the opportunity in their daughters' puberty to relive the excitement of the shaping of their own identity, and we see them trying to give the impression that they are their daughters' friends. And a lot of fathers hear a voice when they face their child's puberty saying *"youth isn't over yet, love is in the air"*, and decide to have affairs with younger women.[31]

Each subject of development has its own story with functional patterns, so **Part 2** of this book also gives parents the opportunity to relive the story of their development in an adult way.

---

[31]Example in the chapter on a safe base.

15 Effect of Relationship between Partners on Parenting

Parents who live and parent with their partners experience their child's growing up as an important stress factor in the relationship with their partner.

During puberty, the balance in the relationship between partners has already been established: either both the mother and the father are present in parenting or just one of the partners.

At our workshops, we often encounter cases when the father has been withdrawn or removed from parenting. This has its own story and meaning, which are connected to the delimitation of roles as parents and as partners.

Setbacks in the dynamics of the relationship between partners are usually reflected in diminished ability to carry out the role of parents in a functional and connective manner.

Fights and disagreements between partners which stem from their mutual relationship are usually transferred to parenting.

---

(20) Non-functional Relationships—safe Balance

At first, a couple came. For couples therapy. A very passionate relationship. In love and in war.

She constantly complains because things don't go according to her expectations. He hits the roof, insults and withdraws. This has been going on for a long time and is gradually becoming unbearable. They both realize what they are doing to each other, especially to the children.

When they were attending therapy for a while, the balance in the family began to change, the children became rebellious, they fought with each other. They complained that the children talk back and never do what they have to do. They seemed appalled that the children would start using their patterns they used in fights between them.

Children get accustomed to the balance in the family, whether it is functional and safe or not. In the environment where they live, they assimilate the survival strategies which offer them safety and often also comfort.

We agreed that all of them should come in for a family discussion.

The father, the mother, fourteen-year-old Emma, eleven-year-old Ava.

The father and the mother honestly wanted to hear what was really happening to them. Fourteen-year-old Emma mentioned that she was tired, that constant threats with a divorce were driving her to despair, that her parents should do something, get a divorce or straighten out their relationship, that she was nervous because there was no peace in the house, that demands made to her should be clear because she never knows where she stands, that she felt sorry for her younger sister, she said that she'd survive, but that they had no idea what they were doing to Ava... If they are to divorce, she's going with her dad. She gets along with her mom just fine, she can talk to her about everything, but she can't stand her constant bad mood... All these sentences were accompanied with tears, even though Emma was was very mature and grown-up about it.

Ava's story is shorter. She cries all the time, letting everyone know that she is afraid of the divorce because she loves both of them, because she doesn't know who she should go with. That she only wants mom and dad to talk calmly, and that she doesn't know what to do to make that happen.

When we heard all these stories, everybody was crying, the parents were obviously shaken up. Until we hear such confessions, we never really know what we are doing to our children.

With the relationship with their partner, parents create an atmosphere which affects the functioning of the whole family system. Our experiences confirm that better mutual understanding with a permission to be different and greater empathy between partners brings about a change in all relationships and in the atmosphere in the family. There is less tension, and more willingness and openness for everyone to have their say about important topics and for other family members to actually listen to, and hear, them. The most surprising, however, is that parents, following a change in the relationship with their partner towards a better connection and bonding, speak about automatic changes in the behavior of their children, especially of children who are not teens yet.

A more connected relationship between partners means less tension, less deadly habits, more peace and tolerance, which creates a more tranquil, safer and healthier environment for children to grow up in. It also gives children the feeling of safe attachment.[32]

---

[32]Dallos, 2007.

PART II
Connecting with the Important Developmental Needs of Teens

As adults, we must know the developmental needs of our teens. Each period of development brings a different set of demands to help us make the next step forward in life. Growing through the transitional period between childhood and adulthood, young people become equipped for independent life in the world of adults. This requires skills which can't be learned at school, life skills. Parents no longer have the opportunity to supervise development, and we don't know what the future holds. Our job is to help our children enter independence with an awareness that they are equipped with self-esteem and a feeling of safety.

In addition to knowing the key developmental needs of our children, they also need us to respond to their needs as the people who are most important to them, and to give them feedback which creates a safe environment in which to grow up. The most important message growing children need from their parents is that we care about them.

What are the needs of growing children?

The parents' problem when identifying needs is that they don't distinguish between needs and wants. Teens say that they need plenty of things: from a high-performance mobile and all that i-stuff, headphones, computers, and sports equipment to clothes. Material things are just support for their needs, and constitute wants. Needs require skills and equipment for life, life wisdom. Wants change and may be put off, while needs can't be put off. This is especially worth emphasizing at this time, when *to have* has become a greater value than *to be*. Even if we can't make all teens' wishes come true in a short period of time—also because some people face financial distress—we can still meet the needs which will help our children survive in the long run.

137

If a teen pressures us into buying him a new bike so he can go out with friends, we need to know that socializing is, in fact, their need, that they really need experience which can only be gained in contact with their peers. A need is also that teens appear self-confident in front of their peers. But the bike? That's a want. A bike may also be a need (perhaps it's the best way to get to and from school), but its brand and equipment are wants. Skills important for wants mean that we know how to delay their satisfaction. A want may also be satisfied later, not immediately. In any case, satisfying wants isn't the parents' obligation, but it is a great opportunity for teens to participate, adding their own input and contributing their share. This way, they learn skills and gain an important experience—that adults are responsible for satisfying needs.

If a teen wants a motorbike, this is his want. It is absolutely connected to his developmental needs, which are related to the fact that he wants to feel independence, that he has to know how to take responsibility, that he has to know the boundaries, how to take care of himself and his safety, and be sensible to other people. So a motorbike can be a great opportunity for the teen to learn how to be independent, and to see that parents are there to support him.

Because teens and their parents don't see eye to eye about the definition of developmental needs, complications arise in the want area. Teens usually conclude: *"Because you didn't buy me what I wanted, I don't matter to you, you don't understand me, you don't understand my vital needs, and you don't care about me."* Knowing developmental needs will enable us to avoid communication traps and bring more certainty into our decisions.

The awareness that experiences in the period of growing up shape the identity of future generations of adults is a responsibility also for those of us who convey important life messages. The messages we convey depends on our choice and values.

The selection of titles in this chapter is based on practical attitude and experience, our values and beliefs. Most often, parents put school and everything related to it first. According to our plan, this topic appears in the next part. There are many other skills we need in order to live independently, and which we don't learn at school. Many aspects of growing up are ignored and neglected by our elementary school, but are important for our children's lives in the future. Therefore, we describe the areas of needs of growing children:

first, because we simply can't ignore those areas, and second, because we wish to point out their mutual connection and interlacing.

People are more social creatures than we might realize. We need other people, we need responses, we need bonding and safety. Learning social skills[33] is our opportunity to change the direction of our mutual relationships towards our civilization, taking an essential step forward.

We can't imagine functional mutual relationships without the ability to empathize. In this chapter, we attempt to sum up what people need to be able to meet our needs in contact with others. This is a completely different knowledge than we know from our everyday conversations, knowledge which shapes conscious attitudes to the world and to people. From the awareness of safe belonging to our family, the awareness that we can make it alone, that we have the permission of others to do just that and, within ourselves, to be aware of our self-worth and sense of acceptance.

And another important note.

This book contains plenty of stories with effective and useful solutions that will inject some hope into any situation. The stories are all true and verified. But remember: Everything described as having worked, only worked when parents were connected to their children, when they worked towards the safe connection described in **Part 1** of this book. Therefore, if the outcome is negative, this first part should be reread, again and again.

---

[33]Goleman (2006).

1 How to Set Boundaries: We've Tried Everything, But Nothing Works

The situations in which we become most aware of the importance of respecting boundaries in life are human tragedies. We are hurt when accidents happen because someone ignored speed limits or because of alcohol or other intoxicating substance consumption, when we hear about tragic stories brought on by the disregard of the borrowing limit when the economy collapses, when divorces in our families happen because partners didn't respect the boundaries of fidelity or crossed the line when flirting with other people. Boundaries exist so that society can function, so we have the freedom to create and reach beyond narrow-mindedness. The boundaries that ensure functioning are vital, and our job is to pass them on to our children.

Knowing boundaries means ensuring safety. Boundaries are like a wall— if you put us into a dark room where we don't know where the walls are, we will wander in discomfort until we reach a wall. We may compare the sense of security in knowing where the walls are to the sense of security in knowing and being aware of boundaries.[34]

This applies to both parents and children. It means that we know where we stand. The boundaries we need are the boundaries of stability. Parents often confuse the boundaries of safety with the restriction and obstruction of freedom. This is not the same. Living safely with boundaries enables us to be creatively free.

Boundaries are something that change with development. When our teen was a few years younger, his boundaries were narrow, but now they need to widen. This runs parallel to the development of responsibility.

Our job as parents is that our teen internalizes a healthy attitude towards boundaries, and learns to respect them as part of his self and self-discipline. Without respecting boundaries as a skill, the child will have problems achieving balanced adulthood and independence.

Boundaries may be rigid or flexible or non-existent. Boundaries are what works in life as a boundary, not what we imagine or want it to be. If we wish for our children to come home from school at a particular time (which we deem a boundary), but in fact, they arrive as they please, the boundary only

---

[34]Dallos & Draper (2015).

exists as our wish, but not in reality. Boundaries live in family life as a pattern. Our own patterns and experience carry the messages about our attitude to boundaries, and how we were taught about such attitudes. But this has already been discussed in **Part 1**.

Parents who come to us are often at the end of their rope, because their boundaries aren't respected. Most of these parents didn't know how, or didn't manage, to set boundaries for their children when they were younger, and to adjust them to changes in boundaries as they were growing up.

There is a myriad of sad stories about failing to set boundaries, but there is also a plethora of comical stories about the same subject. We need to be aware that teens have power. And that they can beat us with it, if we start a war with them.

Do you know the feeling when you prohibit your child or don't allow him to do something, and the child doesn't respect that at all? We get the feeling of powerlessness, being lost, and one big important question arises: *"What should I do?"*

Do you know the feeling, when you just want to slap him and you feel like this is the only way to clearly show: *"I'm serious!"* Do you know the feeling, when you constantly struggle to bring the child up "right," and for him not to suffer too much? You feel fear, worry and doubt.

People with safe but flexible boundaries feel more safety and trust in their relationships. Their value is to stay connected and bonded. The term "flexible" doesn't denote giving in. It is about talking and coming to agreements which, during puberty, becomes negotiation. But we still preserve clear rules and boundaries.

Children like to respond to the energy their parents or adults radiate, and when they assess that we carry fear or doubt, that our demand won't be realized, they are more than happy to oblige. Such fear brings out our powerlessness, and we can see children who do what they want—regardless of their age, and parents who shrug their shoulders in their powerlessness and say: *"What can I do? We've tried everything..."*

A clear boundary is like a frame that determines the area we know and where we are safe. In this area, we know what the world is like, what the consequences are if we misbehave, and more importantly, we know that we carry our share of responsibility for wellbeing in this field.

Let's take a look at a typical story of a father we will all remember from when we were growing up.

---

(21) Hanging Out

It was a relaxed kind of day. My wife and I were having coffee in the garden, talking about how great our life was. Then our fifteen-year-old son joined us. I felt that he was slightly tense and nervous, and I got a feeling in my stomach that the tranquility was over for the day.

"What is it, son? What's bothering you?" I asked.

He looked at me softly (such manipulations sometimes work, and this is always the first thing they try.), and firmly uttered, I don't know, a question or a statement—fact: "I'd like to stay out until two in the morning."

My wife and I looked at each other, shocked. I asked him if he could leave us alone for five minutes.

When he left, we talked about this jaunt, what we wanted to know, and produced a joint story. (At this point, I'd like to say that we don't necessarily have to agree. It's just that the story must be the same so that we can both stand by it.)

When he got back, we just said: "We allow you to be out until 23:30."

You probably know the reaction that followed. A myriad of horrible words, an inappropriate tone of voice, uncontrolled dynamics of his body...and a walk-out from the scene. For a while. Then he returned, and started begging (these are techniques engineered to test a parent's patience), looking softly, promising...

"You won't achieve anything this way, son. I want to know where you're going, who you're going with, who I know, what you're going to do there..."

Then a few more sentences on invading his privacy, his right to be free, etc. We just sat there, in silence, looking at him nicely. Our gaze clearly said: "It doesn't matter what you think. Until we have this information, we aren't budging."

Our son slowly calmed down, provided us with the information and, in the end, repeated the fact that he wanted to be out until two.

"Midnight," said my wife.

"One, pleeeeaaaase."

Silence.

"Okay. Can I stay out until half past midnight and you come pick me up. This way you'll see if I'm okay. This will buy me an extra hour for next time."

We agreed with this suggestion, and observed the happiness in the eyes of our teen. He fought it out, he set the time, we trust him...yeeeah!

Related Topics
Attitude to Authority | What to Do with Rules? | Taking Responsibility | Autonomy and Individuality | Power Struggle | Addiction, Dependence

Within the Scope of Awareness

The skill of setting boundaries is connected with our personal experience. Did we feel safe with the way our parents set boundaries for us? Were the boundaries too rigid and prevented us from living? Were the boundaries chaotic?

Boundaries can be flexible, more or less closed or open, loose or rigid. But it is essential that they are clearly and firmly defined.

If we experienced the setting of boundaries as violent or aggressive, we often adopt the principle: *I won't do that to my child.* And while we justifiably renounce the use of violence and aggression, we overlook the need to set boundaries. These are also patterns with which we shape our image of authority. It involves many beliefs we have developed as a generation which was raised with more aggression, abuse of power, and violence. Setting boundaries isn't aggressive, it is persistent, consistent and determined. It is about our internal attitude: are we comfortable with giving in, or with standing up for ourselves (being assertive) and setting clear boundaries?

Many parents face an internal dilemma: *if I constrain my child too much, he won't like me anymore.* Setting boundaries isn't the same as constraining. Many dilemmas of parents who want their child to develop freely arise from this, but often end up with the popular diagnosis of ADHD (attention deficit hyperactivity disorder).[35] Boundaries are related to the clear structure of everyday life. What does that mean?

---

[35]This doesn't apply as a general rule, since the ADHD issue can't be simplified to only one factor. Our position stems from experience, since we have dealt with many cases in our practice when hyperactive behavior was linked to the lack of clear boundaries and a first structure. When parents managed to set boundaries and enforce them in their everyday lives, their children's hyperactive behavior "miraculously" faded away.

Parents bring structure to life all the time by carrying out certain tasks which are self-evident and which we don't negotiate about, because that is just the way it is in our family. This is more easily achieved in younger children than older ones.

Structure is related to repetitive rituals, and is a pleasant experience for our children, who take it for granted. Rituals and behaviors we don't negotiate about and don't explain, they are just there. Just like we introduced, without negotiations and discussions, the rule that we use cutlery when eating, that we use a spoon to eat soup. And that when we use the toilet, we behave hygienically, from using the toilet paper, rinsing and cleaning the toilet to washing our hands. This is self-evident and part of the culture of living in our time and space. A clear structure contains the rules we have introduced which work. The emphasis is on the fact that something works—not what we want and what we argue about every day, over and over again.

Structure and related boundaries depend on what we can do. First, about ourselves. If we have an idea that our children should respect the rules about eating at the table designated for dining, the question is whether our behavior defined this table as a dining table. Is this just one of the possible locations which we choose on the basis of vague rules?

The idea of respecting boundaries and rules, first and foremost, stems from our experience of everyday life at home.

When we recognize in our teen a developmental need to widen the boundaries, we respond. However, widening boundaries in no way a means abolishing them!

Unfortunately, parenting issues are never simple, they are mostly connected with something and multilayered. In the case described above, the connection with focus is of great importance, as our teens always try to sidetrack us.

We need to think about what wants and needs are. What is our parenting goal? Are we aware of boundaries? Is the boundary clearly delimited in our awareness? (Until when can our teen stay out?)

Is this boundary adjusted to our teen's wider needs?

Is this boundary safe for us, do we feel comfortable with it? (The teen's argument that all his peers can holiday with their friends alone, which worries us, won't put our mind at ease.)

Can we persist with negotiations? (We stand less chance of being successful by using power or fighting than by cooperating.)

Respecting boundaries comes from experience when violation brings expected and predicted consequences. Every child will test our seriousness when we set a certain boundary. So we need to be ready, and we need to know what our next step is going to be to protect the boundary.

The story about boundaries is linked to another topic which gains momentum during puberty—attitude to pleasure. A very important skill is to delay immediate satisfaction of a certain need to the appropriate time. It is about the interlacing of the functions of self-control, control over your feelings, and intellectual abilities.

Tips and Solutions

Our job as parents is to distinguish between wants and needs. If we look at the story more closely, we can clearly and swiftly recognize our child's wants. It isn't our job to make every wish come true, and it is not a good life lesson for us to do so. On the other hand, the realization of, or help with the satisfaction of, needs is our responsibility and duty, as this way we help our child to become more independent and self-confident.

What is a want in the story above?

Going out for a concert with friends.

What is a need?

The need to socialize, have fun, trust in parents and be trusted by parents, the need for experience, the need to make one's own decisions (independence and autonomy). And first and foremost, for parents to keep their authority over the setting of boundaries.

When parents insisted on their son coming home early, they restricted the satisfaction of the want (you can't have everything immediately), with which they conveyed the message that trust is built in several steps. In the end, they accepted their son's suggestion about when he should come home, and of course, the privilege he would have if he came home "okay." Okay is in quotation marks, because every family has their own criteria about that. What is "okay?" Can he have one beer or no beers? You need to agree on that in advance. Rules and boundaries must be heard and be clear. If they aren't, and you say to your child that he didn't stick to your agreement, you lose your opportunity to negotiate. Not only won't you trust him, but he also won't trust you. That is when your teen says that you are "screwing him over." Wise parents learn from experience to check that their teen heard and understood their rules and boundaries with a simple question: *"What do you think of that?"*

Let's go back for a bit. The son suggested an earlier hour, and his parents agreed. In spite of everything, he got a feeling that he determined the time when he had to be home (independence), and that it wasn't easy and he had to try hard (very little possibility of him being late).

What will happen if he is late? That is a consequence of not respecting the agreement. The teen must know that in advance, so that he can choose between the privilege and the consequence.

We favor the principle that teens choose both themselves.[36]

The following question opens up for some people: *"Son, what will happen if you pull a fast one, if you won't be at the agreed place or if you are late?"*

Answer: He determined the consequence. If he adjusts the consequence so that we aren't satisfied with its effects, we can correct it to be more educational. An example of a consequence of disregarding boundaries:

Teen's suggestion: *"Next time, I'll be home an hour earlier."*

Consequence determined by parents: *"We won't negotiate for a month about being out after eleven pm."*

Parents have the authority to determine the rules of the game: take it or leave it. It seems that consequences bring less comfort than privileges. From our experience, most such agreements are observed. The teen won't be late. The balance is disturbed in families where consequences never happened to the children when they were growing up, which in turn has to do with how parents were brought up.

In such cases, we speak of the severe distress of parents, and things that should have been set a long time ago should be set. Children fight this and sometimes huge battles arise. Parents can overcome such situations with professional help, if necessary.

---

[36]More information on the principle of choice and consequence is in one of the next chapters.

2 What to Do with Rules? Keep Them, Drop Them, Change Them?

Rules are directly related to boundaries. Every family has its own rules, usually unwritten, which develop with time and are part of every segment of family life. These are rules on accepting agreements, solving difficult situations, the manner of communication, on the way we feel and think, on the use of power, behavior at home and outside and, last but not least, rules on how to respect rules—do we respect them at all, and how.

Rules are usually repeated, and ensure predictability and safety in life. They also create the spirit of family life and connect family members, as well as define the family's identity. By having rules on how to live together, families create stability. Certain rules are more visible, others function without us even being aware of them. Some rules are more easily negotiated, while we don't even begin to negotiate about others.

Rules change with developmental changes, and every family has its own patterns for following such changes. In some families, rules are rigid and difficult to change. A change is a threat to well-being and brings chaos. In other families, rules change in a soft and safe manner, with calm agreements.

A change reported by parents of teens is an impression that the teen wants to demolish all existing rules in the family. So, what should be done with rules and teens?

Attitude to rules takes shape in families long before there is a teen in the house, and he learns his attitude to rules by living with us.

Have we been consistent about rules so far? How did we, years ago, introduce the rule on children sleeping in their own beds and not coming to their parents' bed at night? How did we later introduce the bedtime rule? If we introduced the bedtime rule in a way in which words said one thing, but something else was actually carried out (in violation of the spoken rule), then we let our child know that rules don't have to be respected.

Did we introduce rules during family rituals?

Which rules need to be adjusted for our teens, and which ones need to be changed?

Which rules are our whims, so that it wouldn't be reasonable for us to stick with them?

147

(22) Rules to Stick to at the Table

We are a seven-member family. At our house, it's always very lively and loud, it can be merry or very stressful.

We perform a ritual in the form of a common meal, which means that, no matter what, I make sure that we gather at the table at least once a day. Sometimes that's lunch, sometimes supper. I believe this means a lot to all of us.

My stance is that we live what we eat, and that it's very important to eat in peace. I do my best, and always cook with love, and it hurts me if I don't feel respect for the food I've prepared, and for our stomachs.

Three of my children are teens, the youngest two are about to become teens, and the dynamic is really hectic. A lot of wisecracking, small conflicts (who's got whose sweater, socks...). My husband and I noticed that such a dynamic occurs more and more often during our meals. The tension was rising, the children were tossing all kinds of inappropriate labels at each other. I was growing increasingly nervous, as was my husband. One of us raised our voice. The children looked in amazement, pounced on us, and all hell broke loose at the table.

I couldn't stand it anymore, this feeling of tension after each lunch, my stomach hurt, our common meals began to infuriate me, they became a burden.

I said politely several times that I couldn't eat in such an atmosphere, that I didn't feel well... Nothing changed.

Then my husband and I made a silent agreement. As we were sitting at the table, he asked for attention and told them:

"Mom and I deserve to eat in peace, we love eating together with you guys, as soon as you start with arguing, we'll take the salad bowl and eat in another room. This is what we need and we are not backing down from this!"

The atmosphere at the table was calm and pleasant for a while, but then, of course, someone said something which another one took personally, they set up, as always, two or three camps, and KABOOM.

My husband and I got up, silently, took our salads, and left. After a while, silence fell upon the kitchen. We were eating in another room in heavenly peace when they came, promising that they would respect our rule about not fighting during lunch.

We didn't go back to the table that day, because we wanted to show that we were serious and that the rule was really important to us. The children were left without the salad they love, while we were full like we hadn't been in a long time.

Naturally, energies still rise sometimes, but it is enough if I say: "We're having lunch, please, stop."

So, for us to be able to eat lunch in peace, we never discuss unpleasant stories, not even school, during our meals. We talk about fun things, success, we tell each other jokes... After lunch, our ritual is to remain at the table and that's when we solve complicated issues.

Related Topics

Where Are the Boundaries? | Attitude to Authority | Part 1 of the Book | Power Struggle | Taking Responsibility | Attention-Deficit Disorder, Hyperactivity

Within the Scope of Awareness

Instead of insisting on rules and their observance, which quickly results in authoritarian parenting, the abuse of power and the dynamics of inferiority, we should instead focus on our needs. Many needs are satisfied in our everyday lives. Eating is one of our needs. In the story described above, the need of family members was not to get upset and irritated during lunch. Lunch is a ritual. And each ritual has its own unwritten rules. The family learned that a long time ago. The rules determine how family members should behave when eating, with every person having their role. The rule the teens tried to change was the possibility to resolve mutual tensions at the table, which meant trying to start a game where camps would be formed and a power struggle would begin. The opposing rule (and boundary) the parents introduced was: the atmosphere during lunch is tranquil, lunchtime is dedicated to connecting, we want to enjoy food, stress and burden free. More difficult subjects can be resolved after lunch.

This family has plenty of other rules, for example where the dishes in the kitchen are stored, how to squeeze toothpaste, which bowls are used for cat food, how to tidy up after yourself in the bathroom, how to tidy up the room where they leave shoes and coats, is it allowed (and when) to eat outside the dining room, etc. These rules are constantly violated. The parents' response to the violation of "petty rules" largely defines the atmosphere in families, and the children's belief about their parents' intolerance.

In families where violations of rules are unacceptable, where violations lead to catastrophic reactions, and the defensive (reactive) belief develops that you mustn't say anything, that openness is something that will be sanctioned. As children enter their teens, such families face rebellion and more violations of rules which, along with intensive emotional dynamics, can result in intensive violations of boundaries.

A family is a system which regulates itself with its own rules. Rules are made and they change in every period of development. Each period requires different rules and adjustments to the needs of family members, meaning that each member and the family as a whole need to adjust. Rules and responses to them arise from learning by trial and error. We adopt certain rules from our parents, while others were transferred from the culture and the environment we live in. Some rules are shaped anew. The family system arranges, through rules, what is allowed and what isn't. Every family makes its own rules, which are typical of the family. Rules aren't written, they are more guidelines shaped on the basis of repetitive experiences. Rules are manners of behavior of family members in certain situations which turned out to be the most functional. Therefore, rules can't be unambiguous, we can't be sure in advance, or determine what is right for a certain family and what isn't.

Let's imagine that we are visiting a family with completely different habits and rules than we are used to. In some cultures, family members respect a rule – what is presented as a habit - that by entering the house, they change shoes for slippers. This is a rule which regulates the behavior of all family members, and generates various responses and dynamics among family members. We can't even begin to discuss the reasonableness of this rule, since every family has its own reasons to introduce or not introduce such a policy. We may not know the rule, and when we attempt to overstep the boundary about not being allowed to wear shoes inside the house, the mother lets us know, clearly and decisively, about the rules in the family. We may be offered slippers when we arrive as a guest, letting us know that there is a habit (rule) in this house of changing into slippers. Slippers may simply be in the hallway, and we don't know whether it is optional or necessary for us to put them on. We face a dilemma: if we don't put them on, will they say anything? Or will they silently put up with us breaking the rule, making us all (them and us) uncomfortable? Will they dare say what the rule in their family is about wearing slippers? How important is this rule for this family? It may be an opinion the parents have prepared about wearing slippers, as opposed to a practice in the family. It may be people's negative attitude to wearing slippers. Some people may find this habit intrusive. For some people, baring their feet is a greater invasion of their privacy than taking off their clothes. For others, wearing slippers is an outdated, narrow-minded habit which violates the criteria of good taste. However, when we try to rationalize habits that for us are strange, we are engaged in a hopeless enterprise. Is wearing slippers a sign of feeling at home? Is this a way to make a visitor feel more at home? But how can we engage in something that, for us, feels so strange, while remaining respectful? Should we, before each visit, prepare a list of possible arguments for and against wearing slippers? We can simply turn a blind eye to opinions and possible outcomes, disregard all of the aforementioned, and simply introduce a new rule when we visit. Are we conventional or unconventional? In awkward situations, we can save ourselves by being respectfully curious: *"What is the habit in your house about wearing outdoor shoes inside?"*

The rule may also be adjusted to various ages. The rule may not apply to young children. Certain behaviors of family members about taking off their shoes may be related to the rule. Do we take them off anywhere, or at a clearly defined and agreed place? When family members break the agreement about taking off their shoes, we can see the importance of the rule for the functioning of the family system. Do parents respond to children's violations, and how? Do children remind their parents that they are breaking the rule? How do they communicate, in this case? Is it unacceptable to break this rule? Are there double standards about this rule for different family members? Are there double standards for family members and visitors? Do parents unconditionally require their children to wear slippers, while they allow guests to choose whether they will wear them or not? Which messages do family members convey to one another about the rule? Do parents remind their children to put their shoes in the agreed place, but children disregard them, and then parents silently put the shoes away for them?

The seemingly unimportant and marginal rule is related to the very hectic life of a family. Establishing a rule may also be a pattern communicating the way family members function with each other.[37]

Tips and Solutions

The idea to prevent our teen, by ordering him, from doing something what they have fought for within their idea of adulthood, which hasn't been a rule in the family thus far, usually doesn't work. Using the word "rule" when communicating with a teen is not a promising path.

Also setting rules (as we set them years ago) and children obeying them doesn't lead to good solutions. If rules are communicated to teens using our position of power, they may experience it as an invitation to fight. And they will always respond to such an invitation. So what's the best way?

Rules (which will not be called rules, but rather "needs for life") are accepted by teens because of bonding, the sense of belonging, connection, because it is in our awareness that we care for each other. We have learned this first-hand, and it has always been our starting point.

All parents are concerned that their children won't respect certain important rules. And then our fears gathering around certain rules give rise to our horrible images or movies that we play out in our heads.[38] Sample fantasies: that our child will hang out with bad people, that he will stop learning, that he will disregard us, that he will just take off, that he will start taking drugs, become homeless, a delinquent, a deadbeat...

Based on these fears, we start pressuring our children in everyday life, when they don't put away the food they have eaten in front of the TV, when they don't turn off the computer at the agreed time, when they don't put their shoes in the agreed place, when they don't bring their clothes when we do the laundry, when they don't study and do schoolwork rationally... (Because we continue playing out the fantasy in our heads, creating the

---

[37] An important subject of the systems theory, cf. **Dallos & Draper** (2015)

[38] As we mentioned in several places in Part I, eg. under the title *Parents' Intrusiveness.*

belief that: *"if he can't respect the minimum rules of family life, how will he respect critical rules."*)

And we so launch an attack led by our fears and distrust, which lands us in the area of genuine disregard. This way, we lose the connection and show ourselves to our teens as someone trying to assert power. In such cases, the effect is usually rebellion and disregard for our intentions. This is the case for numerous parents who have chosen the path described. When they sought our help, the path out of the world of the disregard for rules with severe consequences took much more hard work, and was much more painful for everyone.

We also need to decide which rules are more, and which are less, important (in the long run). Our long-term connection is probably more important than a tidy room or messy clothes. Also the rule regarding how (and how much) a teen should study relates to our fantasy about studying. The fact is that we can't study for them. We need to answer the question of whether we will insist on our rules which don't make any sense to our teen, and are our whims, for the price of connection.

However, there are rules which aren't negotiable. These are rules which refer to our values. That we survive and afford goods by working, in an honest way. That we don't destroy our health. That we respect other people's possessions. That we keep up our personal cleanliness and the cleanliness of our home. That our home is our safety zone. Families differ in this respect, determining their values as they see sensible.

---

(23) Rules known in advance

 First day of high school. The son brought home an enrollment certificate, and I told him: "You'll need this certificate in several copies, one for your student ID, one for your monthly transportation pass, one for the student job center, and one for free accommodation in this family."

My son was really excited about the new things of the first school day, and only asked, after a while, what I meant by "free accommodation".

The answer was clear: "You can live in this house for free, as long as you have a valid enrollment certificate. This will apply until you finish your studies. We'll give you one year, if you ever fail. Once you don't have an enrollment certificate, this means that you have to contribute your share to living in this house, to the costs of living, meaning electricity, water, municipal utility services, etc., and food. To be able to do this, you'll have to earn money. You also know that, without an enrollment certificate, you don't have a scholarship, and we have no intention to give you money for all your needs."

We didn't discuss this issue again, and even when he had to re-sit his exams and passed them, the first thing he did was to show us his enrollment certificate.

This is an example of when the child took the rule seriously, because it was articulated unconditionally, and it wasn't just his parents' whim. It was based on his experience that his mother was serious about it. And the rule was defined in advance, at the beginning of the school year, when there were no issues and doubts about school performance, handled calmly and without agitation.

Royal Path to Learning How to Be Responsible and Preserve Our Authority

The way we respect rules is related to the creation and preservation of our authority.

Our experiences have taught us that it is more effective if we talk about rules with our teens in advance, and present them as their choice. Instead of using the logic: because you broke the rule, you're in for a punishment (or a consequence), the logic based on choice and mutual agreement is far more functional. Of course, parents are the ones who must set boundaries and rules. But the pattern is always the same: *"You can choose between behavior A and consequence A, or between behavior B and consequence B."* Consequence A is usually linked to more comfort, and aimed at healthy development, but also requires hard work. Consequence B offers a simpler and more comfortable path, but it is less favorable for the child's development, and significantly less pleasant for the child.

Table 4: *Choice Boxes*

Choice 1	Choice 2
Behavior A (you do your best) **Consequence A** (comfort)	**Behavior B** (you pursue comfort and don't try hard) **Consequence B** (discomfort)

As most complications and fighting spirits occur in such cases, let's take a look how we can carry this out in a concrete situation.

---

(24) Choice instead of Punishment

 The children could hardly wait to watch their favorite TV sit-com on Monday night; all their peers watched it, and it was a common topic of conversations among them. At that time, we didn't even watch TV during the week, and this included my wife and me. My daughter asked if she could watch the aforementioned series at eight.

Father: "Have you cleaned up the kitchen, as I told you to?"

Daughter: "Not yet."

Father: "Look, you have a choice. It's four o'clock now. Clean up by five and you can watch the sitcom. But you can also choose not to clean up and not to watch."

When, at five, the kitchen wasn't clean, I didn't get upset that she hadn't cleaned up, and that she wouldn't watch the sitcom as punishment; instead, I said, indifferently and nonchalantly:

"You made an interesting choice, not to watch the series at eight."

My daughter didn't say anything, and I know that, deep down, she was mad at herself. She still had to clean up the kitchen.

This way, a rule becomes something that teens experience as the power of autonomous choice. The consequence of their choice also belongs to them. This is the way to teach them what responsibility is. We allow them to feel freedom, independence, the use of their own will. This way, we also

155

avoid being a culprit or enemy in the eyes of our teen, who must be besieged and attacked until he dishonorably capitulates.

The awareness that we are responsible for the consequences of our choices is the awareness we wish for all adults, independent and responsible people, to have.

The choice is ours, and it is related to how we convey violations: do we complain, nag, humiliate, yell, use power...? Or are we, when conveying violations, still in touch with caring habits?

Violations of Rules: Consequences Instead of Punishment

As our children grow up, they get to know our responses. This means that they know whether our words are worth something, or we are just saying something, but then nothing happens.

With our responses to violations, overstepping boundaries, asserting rules, respecting authority in the years before puberty, we build a solid foundation. The quality of this foundations will make our life with the same topics during puberty easier or more difficult. Have we learned to argue with our child? Have we tried to explain things to him, in a friendly way and without conflicts, or has the child had stronger arguments? Do we exhaust ourselves trying to get the child to hear us and see that our intentions are good?

Children don't listen to us, they watch us. Therefore, it is only sensible that violations of rules are followed by consequences. What are consequences?

First and foremost, a consequence means that we respond to a violation.

If we resort to punishment, teens understand that as invitations to power struggles. This usually results in rebellion, and the relationship develops on the battle field, where our persistence is bound to yield. This way, we also choose behaviors which don't preserve our connections and destroy relationships.

A consequence happens on the basis of something announced in advance. So it is a prerequisite for predefined rules. This means that we need to act consciously, prudently, not impulsively.

"You'll get your allowance when you take out the trash."

"Next time you are half an hour late, your outing will be half an hour shorter."

Carrying out consequences requires parents to be consistent, and able to actually carry out the actions they have announced. It is dangerous for us to lose our sanity in emotional turmoil and announce unrealistic consequences: *"If you use such humiliating words when talking to me once more, you won't go out all summer."* Remember that our actions are bound by consequences, as we need to support them. Consequences are "punishment" for parents. Therefore, it is important if we can play our role when it comes to fulfilling the announced consequences.

---

(25) He is Late

 On a night out, a fifteen-year-old son chatted with his friends too long, and forgot about the time. He had never been late before. His mother waited for him at home for a while, but then went to the bar where he and his friends were sitting on the pavement, talking intensely.

"Mom, what are you getting so worked up about?"

"Well, I'm worried about you and play all sorts of scenarios in my head."

"Geez, you can see that I didn't get hit by a car."

The mother, upset and in a slightly raised voice: "Yes, I did think of this and was really worried."

"Mom, c'mon, keep it down."

"I won't keep it down because I was worried sick, and I want you to know that."

"C'mon, let's go home."

The mother walked in front, and her son and three of his friends treaded silently behind her in line. The next morning, his friends came to visit and commented on his mother's behavior: "That thing yesterday was really too much."

Mother: "Next time he's late and doesn't call me, I'll step on the table and howl across the whole place for everyone to hear!"

The mother showed relentlessness and firm determination to insist on the consequences she had presented. No matter what other people think.[39] By doing so, she set the boundaries and the rules that apply to them. We should also note that the mother's word gained credibility with years of the child's experience, when words uttered and announced were always followed by actions.

---

(26) Skipping School

 Students underwent an external assessment of knowledge at an elementary school. A mother had just sighed in relief, when she got a phone call from school. Her son didn't return to school after the first hours of the assessment. She followed the paths and locations of her teen years, and soon met her son, sitting on the riverbank. He asked her, astonished: "What are you doing here?"

Mother: "I should ask you the same question."

Son: "What are you fussing about? Yeah, we had the tests and I was tired. Anyway, I knew you wouldn't let me go home."

Mother: "You know what we agreed. If you need anything special, you can see the counselor and call me. You haven't even tried that."

Son: "I know you wouldn't have let me."

The mother took her son to the car and drove off. When she didn't head home, but to school, he remarked grudgingly: "Where are you taking me now?"

Mother: "I'm giving you another chance to check if I would let you go home."

She walked her son to his classroom, and opened the door widely, so that all of his classmates could see her.

Her son didn't call, he came home in silence.

The younger daughter asked during lunch: "Did Mom really take you back to class today?"

Son: "How do you know that?"

Daughter: "The whole school was talking about it."

---

[39] The parents' weakness is precisely in the area of "what will other people, neighbors, relatives think or say" and, therefore, we give in because of shame, handing over the power to our teens. Their negotiation strategy and their fight for their interests take place in the area of "I don't care what other people think."

What was important in the mother's behavior? She was aware of what worried her—her son thought that by skipping school he'd gain a reputation among his peers. She managed to control her emotions and, instead, she was curious. She remembered how it was when she was his age, what went through her head, what she resorted to. And surprisingly, children didn't even change the location for their truancy.

When she found her son, she kept her role as an adult and a stable person. At first, she explored the child's way of thinking. In spite of his inconsistencies, she remained in the role of a fair adult who gave second chances. On the one hand, she kept her authority, being aware of the power of consequences, while on the other, she gave her son the opportunity to choose. By driving the child back to school, the mother showed that she wasn't willing to negotiate school attendance, but that she was willing to negotiate leaving school early for a good reason. Her son didn't pick the second option, reaffirming his experience of what rules were and where boundaries were.

Persistence in rules and boundaries, which become a way of life, ensures that teens don't overstep boundaries in a direction that would worry us. Keeping rules means that we live with our teens within boundaries which lead to functional outcomes and mutual cooperation, which means respect of the agreed time and of boundaries regarding schoolwork, respect of the boundaries and rules related to the spending of money, the consumption of intoxicating substances, the appropriation of other people's possessions, comfort, work habits, attitude to yourself, your body and health, and to the overcoming of hurdles. Experiences which exceed the expectations described will be discussed in our next book.

We need to take into account that as the teens' brain develops, the need to experience new things, and to raise the adrenaline and dopamine levels occurs. This is most quickly achieved with behavior that oversteps boundaries. Therefore, these needs will be satisfied without harmful effects, if our teens internalize life with boundaries and rules.

3 Attitude to Authority

Respect of authority is a skill needed to develop internal discipline, to live in the hierarchically-arranged world ruled by rules and laws. It is also the path to develop self-discipline.

We shouldn't mix authority as a function and a skill for life with authoritarian attitude. Authority provides structure and safety, while authoritarian attitude suppresses the possibility of free development, autonomous expression, and creativity.

The experience of authority is an internal experience, enabling us to be comfortable with rules and boundaries in our lives. The experience of authoritarian supervision is an experience of abuse and suppression.

In our attitude to authority, and especially when choosing our behavior, parents may face doubts and fears, also discomfort and fear that this means aggression and violence. Some people link understanding authority with memories of restricted freedom. Regarding our own beliefs and past experiences, which influence our behavior in the role of parents, we should consider what we discussed in **Part 1** of the book.

Authority means that we are stable inside, and stand firmly behind our positions, decisions, and behaviors. Authority enables us to feel guilt-free when making parenting decisions, and not to act ambiguously and unreliably. It is important not to enable or open the possibility in our minds that teens would oppose our setting of boundaries, and respect of agreements and rules. This is affected by past experiences which define the level of respect of our authority. If we didn't know how to, or want to assert our authority in the past, our teen will have a difficult time accepting a change in parenting with authority.

Doubts about the use of authority occur in parents when they need to limit, prevent, or insist on agreements which don't sit well with teens. Parents find themselves on a slippery slope, as teens rebel and try using arguments to get their parents to change their decision. Doubts are often connected with unclear recognition of what our child really needs and where the boundary of his pampering is.

Is satisfying needs the same as fulfilling wants? Remember that wants and needs are not the same. Let's take a look at an example of communication between a new teen and her mother.

(27) Kind Mom

When I got pregnant, I promised myself that I'd be a nice mommy, that I'd never raise my voice, let alone raise my hand to a child. I didn't exactly have a beautiful childhood, there was a lot of physical violence from my dad, and a lot of emotional blackmail from mom. (I remember a sentence that used to be said frequently: "I'm sad about Dad as it is, don't you do this to me too...")

So I'll be a different mom, a better one.

That's why I left my husband so quickly. He had overly high principles and determination. It smelled of violence. So the little one and I were left by ourselves. I was convinced I'd make it. I thought to myself that I had to do the contrary of what I was taught, and he'd grow to be an ideal man.

My upbringing approach was kind. I used to explain everything: why we should brush our teeth, why we sleep in pajamas, why we don't eat with our hands. I never forced him to do anything. If he didn't want to go to bed at eight, he went at nine. If he wasn't hungry at two, he ate at half past two. I spent a lot of time being with him, and lost a lot of friends along the way.

When Ethan was ten years old, I felt utterly tired, and began observing our relationship. Everything I did was for him, for his wants or needs (I didn't know the difference), while I no longer knew who I was, what I needed or wanted.

I noticed that my child didn't actually do what I said, didn't stick to any agreements, and that he enjoyed himself more and more, and worked less and less.

My first reactions were expressed in my thoughts: I gave him everything, I did everything for him, I was always there for him. I had mulled over these sentences for a long time until I asked myself: "What if that was precisely what was wrong? Have I created a little egotistical monster?" *I'm sorry, perhaps parents only have beautiful thoughts about their children, but I had many terrifying feelings about mine.*

I didn't know how to help myself. I stopped waiting on Ethan, and he was becoming increasingly dissatisfied. We began fighting. At first, these fights were verbal and later destructive (he broke many of my valuables). His father was of no assistance to me, which was understandable, as I was better off all these years if he wasn't there.

When Ethan was thirteen, he stood above me as if he was going to hit me, because I wouldn't let him go out. That shifted me.

I sought help. But everything we achieved and all the changes I chose, everything was in vain. I always left with questions: "What if he disregards that? What if he doesn't stick to that? What will I do if he doesn't come home? What will I do if he really hits me?"

I didn't know how to be decisive on the outside because, on the inside, I was without authority, full of hesitation and doubts. I didn't know how to say: "Take out the trash!" *in a way that would make him do it. I always said that with a voice that showed my doubt and provided an option for this not to happen.*

I thought I was lost, that this was something that couldn't be learned. Then at therapy, I went on a difficult journey of my fears which caused such decisions. I had to understand where they originated, and that they were my manner of avoiding being hit when I was younger. I always said things as if I was checking whether that was okay or not. I had to accept the fact that I was an adult, a mother, and that I was responsible.

I practiced all the tasks I gave to my son in front of a mirror, together with my therapists, with my friends... When I felt that I was doing okay, I asked my son to come to therapy with me, because I would like to tell him what I had done to cause alienation and the loss of connection between us. I told him that he would give me the opportunity I really needed, because I didn't want to lose the connection with him, that he was the most important person in the world to me. That we wouldn't give him a hard time, but that I needed help so I could let him know what I wanted to.

He agreed.

There, we got the opportunity to tell each other painful stories from the past, in a dialogue. How we felt, that we missed each other. I told him about my decision to decisively demand from him to be home on time, to do the things he needed to do, to clean up after himself, and that I would no longer negotiate and argue. That I knew it would be tough on him, because I had taught him otherwise.

Life didn't get better overnight. It went slowly, in small steps, as if we were learning to walk again. I can say that Ethan became a teen who is friendly and rebels within boundaries that preserve the connection. I believe that this happened also because I set boundaries with my authority, which he knew were there, and he couldn't just move them or even pretend they weren't there.

"Ethan, turn off the computer! It's enough!"

"I'll finish in five minutes, turn it off, and go to bed."

That really happens. I didn't believe I could do it.

Related Topics

Power Struggle | Part 1 of the Book | Where Are the Boundaries? | What to Do with Rules? | Taking Responsibility

Within the Scope of Awareness

Authority is related to how other people, in this case our children, see us, on the basis of our behavior. It isn't related to how they want to see us, or even how we imagine ourselves or want to be seen, and to be responded to accordingly. Authority is a reflection of the beliefs we have about ourselves, beliefs that we carry inside. Authority concerns the certainty of our notion of the values we carry inside. If we are insecure, if we are afraid and doubt that the child will consider our instructions, if we let him violate and ignore them, if we think he might disregard us, all these are mental bases for the messages we convey. Children simply suitably "read" this information and respond correspondingly. So if we radiate insecurity in the role of a parent, our child will respond by confirming that insecurity. If, in our internal world, something happening in any other way than what we believe appropriate (in areas where we don't negotiate) isn't an option, the child's response will correspond.

Our attitude to authority is about the question of whether we feel safe with authority. What are our experiences with, and patterns of, authority from our primary family?

If we experienced our parents' authority as an abuse of their power or as coercion, then we don't feel at ease, safe, and comfortable with the idea of authority. Instead, we withdraw from situations which require a rigid approach in the role of authority, or leave the captain's spot, for fear of chaos. Within ourselves, we mix up the idea of authority with

163

authoritarian attitudes, violence, abuse of power, coercion. Of course, we won't do this to our children, so all we can do is to do nothing. However, authority isn't something that evokes reluctance and rebellion. Authority is the inner strength of an adult, which gives us safety, a power that teens follow because it makes sense—because of the connection in the relationship, attachment to the person, because they feel respect and feel that the person is fond of them, because they see a higher sense in the relationship. Authority is the effect of actions which arise from the quality of the connection in a mutual relationship.

It is also true that authority is established with long-term consistency in our own behavior. Part of it derives from the consistency between our words and behaviors. Especially words uttered thoughtlessly from the aspect of authority, which aren't then followed by actions. Let's take a look at an example.

---

(28) Consistency

The father tried to use his authority to stop his argument with his 14 and 15-year-old daughters about their wish to have a belly-button piercing.

"If any of you has a belly-button piercing done, I'll throw her out."

The smart teens came home next day with stick-on (fake) belly-button piercings. Their father uttered a myriad of words to express his opposition, but the action he had announced didn't happen, because his daughters were still completely unequipped to live independently.

A day later, they came home with real belly-button piercings.

Consistency means that our behavior provides a safe environment for our children, in which they know where they stand. Consistency is the basic support for safety, as it enables predictability. With consistency, we let our children know that our response to a certain situation will always be the same. It is true that it is easier to establish authority with consistency when our child is younger, before puberty. Authority is also related to maturity and the ability to remain in the role of adult. And especially to the quality of the connection we have created.

In spite of this, less functional behaviors may be changed for more functional. In a similar fashion, parents who raised their children without authority can change the established patterns of giving in and inconsistency. Nevertheless, we need to take into account that each change in the system destroys the balance, meaning that the whole system will resent the change, at least at first. The rebellion of teens, when it comes to introducing authority to the system, can be quite dramatic and exhausting for parents.

It turns out that parents, with their persistence and consistency, manage to let their teen know: *Now it will always be like this and I am not giving in anymore!* But before such changes and their firmness can take place, we need to change our beliefs, which is often connected to the emotional part of our own experience with authority.

Tips and Solutions

Consistency or Arguments

"Mom, tell me now if I can go to the movies with Sarah in half an hour. Her dad's driving us."

"Have you taken out the trash like we agreed?"

"C'mon, Mom, do you always have to hassle me? Can't you see that I need the answer now? Tell me already, Sarah's waiting!"

Option 1:

"I know you want to go to the movies and I agree with that. We'll talk about it when you take out the trash. Period."

Option 2:

"Do you always have to blackmail me?"

"Argh, you're so pathetic, do I really have to have the most pathetic mom in the world?"

"I won't let you talk to me this way!"

"You're pathetic, pathetic, pathetic... Everyone can go to the movies but me."

"Look, I just want you to take the trash out."

"What don't you get, can't you see they're waiting—and you always have to come up with stuff."

165

"And you never listen to me and respect what I tell you."
"And I never will, because of the way you treat me."
"Dear me, what have I done to deserve such an ungrateful daughter?"
"I'm off, bye."
"Here's some money, you can't go to the movies just like that."

In the story above, there is the daughter's wish to go to the movies on one side, and the mother's dilemma of how to balance the need to hang out with friends and the need to respect authority, boundaries, rules, agreements, and to impart to her daughter an attitude to work habits, on the other. It is clear that the daughter tries to avoid respecting the rules; it is understandable that the principle of comfort and the need to hang out with her friends are talking her into going to the movies without fulfilling her obligations. But this is precisely the job of parents—to teach our children to distinguish between the immediate fulfillment of a want, and the fulfillment of a want by considering all areas important for us to function in life. Our job (and also desire) is to equip our children to act as independent adults.

In the first option in the case above, the mother is clearly focused on one goal. She has no internal doubts, she doesn't include potential feelings of guilt towards the child, or other thoughts which would hinder a clean connection with a clear intention: the daughter will take out the trash before she leaves.

In the second option, the mother plays the game and pursues the flow of her daughter's thoughts. We can see that she doesn't trust herself, that she is insecure, that she considers other thoughts (what will other people think, how will other people see us...). This option which takes into account other aspects (one of the strongest misconceptions is that the child has it tough in life), in addition to a clear demand and the child's evasion, soon loses its edge and plausibility. It can often be encountered in cases of divorced parents, or children who are sick or otherwise handicapped.

The first recommendation for parents: When in doubt or feeling insecure, we have the right to take some time to think. Sometimes, the only option is to have to go to the toilet immediately. We can always think in peace there. We may also postpone it or use techniques described in the book:

Tip 1: *patience and mirroring (see page 123)*
Tip 2: *determination (see page 102)*
Tip 3: *consistency (see page 165)*
Tip 4: *consequences instead of punishment (see Table 4 on page 155, see page 156)*

"Honey, not only your friends are waiting for you, and they will continue waiting for you until you take out the trash. I'm not asking anymore, I'm ordering you. I'll be sorry for you[40] *if you lose the opportunity to hang out with your friends because of one trash can."*

We can show that we heard what was said:
- *"I'm sorry you feel like I'm blackmailing you, but this still doesn't change my expectation. Take out the trash, and then we'll sort out everything you need."*
- *"Yes, and I can imagine that, in your eyes, I'm pathetic. Bummer that you have a mother like that. Now take out the trash, so your misery is complete."*
- *"I can see your friends are waiting for you. Shall I give them some juice, so that they don't get bored, or would you rather take out the trash?"*
- *"C'mon, sweetie, hurry up, you know there's no movie if you don't do what you have to. We won't argue over a bag of trash, will we?"*

It is important for us not to become aggressive, offensive, and impatient, as this would give the teen power and open up opportunities to rebel. The same goes if we become vague and indecisive. We need to be focused on *our* goal (the mother and the teen don't have the same goal: the mother is confused, the teen shifts her goal from the movies to insults and from insults to friends—if we buy this, we usually get bewildered and mislead). Throughout communication, we need to stay focused on the trash. Then we can be calm, decisive, and even funny. Authority is created with the power we use to stay focused on our goal.

If both parents do parenting, contradiction in their relationship is often the basis for none of the parents to act out of authority.

How do parents create authority, if their opinions or beliefs differ?

---

[40]The statement "I'll be very disappointed" would signify emotional blackmail.

Arguing in front of children about who is right shifts the focus from authority to facilitating ways out. If parents' belief and opinions differ, the most functional thing to do is for one of the parents to take responsibility for leadership and gain full power to see the story through from the beginning to the end. The other parent cooperates as support.

There is nothing wrong with letting our children know that our opinions differ, but that we have decided on a certain action. Then we speak in plural:

"We have decided, with your mom/dad..."

Perhaps it will appear frivolous, but it works. A very effective practice to learn authority is to go to a dog training session. But the truth is also that we don't buy dogs for our children, but for ourselves.

4 Experience of Independence

In order for our children to gain independence, they have to act independent. Independence is the awareness of inner safety that comes from feeling that we are able to survive on our own. This is connected with many skills: we wake up by ourselves, we know how to take care of ourselves, we can cook a meal by ourselves, we can take care of the environment by ourselves, we can manage money and payments by ourselves, we are responsible, we can get help when we can't do something on our own…

Learning to be independent begins at the moment our child is born.

---

(29) Not Independent at University

 He's nineteen years old now, and he's the youngest, his older brothers have already completed their studies. After a year seeking a way out of their anguish, the parents decided to get help.

Their son's success was always above average. In elementary school, he was a straight-A student, especially good in natural science and sports. Even in high school, he had no problems overcoming obstacles that posed unsolvable problems to some people. He learned with ease, on his computer. He was an exemplary, unproblematic, quiet and calm, obedient child, he never caused any problems to his parents. He had his group of friends, they enjoyed marathons of playing strategic games without a break. His parents could see the ease with which he studied, completed the work, and now carries on in this way, all the way up to getting his doctorate. He was popular among peers, who all had somewhat similar talents. A child who was above average in every activity he took up. He also met a girl and they got into a serious relationship.

He enrolled in university. Results didn't follow, and Aiden was growing increasingly bitter. At the end of the year, a surprise. He didn't pass his exams. Realization hit that he didn't have the skills to study at this level, in this place. He spent too much time on the computer. He didn't know how to really study. He didn't have the discipline. He wasn't communicative enough. He wasn't skillful in bureaucracy and, because of his clumsiness, he didn't register for an exam that he needed to take. He wasn't taught work habits at home. This was followed by the realization that he didn't enjoy the study program he had chosen. That he didn't enjoy anything. He didn't even know what he enjoyed, or what to do in life. He didn't know his goals. Perhaps he was most interested in music, but he should finish music school. Should an almost 20-year-old who graduated from high school and has all good grades to enroll in any university, enroll instead in the first year of music school? His parents disagreed. His mother and father were wondering what they had done wrong. They saw the roots in their high expectations, and the fact that everything in life went smoothly for him. They hadn't set clear rules for him, they had yielded, he hadn't acquired any work habits. He enrolled in a technical university. They set some rules and more demand to do housework at home. The story of the last year of high school repeated itself. The boy got another chance. The relationship with his girlfriend ended, and he found a temporary job alongside his studies. Now he is at the same spot where he was a year ago, and his parents realize that he won't successfully finish the year. What should they do with their almost 20-year-old son?

The father is convinced that graduation from university is the most rational way to get employment. Should they make him do that? How?

During conversation, the parents seek reasons with traditional manners, from intolerance to distress, hidden mutual accusations, and great powerlessness and concern. "We feel like failures, defeated." *The father is glum, the mother exhausted, and the son is becoming more and more reserved and quiet.*

"Should we throw him out? We can't do that. We are willing to support him, he should just make it clear what he intends to do with his life."

How else could the parents act?

The father blames himself: "He's just like me. I don't know what I want in life, either. I function if you put me somewhere and give me clear instructions what to do. In such circumstances, I oblige and behave myself. And I'm successful." *Is this the pattern that is transferred from parents?*

Was it because of his past above-average success and the excitement of the surroundings that he has never been able to develop his own opinion, instead maintaining his reputation, and the reputation and expectations of his parents to parents?

Related Topics
Taking Responsibility | Autonomy and Individuality | Where Are the Boundaries? | What to Do with Rules? | Attitude to Authority | Part 1 of the Book

Within the Scope of Awareness

Parents used to believe that by growing up, children acquire the necessary wisdom on their own. And they weren't particularly concerned with questions as to how it would come about. And they didn't worry about what puberty would bring. They had faith in traditional parenting methods, and in the power of tradition. Somewhere along the line of the principle: if every child grows up, so will ours. Life brings different things to different people. But there was no irresponsibility or indifference in this. More faith, if anything.

Nowadays parents have a different mindset; they especially have less faith that things will resolve on their own. The belief that each moment in development could be decisive, and that each opportunity missed could be fateful, is very strong. Therefore, the parenting style of modern parents is significantly different than that of our ancestors. But the desire of all parents, also nowadays, is to raise independent children. As we observe them, it seems as if the burden of modern parenting lies in that we have to "hover" above our children all the time, from their conception to independence (if they ever achieve it). Has he eaten enough (as prescribed by norms for the healthy diet of newborns)? Are your pants wet? Are you wearing enough clothes? Do you have school shoes? Have you learned the song? Do you have money to take on your trip? Will you be careful, so that the saleslady doesn't cheat you? Do you have your bike helmet? Will you look after the money? People in this town steal a lot, I hear. Do you promise me not to drive with people who aren't sober? Will you finally learn to respect the time we set? When will you register for the exam? When will you make arrangements for work? What don't you like about her, she's such a sweet girl? And so on and so forth.

Endless questions with which parents express their concerns and burdens, while teens experience them as intrusiveness, control and excessive burden, though probably also as safety and the feeling that someone (their relatives) cares about them.

Parents who come in for counseling or attend lectures always ask the same questions in their ambivalence: When is the right time to teach our child independence about money; independence about respecting time; when can we trust him to go out alone (and until when should we let him);

when can a girl have a boyfriend and a boy a girlfriend; when can he go on vacation alone?

Most parents' worries are common: consumption of all kinds of intoxicating substances, risky behavior, early sexual activity, traffic and other accidents, bad company, all kinds of violence, giving up responsibilities, and listless vegetation in the hotel called home.

And also how to teach our child to listen to us, respect boundaries, rules and discipline, respect our authority and the authority of other people (teachers), know how to adjust, know how to compromise, negotiate...

When and how do we teach them all this?

The belief stated below often underlies the parents' behavior: *"They're still little before they go to school, let them enjoy their childhood, we won't make their lives miserable and restrict them. At school, they are burdened with other, most often unnecessary, things. That takes up a lot of their time. It's a good thing that at least we can make their strenuous lives a little bit better. In puberty, we no longer have the time to deal with them, and they also don't listen to us and they disregard us."*

This refers to parents who don't want to miss anything, who enthusiastically embark on their parenting mission at the beginning (for the first decade), pressure preschool teachers and teachers in the first few grades of school to ensure their children have the best conditions to make progress; but when the child should produce some results born of all these investments, and this doesn't happen, parents give up, and the most promising child becomes the most problematic.

Growing up is learning. Learning behaviors that help us survive. Living is learning. Our view of learning is, unfortunately, very narrow, mostly due to our school experiences. But learning is so much more than just learning at school. We still perceive learning as the acquisition of pre-prepared information we need to copy-paste as perfectly as possible, and then get a grade or a certificate for this copy-pasting skill. The orientation of the systems that live off grades and certificates further contributes to such a situation. On the other hand, we contribute to it ourselves when we don't know how to make use of all opportunities offered to us on every corner, to learn from our own experiences. Or to allow our children to learn for life.

What is learning from life? It is learning for life: by trial and error. It is an opportunity to make just as many trials and errors as we need to create our own experience. No one can prescribe and standardize for us the number of repetitions, and the manner to reinforce the experience acquired.

Let's take a look at one of the most dramatic headways a person makes when growing up, when he stands on his own two feet as a human being. This is an experience which tags along all the time, as we gain our independence. And, at the same time, it is a metaphor for growing up, with a very powerful message. Some children are more skillful and learn how to walk quickly, while others are more cautious, and take longer to learn how to walk. It is also true that some children have more opportunities to try and walk on their own, but they also fall more often. Other children are (un)lucky enough to be more protected, they don't fall, but their first step is more tentative. Some children crawl on all fours for a longer period and stand up on their two feet more gradually, while others need more time to explore their feeling of standing independently on two feet. Some children begin to walk with the help of their parents or other safety aids, others run into independence as soon as they get the chance. Every person has his own story about starting to walk, every person uses a different learning method and trial pattern, in different conditions which depend on the beliefs of parents or the surroundings where we tried to walk, as well as on our own motives and the manners we use. But all of us who are able to walk learned from experience.

This was one of the first experiences of learning by ourselves and knowing how to apply it in life. We learned on the basis of information that we collected by trial and error, and installed it into our knowledge and experience system. This wasn't information we trusted blindly or learned by heart. This was information we checked in our next attempt: we put useful information into practice and remembered it, while we discarded other information as unsuitable. And we weren't ashamed of it, no one got upset because of it, no one said to us that we had failed, that we were worthless. They waited patiently for our time to come. (Unfortunately, such patience for a child to achieve the next step of development is running low among modern parents.)

So when is the right time to learn how to be responsible?

The answer can be quite simple: when we get the opportunity to learn something on our own. In younger children, this depends largely on the courage of their parents to allow their children to have their own experiences. When do we move them from our bedroom to their own room? When do we let them hold a knife? When do we let them climb a tree? When do we trust them to do something independently?

Do we encourage and support them, or do we pass our fears on to them and safely believe that they won't try anything stupid?

The way teens learn appears like a constant experiment, many times as a provocation. They experiment with their hair color, fashion, belonging to groups with a certain style, with the music they listen to, with views and beliefs, with fields of interest, with career plans... Understanding, and allowing them their way of learning by experimentation, takes a lot of patience and trust. At the same time, we as parents face a task to put boundaries around this that keep them safe.

Then there are also teens who don't show their attempts to learn as provocations or experiments. These are "well-behaved" or "unproblematic" teens who don't feel safe enough or don't have the courage to express their need to experiment. They may appear quite independent, but life will eventually claim the debt of the learning they missed out on. Another option is to gain their learning experience in secret.

There are plenty of situations in which teens can test their independence. In adulthood, life offers a myriad of them, and teens explore them with their unrelenting curiosity and courage. If they didn't have opportunities to learn from experience, especially unsuccessful ones, before, they will only get their opportunities as adults. At this stage, the price is, unfortunately, much higher, and the pain while learning about the truths of life is worse and more fateful.

If we wonder as parents why our children aren't independent, if they don't know how to become independent, they probably lack experience with which they could learn the necessary skills first hand. This issue probably involves us: what we did and didn't allow them to do. How much did our fears control us? As a rule, it is never too late in life to learn, but we do believe that younger people are more susceptible to learning and more flexible while learning. It seems that the question about when we have enough courage is more important than the question about when the time is right. Courage to face an experience, a hurdle, a challenge. These are skills necessary to survive in the modern world.

In a story where parents blame themselves for their child being independent, it is better to focus on more urgent matters. Will parents be able to surpass their strong emotions and frustrations, and see the points in their child's path of development where it went wrong? Can we see which skills our growing child is missing, which made the story of expected success go the opposite way?

Is our children's independence something that just happens, or does it involve patterns and skills passed on to children through tiny and pain-free experiences in our everyday lives?

Independence is not a state or an event. It is a process. A process of learning first passed on by other people and, when we become independent, we continue the process ourselves. That is the content of lifelong learning.

Are unproblematic children a blessing for their parents, or a woe to themselves and their life experiences? Doesn't the rule say that we can't avoid, and that parents can't spare their children, experiences they need for life?

When is the right time to ask ourselves all these questions?

In any case, independence is the awareness we acquire from experience. It is a cluster of skills with which teens are able to do a job by themselves. Saying that the child will have to pay his own phone bills doesn't mean enabling the child to have an experience. Saying that we are worried how he will manage in life, if he is so irresponsible (and at the same time, bear the consequences that are his to bear), also prevents the child from encountering experiences on his way to independence, which are always less pleasant at first, but turn out to be crucial. If we protect our children from unpleasant experiences, so they don't suffer too much, instead of letting them learn independent behavior, we do them more harm than good. Skills that are part of independent behavior: going out alone, asking for help if needed, speaking to a stranger who is competent to solve a certain situation, standing up for yourself, assessing potential consequences, having communication skills, being confident enough to make the first move and to overcome a moment of insecurity, trusting in your own power...

A metaphor of learning how to be independent is how we taught our child to put on and tie his own shoes. We can offer support in three ways.
1. We support him and let him try on his own to just the right extent to give him safety, and teach and help him until he can do it on his own.
2. We tie our child's shoes instead of him, because he can't do it on his own (intrusiveness model). This prevents the child from learning from

experience, leaving him deprived of the experience. This way, he develops a fear of independently tackling the task.

3. We let our child struggle with a task which is too difficult for him (neglect model). This way, he experiences that things are too difficult, and trying to solve them on his own puts him in distress without safety. The child develops the manner of withdrawal from situations where he should be acting on his own.

Tips and Solutions

Children strengthen their awareness of independence with experiences of everyday household chores. This is possible when they clean the kitchen, mow the lawn, fasten a painting on the wall, fix a computer, wash the car, cook a simple dish, walk the dog, take out the trash, vacuum the stairs, do the laundry on their own.

Parents who don't know how to occupy their 15-year old or older child, whose only responsibility is school, lack ideas of how to achieve this goal. But there is a way. We can always do things together with the child. Our goal isn't the quality of the work done, but persistence to the end, and not giving in to their provocations, which they use to try and get out of work.

A father who had problems finishing a job with his children colorfully described the pattern from his primary family which still had great influence.

---

(30) Parenting Without a Goal

 My father used to always make me help him do stuff in the afternoon. I always did something wrong, he got mad at me, he humiliated me, said that I was a good-for-nothing, and finally he chased me away. Once my friend and I were preparing for a singing performance, and we were practicing, accompanied by a guitar, at our house. In the middle of our enthusiastic practice, my father turned up in my room and told me, irritated, to help him with something. My friend began putting away his music sheets and his instrument, but I whispered to him: "He'll chase me away in ten minutes and we can continue." And that was exactly what happened.

When I was married, I used to constantly complain to my wife that the children only have regard for her, and ignored what I said. The scene when I was yelling at the children, who were in front of the TV in the living room, to put away their leftovers, humiliating them and scolding them over what a mess they had made, took place yet again. The children continued watching, without a response and completely indifferently. I went to complain to my wife, who asked me about my goal: to convey my opinion about the children or to make them tidy up the room. I went back to the children with the idea that the tidying up would happen, stood in front of them, and announced with a voice that allowed no doubt that we would clean the room together (including me).

Enthusiasm in cooperating also stems from connection and the quality of the relationship. We get our children excited to work (also schoolwork) through the sense the child sees in his connection with us, and not in the content of work. Another necessary skill parents should have is trust. First, we need to explore how we feel safe with trust, how much our parents trusted us when we were growing up, how many opportunities we had to learn from experience. Did we feel safe enough to learn from life? Did our parents oppose, and did we have to extort such experiences? Were our parents too worried about us and prevented us from getting the experience of independence?

We always wonder whether our children are old enough and equipped enough to let them act independently. A story about a new teen going on a skiing trip, alone for the first time, describes some of the aforementioned.

(31) Alone on a Skiing Trip

 Twelve-year-old: "Mom, can you give me a ride to the ski slope?"

Mother: "There's no one today to go with you, and you can't go alone."

Son: "Why not?"

Mother: "Well, you aren't old enough or responsible enough. You need someone to watch over you."

Son: "Can you please explain what's up, what you're afraid of?"

Mother: "Let's say something happens to you, you'll be lying some-where and no one will know where you're from, no one will be able to help you, and you won't be able to call for help."

Son: "Okay. Then explain what is the difference between this and me going to the store alone, for which I've been old enough since I was four, a car runs me over at the intersection and I lie there the same way as you've described in your movie?"

The mother mulled it over, talked to her husband, and said to her son: "You're right, but I'd like you to hear me that I'm worried."

Son: "Yeah, Mom, everything's gonna be fine. I'll be careful and won't push my luck."

After two hours, the mother called her son who, enthusiastically, answered that he was taking a chairlift with someone to whom he was explaining things about their country in a foreign language (which was his most hated subject at school), and that he was having a great time. He came home and con-firmed with his behavior that he was independent. His mother was at peace, in terms of his skills.

Most topics of independent behavior suggested by teens at the begin-ning are related to the duration of their night outings. Because of their own fears and insecurities, parents engage in arguments about what is right and what isn't. Such stories aren't only about independence, but also about gain-ing trust, which is a mutual effect of the parents' and children's behavior. These stories include other topics like boundaries, connections, sincerity... When speaking about parents' trust and risks, the level of risk is related to our responsibility in the role of parents. We will risk up to the point where we feel safe. If we take a risk beyond the safe boundary, we are irresponsible.

---

(32) Trust and Independence

 Sixteen-year-old: "Can I go to a concert in a town nearby with Mickey and Jimmy, and stay until 2 AM?"

His parents face the dilemma of whether the boy is indepen-dent enough. All their security questions (with whom, where, until when) have been answered. There was just the dilemma of whether the boy's limits concerning alcohol were sound enough. Prohibition would be a declara-tion of war, while allowing him to go would be risky.

"What will be happening there?"

"A band from Belgium is coming, they're very interesting, and their gigs are really great."

"Okay, you know our deal about alcohol. I'll pick you up at two at the main entrance."

Parents who pick up their children after the event, at the place of the event, convey several important messages. They remain in the role of adults who care about boundaries, and they will see for themselves the child's actual state and his sticking to their agreements. On the one hand, the message is: when you show your share of responsibility, and we are at peace with it, we will be ready to negotiate your next step to independence. This is the point with several possible outcomes. Our teen could fight our right to check on him. Many children come home with a cab late at night, their parents are already asleep, and checking up on the truth is missing from the story. Other stories develop towards the teen's raging rebellion to the ide of his parents showing up at the end of the party. They deem their parents conservative, panicky, controlling... A popular phrase: *"Nobody else's parents come to wait for them, I'll be the only idiot there, as if I don't know my way home."* In this case, it isn't about the content, but about the rules and conditions parents set. We can apply the principle that certain rules are non-negotiable. The child can choose on the basis of the take-it-or-leave-it principle.

There are less risky ways to give children the opportunity to learn how to be independent: teach them to pay their own bills, buy their own clothes, live alone when at university, work during vacation, babysit, be active in volunteering.

When is a teen independent enough to drive a car?

There are regulations about when a person can pass the driving test. There are regulations about how to act in traffic. This is also an opportunity to define the rules and boundaries about car use and safe behavior on the road, in advance. A few examples presented by parents at our workshops:

"You can take the car as long as you ... / when you... / on condition..."

"We'll pay for car registration and insurance, but you'll have to earn the money for gas."

"If you have an accident and you're found guilty, you'll bear the costs."

"If you have an accident, and you're found guilty and under the influence of intoxicating substances, you'll bear the costs and pay the same amount to us."

5 Taking Responsibility

When you're living or working together, unreliable people cause a lot of problems and discomfort.

The most common occurrence is that we agree on something, but then something unexpected happens. We agree that the bus should leave a 6 AM. At that time, most participants are already on the bus, but one participant arrives at ten past six. We agree at work to each do his or her task by a certain deadline. When the deadline comes, one person is late, the work hasn't been done. The consequences may include damage felt by the whole team. At work, there are usually consequences we are aware of, and we accept them beforehand.

For us to feel safe in society, we need responsible people we can rely on, people who know how to bear consequences. Teaching children how to be responsible is part of the process of gaining independence and, these days, one of the greatest parenting challenges.

---

(33) It's other People's Fault

 As a child, I was very obedient and never dared break the rules. Other people told my parents what a well-behaved child they had, while it never even crossed my mind to assert my own will. When I did something deemed an offense, I was beaten. I placed such events in my memory of catastrophes in my life. I saw myself as a victim of other people's unreasonable behavior. Physical punishment always made me think about how unfair parents were, and how difficult it was to be a child. I never had the chance to think about my own share of responsibility and consequences arising from it. So I learned, with the support of moral education at church. I assumed the image of a "beautiful soul:" I tried to meet all other people's expectations. So other people became the most important point in my assessment of myself and the world. Whenever something went wrong in my world, I blamed other people. I trained myself in minute detail.

I went to high school by bus and was usually late. My classmates admired me as the master of excuses. "The first bus didn't come at all, the second one didn't stop because it was packed, only the third one stopped. / I was

just outside school when I remembered that I had forgotten to turn off the hot plate on the cooker." *What all these excuses had in common was the absence of personal responsibility: the reason was never my reckless time management, but external factors. In situations with my peers, in which someone had to take responsibility, I chose to withdraw. Therefore, I wasn't equipped with the experience of confrontation and with other skills to boost my self-esteem and strengthen my position in society. I became a loner who only hung out with the chosen few. An environment with no stress related to responsibility was my safety. When I should have admitted my share, I resorted to hiding and evasion. I preferred to live in my fantasy world, devoid of responsibility.*

The behavioral pattern to avoid taking responsibility became part of my personality structure.

As a father, I withdrew from parenting at the beginning of my child's puberty.

My wife and I sought help because our 15-year-old son quit school midyear. The reason were his teachers, who hadn't tolerated his inappropriate behavior. And he was in a class where other students affected his inappropriate behavior. In our eyes, our son was a victim of an inadequate environment and incompetent teachers, including school counselors.

At home, our child had problems with the computer, especially with distinguishing between schoolwork and pleasure. He spent all night on the computer. My wife complained, but he disregarded her, while I was glued to my screen all night, too. When my wife asked me to help her set some boundaries for our son, we fought, and I concluded: "You're always the smart one, deal with the situation yourself."

When discussing the situation with our therapists, we established that my wife always took responsibility for our son's violation of rules. I was mainly very intolerant of violations, so my wife protected our son and kept his violation secret, from the very beginning. This way, the child didn't gain the experience of respect for authority, and he never bore the consequences of his actions. It seemed that, in his world, only the pleasure program existed, which was stubbornly gaining momentum.

Related Topics
Where Are the Boundaries? | What to Do with Rules? | Attitude to Authority | Experience of Independence | Part 1 of the book

Within the Scope of Awareness

Responsibility is a skill children learn when they have the opportunity to face the consequences of the actions they choose.[41] When children are the actual owners of their experiences, when they choose their behaviors so that they can learn from consequences, especially errors, this is the best basis to learn how to be responsible in all situations.

Bearing consequences in circumstances when I discover that I made the wrong decision takes power and resilience. The power to recognize myself as the person who made the wrong decision, not to search for the influences and responsibilities for it outside myself, and to know how to recognize, and make myself aware of, my share of responsibility for consequences. The awareness that I bear my share of consequences, and not guilt, is the next foundation for responsibility to function in practice.

As children learn responsibility, the parents' role is to gradually equip them with skills that allow them to bear the consequences of their choice of behavior.

What prevents us from leaving responsibility where it belongs?

Our past experience didn't teach us to distinguish between the ownership of our experience and the ownership of another person's experience. We assume other people's emotions, we let stories that cause us pain to get to us, we plant our emotions onto others, we transfer responsibility outside ourselves... The crucial question is how we learned responsibility in our primary family, which patterns are included in our experience of this kind? Do we protect our children from the burden of bearing consequences and responsibilities because of our own unpleasant experiences? Do we ignore consequences?

Part of the influence may also be shame, which plays a rather decisive role in this story.[42]

When a teacher calls parents to school and tells them what their child did, they cave in under pressure. They raised the child with the best of intentions, but now he is doing things to them. Very few parents are capable of saying: *"This is my child's experience, it's his, I'm not responsible (to be blamed) for it."* If we succumb to the feeling of shame, we will do everything to clear ourselves

---

[41]Cf. Cline, F.; Fay, J. (2006).
[42]Hart, S. (2008: 202ff.)

of such shame, depriving our child of an experience which will teach him something. Bearing the emotions which are the consequence of a chosen behavior is an experience which builds responsibility.

Children don't study, they get bad grades, and consequently, they strain their relationships with their teachers. What usually happens? Parents put worries on their own shoulders, they don't sleep, they contemplate, seek help, seek someone to tutor their child, organize additional learning for their child, make arrangements, go to school where they listen to difficult stories, bear shame, the feeling of powerlessness, despair, financial burden... What about the child? He stands by, calmly, for his parents to solve the issue.

Responsible teens mean less disappointment and more tranquil lives for parents. The parents' faith in their children being able to bear the consequences is put to the test. The principle of functioning follows a self-fulfilling prophecy—if I believe that my child won't violate my trust, he really won't. If I doubt that, he will do something to indulge my doubt.

I have chosen to postpone work, which has a deadline, and the consequence is that now I'm running out of time, I'm grumpy, I fear that I won't be able to finish, I'm in a hurry, and I'm aware that this could affect the quality of the product... The responsibility of an adult will perceive the consequences as the direct result of a previous choice. An irresponsible mind will seek opportunities to attribute the reasons for the consequences (not feeling well, fear, panic...) to external factors or persons.

When we agree to do a chore or task, we paint a picture in our heads as to how the story will unfold, we make an internal implementation plan as a script which involves our picturesque images of the course of action. Part of this script includes concrete chores which can be clearly defined. Can we define them for ourselves? Can we define them with regard (and empathy) to others? Perhaps we don't even make one, perhaps there is no room in it for the person with whom we made the agreement? To define means to accurately anticipate the course of action. Do we have organizational and logistical skills which we can use to plan a certain chore by phases? Are we even aware of this?

Each chore consists of individual procedures in a certain sequence, and at the end, we attain our goal with them. If we go shopping, we first need to decide when we will leave the house, be aware of the needs we have regarding shopping at the market (this usually already includes an idea about what we will eat that day), decide which clothes to wear, check other things we need depending on the weather, decide on the means of transport (on foot, by bike, by public transport, by car...). There are always changes in life which surprise us, we always find ourselves in a situation we don't expect. When we are about to go to the market on foot, a mailman stops us and confuses us with an unexpected and unpleasant delivery. We are held up, shift our attention, put down the things we prepared for our shopping, and leave without everything we need. When we discover at the market that we don't have our wallet, is that the mailman's fault?

Taking responsibility in relationships is related to the ability to empathize with other people. When we make agreements with other people, the space we give to another person in our world is crucial. How much space do we give to our needs, and how much to the needs of the person with whom we made an agreement?

Tips and Solutions

The most effective school of skills is a lecture on choice boxes and the consequences, which was described under **Tips and Solutions** in *Chapter 2* of this part of the book *(see "Table 4: Choice Boxes" on page 155)*. Perhaps just a note to go with that, about the absurdity of punishment just for the sake of punishment. *"Because you didn't do this, you'll be without computer games for a week, you won't go out for a week..."*

Learning how to be responsible can take place when we have the opportunity to connect our experience and our choice of behavior with the logical consequences which occurred. What are logical consequences? These are consequences which happen in real life, and which we can anticipate. They are announced and really happen. This also means that we, as parents, are consistent in our forecasts, and we manage to keep the structure solid.

For you to have an idea what this means, here are a few everyday examples.

(34) Where Does Responsibility Lie?

Before going on a trip, we should warn the children that they are responsible for everything they will need on the trip, so they should take care of their ipods, music players and other things to entertain themselves. Naturally, as soon as we leave the driveway, we hear the well-known tune from the back seat: "Where's my...? Where are the batteries? Who's got my...? Why isn't ... in the car?" The logical consequence is that teens bear the consequences of their own non-presence, of not really hearing us, of feeling the burden of deficiency for himself. This is a very appropriate opportunity for us to unknowingly assume the burden of responsibility: we jump in with our moral speech, start arguing about who is responsible for the situation or even—just to keep the peace in the car—go and get the things they forgot. The logical consequence is that we drive off in silence and let the experience work by itself. Let the action speak for itself. If I forget, I bear the consequence, I don't get a treat. The important message which develops the necessary skill is: I am responsible for the consequences with my choices and my behavior.

If I don't put my dirty clothes in the laundry in time, the consequence is that I can't wear them when I need them. If I choose not to go to the shop to buy some milk, I can't pour it over my favorite cereal for breakfast. If I don't fill my camera or phone in time, I can't have my dad's full battery. If I don't hang my wet clothes or shoes to dry in the evening, I can't wear them next day. If I didn't go to my friend's house to get my forgotten sleeping bag, I can't go camping. Recurrent stories, with more or less painful consequences.

As we listen to complaints about bitter destiny, where first experiences of responsibility cut through the gentle personality, our knowledge from Part 1 of this book, about reflective function and empathic responses, will help us survive this more easily.

There are plenty of cases on how to learn to face consequences in our everyday lives, but perhaps we don't know how to use them, or teens successfully skip them and, sooner or later, we are faced with teaching them about responsibility connected with school. The story is usually entitled: should parents assume responsibility for schoolwork, which is the child's job and duty, when the forecast is critical or would we risk the child failing and experience first-hand what we wanted to communicate to him with our endless verbal outpourings.

(35) Deal Between Sisters

 As early as in the elementary school, Amy showed signs of hatred of independent schoolwork. She was the youngest in the family, so she made a business deal with her sister, who was a straight-A student: in exchange for mandatory household chores, her sister would do her homework or write a seminar paper for her. The system worked until the last few grades. In the last grade, Amy finished schooling by learning at home, and with exams agreed in advance. She enrolled in high school with a new zeal, but without suitable work and learning habits. Her mother discovered, soon after midterm, that the story of constant adjustments and evasion persisted, and that she wouldn't be able to keep that up for the next four years. She talked to Amy's father, and they decided not to control her anymore—with her being aware of the consequences. They told Amy about it: "You're old enough to be aware of your responsibility for independent schoolwork. You've chosen this school yourself and decided to finish it. We've decided that, from now on, this is your concern. We will no longer push and interrogate you about whether you've done your homework, whether you're ready for your tests, whether you regularly work on your projects. This, of course, doesn't mean that we don't care, we're just transferring the concern from us to you. We'll always be here for you if you need our help or encounter any problems. But we are afraid that you won't be able to cope with this freedom and responsibility, and that your school story will end up in you flunking."

Amy got upset that they had such low opinion of her and underestimated her. "It's great that I'm free, but I'll prove to you that I can successfully finish this year by myself without your help."

For six months, her mother observed her progress, which would be most appropriately described as speeding down a rollercoaster. The week before school was out, Amy was driving home from school with her parents and shed bitter tears on the back seat.

Father: "What's wrong?"

Sarah: "I'll flunk the grade."

Mother: "Hello! We've known that for the past six months."

Sarah: "If I'd felt that for at least the past two weeks, I might have been able to solve things."

Father (with a completely calm voice, like mother before that): "Yes, unfortunately."

Sarah: "And I'm a loser now, only the worst losers flunk!"

Mother: "If you feel bad now because you'll flunk the grade, let me prepare you that there will be consequences you'll have to bear and which will be even tougher. To begin with, we won't answer to relatives who will ask about your school. You'll do that. And you'll work during summer vacation. And another package will follow next year, when your classmates and friends start their second year of high school. Imagine the first school day, when they'll be made fun of for being a freshman. You've got all this coming, you'd better brace yourself, because it's going to be very tough on you."

Time ran slowly that summer, and Amy was facing the consequences just like her mother had predicted. She endured all the predicted events, and at the beginning of school year, she decided to make radical changes for the better. She listened during classes, which could be seen from her notes equipped with dates, she was no longer absent from school, she regularly did her homework, she told her parents what she was learning, she pinned a paper with the planned tests and titles for home reading on the notice board at home. She didn't become a straight-A student, but she saw to it that she did her schoolwork independently.

It is important that her parents trusted the correctness of their decision, which could also be understood as irresponsible behavior. But they were focused on their goal, to show their child the consequences of her own choices and face her with them. More on this will be presented in a special chapter in our next book. The attention in the parents' response was constantly focused on how they won't take any responsibility on their shoulders. The parents' awareness contained only one thought: what the consequence was and who its owner was.

6 Autonomy and Individuality

The period when our children are growing up is one of the most difficult times in family life, as parents face unknown experiences. It seems that growing up is a test of parents' past work. We all wonder fearfully what our parenting achievements are. The most difficult thing for parents is to accept the development-related fact that growing children are no longer obedient beings. A teen in the family is a change that requires altering the functioning of the whole family system. This is a development-conditioned change towards releasing control and opening to independence. We all accept that rationally, but it is harder to realize it in habits and patterns in our everyday lives. A growing child doesn't communicate it in words: *"Hey, parents, I'm an adult today, I have my own views, I have a huge need to be independent, to try all things in life, so you should step aside."* All these messages enter a family through conflict situations, bad decisions, unexpected changes, and rebellion.

Developing autonomy is one of the child's basic needs in this period, and every child paves his own way to get there. Family members become less important in the child's eyes, his interest in focused on the external world, and his peers become the most important people to him. However, that doesn't mean that parents and family members are no longer among the most important people, that they don't influence the child anymore.[43] Quite the opposite: only if a growing child receives his parents' firm support, can he safely experiment and test the limits to his new developmental impulses, and this way, develop his own autonomy. Researchers[44] mention three important areas of development: emotional autonomy, behavioral autonomy, and the autonomy of the value system.

Individuality means that we differ from other people and that we are special. Being aware of individuality significantly contributes to the shaping of personality. Individuality is our attitude toward ourselves related to permissions we give ourselves to be special. Individuality is a characteristic that separates us from the crowd in which we would be immersed and dependent on without our individual mark.

---

[43]Lerner & Steinberg (2004: 95, 354).
[44]Steinberg (2013).

In the history of mentalities, the so-called "sexual revolution" in the 1950s was a social movement of young people which brought changes precisely by allowing individuality to be expressed. Now this is something we take for granted, and no longer has our emotional attention.

However, the onset of individuality is, from the standpoint of development, still something that can heavily swing the balance in a family.

---

(36) Own Style

 Adrian was slightly over twelve. He always wanted to be something special, when it came to clothes. Now he wore skater pants, sagging to the middle of his behind. His father was ashamed of his son's half naked behind, when they strolled through the town together, so he visibly lagged behind the others. Adrian kindly pulled his pants up a few millimeters. His father thought about the period when he was growing up, his own fights about wearing jeans at church, the period of long hair and sticking posters of his idols on the walls of his room. The story is now repeating itself, and he is calm about it. He also remembered that he had read somewhere how important it was to accept our teen's style, and that parents should ease up on issues which aren't life-threatening.

At the same time, Adrian was going through photos in the family album and found a group picture from the second grade. He adored tiger print back then, and a family friend had made him tiger print pants that he wore day in, day out. The twelve-year-old was checking out the photo, and said: "How could you have dressed me like this!" His mother reminded him that he had wanted those pants so badly and that she hadn't been all that comfortable with the idea. The mother's story was also confirmed by the family friend who made the pants. Adrian was just silently shaking his head.

---

(37) I'll Move Out

 When he was fourteen, Josh announced to his parents that he would like to move as far away from home as he could. He said that he would enroll in the high school which is the furthest away from his hometown. His parents listened to him, without saying a word, but at the same time, they thought about providing him with the most educational experience, where he could put his independence to

the test. Then an opportunity came along: he could go on vacation to their friends' house in Spain.

"Would you like to go on vacation to Spain, alone?" *mother asked Josh.*

"Sure, I'd love to. Spain, cool."

The mother knew that her son had painted in his head the picture of Spanish beaches and adrenalin-filled life there. The friends were, in fact, older people living in a remote and lonely place on a large estate in Andalusia. They were self-sufficient. The place was about 50 kilometers away from the Mediterranean coast and an hour's walk from the nearest village. They agreed with these friends for Josh to stay with them for six weeks.

The family took Josh to the airport, and the boy embarked on the first real test of his independence.

The friends had no phone and no internet. The only way Josh could communicate with his family was by walking to the village and then calling them or writing them an email. He slept in a tent, and since the friends were still building their green home, the standard of living was much lower than at home. Josh's messages his family received described the horror of his life there, and his younger brother even commented that their mother should go get him.

The parents talked to their friends, who reassured them that Josh was in safe hands. He showed some initial rebellion, he didn't even speak and maintain his personal hygiene for a few days, but he calmed down and adjusted to the circumstances. He joined them at work on the estate, they went places, visited their friends, and went to the beach. Josh spoke Spanish the whole time and he returned home a changed person. His parents perceived him as an adult.

After he returned home, he was happy to be in his domestic environment, he even said that he had missed home, but his behavior showed some obvious changes. It wasn't hard for him anymore to go to the pantry and serve himself, which used to be an endless subject of tension.

---

(38) "Do not Enter" *(On The Door Of The Teen's Room)*

Parents, rather lost, come in for counseling. Their son, their only child, began acting strangely. He stopped talking, began hiding things, even lying. He wouldn't let them into his room.

Mother: "What have we done wrong? He used to be so sweet, he told us everything, he told me about friends, about what was going on inside him, about what he was thinking, he loved going places. He didn't have any secrets. We were like three friends. Now, he has the nerve to swear, like »*fuck off man,*« and even worse. I'd rather not say. He jams a chair under the doorknob."

Father: "He's driving me nuts. He has no right to lock anything, it's our house. We'll go where we please. He can't claim, take, our stuff. We'd like to show the kid that things can be the way they used to be, or we'll find another way to sort out the mess. And he won't be leaving any hostile messages around the house. He put a sign on the door: »*Take a hike, woman!*«"

Mom (in tears): "How could he do this to me, to us? I could go on. There's mess everywhere, oh my god, his room, he leaves behind everything, he doesn't stick to agreements. As if something stung him at night, and our greatest enemy moved into our house."

Related Topics
Part 1 of the Book | Trust | Where Are the Boundaries? | Taking Responsibility | Experience of Independence | Attitude to Physical Development | Teen Love and Sexual Maturity | Shaping Self-Esteem, Self-Image | Power Struggle

Within the Scope of Awareness

The need of a growing child is to become autonomous, which is shown on the outside as the family stepping into the background. This doesn't mean that we aren't important or that we can just withdraw. It is important that we allow the child to gain life experience.

Autonomy is expressed together with independence, and is related to decisions we make for ourselves. Autonomous behavior comprises the ability to manage yourself, responsibility, independence, and making decisions. Autonomy exceeds independence in decisions that refer to independent moral judgments.

The experience of consequences of independent decisions leads to the experience of being able to manage yourself, which will be successfully used by adults in important fields: care for health, the future, career. Autonomy concerns the fields of feeling, behavior and values.

It is important that we, as parents, aren't intrusive, that we don't force ourselves into the world of autonomy of young people since, in this case, responses may be unfavorable.[45] This means that we let them make their own decisions, which enable them to feel the importance of independence, that we don't restrict their living space with our "correct" advice and solutions, with what is right in our opinion, how something must be done, that we don't manage them... This is an important process which requires us to gradually abandon control, a process which lasts from the beginning to the end of puberty.

Leaving space for growing children to develop autonomy is also hindered by the changed parenting ideology of modern parents. We grew up in the atmosphere of our parents taking care of our fundamental needs, our career projects and employment, while we had to take care of our individuality on our own. They said, back then: *"If you don't go to school, you'll have to work in a factory. You've made your bed, now lie in it."* In today's parenting ideology, a child is treated from birth as a project his parents gradually lead to a successful conclusion. We don't speak about it, it is conveyed by our everyday behavior, with which we express to the child our concern for his future. Parents are obsessed with allowing their child to develop all possible potentials, and panic when they just think about missing or overlooking something. On such a beaten path, children don't feel free, and in their teens, this is one of the greatest hurdles in the development of autonomy. Therefore, growing children seek the most drastic ways (apathy, depression, problems at school, eating disorders). As children develop their autonomy, parents may use the principle of choice *(See page 154)* to enable teens to be more aware, and assess things on the basis of life experience—with the crucial addition of the experience of responsibility.

There are general options for teens to have their space for intimacy and individuality. A room they can equip according to their own taste, a nook, their own intimate space. Respect of privacy also means that parents don't browse in secret through their teen's phone, read their diaries, browse their computers, open mail addressed to the teen.[46]

---

[45](Dallos, 2004), Cf. also in the chapter about eating disorders in the Volume 2 of this book.

[46]If we are worried about the abuse of computers or otherwise, we choose a way to check things that preserves the teen's need for intimacy. This is discussed in a special chapter on addiction.

Having one's own individuality is a developmental need expressed by teens by searching for their own style, which sometimes really embarrasses their parents. Searching for style means experimenting with various imagined identities, where teens act in the world of their social environments. This includes imitating various currently-trending styles, belonging to a certain fashion group, setting your own identity, which tries to convey something opposite to style and value criteria of parents.

When seeking their own identity, role models play a decisive role, which is discussed at the end of **Part 2** of this book. Role models are people teens imitate because they have something teens need. Such a need is unconscious, and mostly related to a person who enables teens to have safe attachment. First and foremost, these are, and should be, parents. Next to their parents, teens explore what it is like to be a person who is respected in their world.

Another important thing: growing children equate their style with their personality. So if we comment on their latest fashion style with a bit of non-acceptance, the teen will understand the message as: *"I'm completely inadequate, unacceptable for my parents."* And he will choose his own suitable counterblows.

Therefore, it is very important how we explain to ourselves the behavior of our children. Namely, our view defines our response. Depending on our responses, our teen very explicitly shows us the feedback principle, which strengthens or reduces certain behavior. The more we try to change the behavior, which is part of our teen's autonomy and individuality, with intrusiveness or prohibition, the more such behavior will strengthen. The same holds true for beliefs and values. Extreme cases are stories where teens rebel and, in their fight for autonomy, choose partners or friends their parents deem inappropriate. Parents' attempts to restrict contacts generally enhance relationships which were, in their core, non-functional and would unravel in a different way on their own.

If exploration of gaining an independent identity is seen as a whim, as if the child exaggerates, makes things up, fantasizes, we see his attempts to gain independence in his style as uncalled for or inappropriate behavior. Then we will respond, according to our understanding, with the message our teen will understand as if we don't permit him something he deems most important. And in this, we have absolute power.

Can we see a special style our teen has come up with as his expression of the need for individuality, his own expression and own identity?

How can we perceive the indicators of independence and individuality, special features children use to express themselves, which differ from our values?

When parents lose their focus at the first resistance, we often ask them about their image of their child in ten years' time. Will this resistance be a disaster, or are other things also important? Perhaps we can find in this an opportunity for the experience that the teen can overcome his distress on his own? We can also discover positive things. Perhaps more important than the grade in English is whether we can trust him to persist, to have a limit, to know what his goals are? All this can be more important than grades, or than the shame he brought on us. It is worth giving the child an opportunity to get an experience from life.

Growing children articulate their need for autonomy as: *"You don't give me any freedom, I need freedom, you're suffocating me..."* Parents usually understand this as: he doesn't want any control, rules or boundaries. The teen's developmental needs and our level of trust, the power of authority and of boundaries we have set, meet at this point.

What are our experiences and stories regarding autonomy and individuality? Which messages from these stories are patterns which recur in our parenting beliefs and behaviors?

Because of certain circumstances in their lives, teens can be especially tightly connected to one relative, and in this relationship, subordinate and non-autonomous. This can also occur in the relationship between twins. The task in the teens' development (with parents having the opportunity to influence) is that, in such relationships, teens become autonomous and follow the path of developing their own individual personality.

Tips and Solutions

We can add to the first two stories also the story on makeup from the chapter entitled **Attitude to Physical Development** (See page 232) These stories already include solutions. Common to all the cases is that the parents didn't use the strategy of opposing the expression of individual needs but, at the same time, they maintained clear boundaries. In all the stories described, initial passions calmed down according to the principle: *first permission, then restriction.* Without damage, we can let adolescents (and younger children) have their freedom about their fashion style, arrangement of their rooms, lifestyle... When teens get the permission from their most important subject in terms of values, they are also willing to accept boundaries.

---

(39) Quiet Sunday Lunch

A family was having Sunday lunch, and the oldest, a fifteen-year-old, announced that he would have his lower lip pierced.

His mother thought that she was ready for anything, but not this. The notion of piercings and tattoos on a developing body was most certainly not compatible with her values and principles. This time, it didn't occur to her that she could buy some time to think by going to the toilet. She tried using humor to divert the importance of the topic, and counted on her husband to help her.

"You'll have a hole in your mouth and you won't be able to blow up balloons for your kids." *The son rolled his eyes.*

"When you eat, soup will be leaking through the hole."

The son was becoming increasingly upset and impatient, the mother was lost, while the father was staring at his plate, indifferently. Finally, the father's voice could be heard. He had, meanwhile, been madly thinking about how not to use the word "no:" "Well, you can have a piercing when you bring me a certificate proving your full-time employment."[47]

The son mumbled something, and grumpily stormed out of the kitchen. And this was the end of the story.

---

[47] The father's argument was completely absurd and unreal, but here, the structure that allowed the field of the teen's autonomy, preventing fight and opposition, is important.

When the son, at eighteen, announced to his parents that he was getting a tattoo, they talked by listening to each other's arguments.

Everyone had their own beliefs, and the son listened to the second thoughts of his parents, but the final decision was up to him.

Where (how—when—to which point) can we let our teen make his own decisions, and independently control his life?

In the story about the teen's idea to leave home **(No. 37)**, the parents offered in advance the opportunity for a comparable experience. This is a fine example, showing that the need for autonomy is related to responsibility, and that freedom depends on maturity. Functional skills used in adult life are learned gradually, with small steps in safe environments. This is also the preparation for independence. Teens can't become autonomous without their own experiences in safe environments.

A common topic related to teens' independence is a purchase of a pet that teens want, as justifiable support for their emotional experience. This is also a great opportunity for them to learn how to be responsible, to care for another being, to provide emotional support... On the other hand, the question of who will care for the animal pops up. Teens guarantee that they will do it. But parents know stories where such guarantees turn sour, and the care for the animal is left to them. A father who didn't want to argue whether his daughter would care for the dog or not simply enabled her to experience it in advance. *"Here's the leash you'll walk it every morning for the next two weeks. When I see that you're prudently and consistently doing it, I'll know that you're really independent and responsible enough to care for a real dog."* They say that there wasn't a pet in that house for quite some time.

The third story **(No. 38)** combines several influences. It is evident that the parents take their son's behavior personally, as the consequence of their influence. The parents' awareness reflects that they aren't ready for a developmental change. They fight it because it requires them to change their old parenting styles. In their defense, they cling to the "all or nothing" principle. ("It will stay the same as before, or there will be nothing.") At the same time, they can't set a boundary between intimacy and humiliation. It is sensible to see which patterns are included in the field of intimacy in

197

this family. Does the rule that you have to knock before entering the parents' bedroom apply? Do they respect privacy, and how?

The child's behavior contains a message which invites the parents to teach the child internal control, instead of using external control. This means creating a safe environment to allow the child his own experience, trust, clear boundaries and consequences, to learn how to be responsible. In brief, topics already described in other sections.

Learning autonomy, searching for individuality, and gaining the experience of independence no longer follow the "all or nothing" or "black and white" principle. There are various fields, some safer, some less safe; in some fields, you can withdraw with your worries sooner, in others, later; in some fields, we feel safer with our teen's experiments, in others less safe. The principle of learning and strengthening trust goes from less to more. So it is sensible to start with less.

Fields where teens gain first-hand experience and experiment risk-free are: shopping for clothes, choosing a hairdo, choosing friends, choosing styles (music, art, aesthetics), putting decorations in their room. The parents' job in these money-related choices is to set boundaries.

"Our contribution for your clothes is X dollars.[48] *You can choose. If you need more to satisfy your needs, you'll have to provide the rest."*

Then there are other fields where we, as parents, have the right and duty to be informed. One of such fields is attitude to money. Having one's own money and managing it independently is a necessary experience which facilitates the development of autonomy and independence in the field of economy. Independent money management is a field of learning placed between external control and autonomy. Our right is to know how our teen spends his money, while the teen can test various money management strategies from spending it regularly on goods he needs at the moment, to saving it for more valuable and durable goods.

If the teen saves large sums, and he can spend them on certain goods, a dilemma occurs between allowing autonomy (*"I can buy a four-wheeler or a computer with my own money"*) and the risk of exceeding the boundary. We protect ourselves by predefining boundaries.

---

[48]Every family determines its boundaries and rules. Experience shows that the principle "less can be more" applies.

7 Power Struggle

Parents experience the need for power in the period of growing up as a fierce and dramatic change. All of a sudden, the once obedient child begins rebelling, powerful changes in words the teen uses when speaking make our heart ache, gestures are abrupt and provocative. We are familiar with periods of stubbornness from the past, but when the teen becomes aware of his potential power, parents get scared, and in their responses, they may quickly find themselves on the battlefield with their teen.

(40) Power Struggle around the Computer

It was at the beginning of the holidays. Mother and father came, concerned, with a hard disk from their son's computer.

"What should we do? Thomas, our 15-year-old son, suddenly became closed, anti-social and the computer is his whole world. He could play games all day and night. Meanwhile, our world is running around, arguing and extortion over how long he can use the computer. We are both very pre-occupied with our jobs and, during the day, we cannot control him. Particularly now, during the holidays, he is home alone and hanging out on the computer all the time. He does not even respond to friends who call him.

First, I took away the computer cables. But he went to a friend and brought other ones. Then I changed the password, but in two hours he was in again. I don't understand, but he somehow installed a camera above the keyboard and cracked the lock. We are completely helpless against him.

Now he's become rude to us. Every time we force him from the computer, he is cursing, pounding with doors. And yesterday he told me words that really hurt me. I cannot allow or tolerate such way of communicating with me. I'm taking back authority, and saying that enough is enough. Now we are here, without any idea what to do. I removed the hard disk from his computer, and it is here in my bag. I would like to see him now, how'll find a way around this! But I'm scared that he can cross all the limits and do some harm to us. His attitude is:

you are doing something bad to me, I will do the same to you. He tries to be equal with us, without respect."

Taking the computer away, or a power struggle around prohibited access to the computer, is a lost battle in advance. We are in the field of previously-discussed topics: limits, learning responsibility, creating the connection, authority. How can we step out of the power dances that you can see in **Part 1** of this book (Chapter 7), where we described how we can be caught in such "dances" (*"Punishment and Abuse of Power,"* on *pages 92 - 94*), and reconnect, despite destructive behaviors.

When parents in *Story 40* step out of the dance of power, then the son saw that he had the chance to deal with power on his own property, and the vicious cycle stopped. Instead of the computer being the central point of the parent-child relationship, they focused on how to build and keep a lasting connection.

---

(41) When Does Parents' Power (lessness) turn into Violence?

They came to our workshop on communication with teenagers, on the recommendation of a social work center. They brought a story about their daughter being taken away at the beginning of her teens, because of the parents' violence. They were struggling to get her back, but were completely lost. They simply couldn't find the essence around which the dynamics of relationships in the family revolved. They got stuck in marginal events, because they couldn't see the logic or understand which forces led the game which resulted in their violence against their daughter.

At the workshop, they faced their patterns and experiences from when they were growing up. Parental violence was the prevailing factor in these experiences. The woman's mother told her to do things which were too difficult for a ten-year-old girl, and she didn't feel like she had a free childhood. Her need for play wasn't met.

The man described his growing up as being in a labor camp. His father conditioned his relationship with him. He didn't allow any autonomy. It was always the way his father said it would be, and he didn't consider his needs. Parenting was based on intimidation and ruthless disciplining with suppression. If the child cried or was stubborn, his parents poured cold water over him, suppressing the unacceptable behavior. John said that his father had put a book on the table for John to learn a foreign language, and demanded for him to do so, but he hadn't even considered that John didn't understand the subject and couldn't learn by himself. He got external help for his daughter, but she still wouldn't learn. And this was driving him nuts.

John and Vera strongly believed that parenting means directing a child according to the parents' ideas, which, when the child is no longer obedient, is settled with coercion. They weren't able to consider that there are sensible reasons behind no matter how unusual a behavior, and that most children aren't aware of that. So John didn't see that in his relationship with his daughter, and he was led by what he believed was right, but he wasn't able (the same as his father) to think that the child might have other reasons or sense or needs.

After such experiences, both partners talked about the circumstances that provoked violent behavior in them. They understood that they chose it because of powerlessness. Their daughter had problems at school, she didn't understand how to read and write basic mathematical operations. At school, they hinted that their daughter's abilities were lower, and suggested she be transferred to a school with an adjusted learning program. The parents took that as something shameful. Especially the father decided to try as hard as he could to wring the knowledge out of his daughter. He believed that he would achieve this with repetition and brushing up on her knowledge, which his daughter couldn't do. The father chose violent behavior as a way to coerce his daughter to do more schoolwork.

The experience of meeting the emotions of the child suffering violence enabled the parents to open up an opportunity for a different view. In their world, a conflict of values was taking place: connection and connectedness on one side, the duty to give their daughter education to see her to independent life on the other. The emotional experience helped arrange their hierarchy of values. They allowed the possibility that their daughter truly couldn't cope, and that schooling at a school with an adjusted learning program would be less stressful for their mutual relationships and for the child's healthy psychological development.

(42) When Teens are Violent to their Parents

Kathryn lived with her mother after the divorce. Her father blackmailed her mother, and threatened her with taking the child away, over and over. Her mother was insecure inside and her parenting was permissive. Kathryn slept in her bed, even when she was nine, when her mother's new partner moved in. The mother solved her difficulties with Kathryn's willfulness and stubbornness with threats that were never followed through. This developed and strengthened Kathryn's belief that she had the power. The new partner was also indecisive about his role, as he hesitated between not being the biological father and not having the right to parent her, and being aware of the necessity of boundaries. The whole system between was without any effective manner to teach Kathryn how to be responsible, through firm boundaries and clear consequences.

When Kathryn was thirteen, the partners faced difficulties, and her mother started using exits, both as a partner and a parent. Kathryn lost her feeling of fundamental safety, and repeated her mother's pattern. Her mother watched helplessly as Kathryn escalated her violent behavior. At first, she destroyed things around the house, then she usurped her mother's favorite items which she gradually destroyed, she tortured their cat, and finally, she physically attacked her mother.

Life in the house became unbearable. Kathryn completely slacked off at school, and announced that she would stop going. Her mother sought help, from her personal psychiatrist to a social work center, psychological help for her daughter, toyed with idea of placing her daughter in a residential care institution or foster care, or sending her to her biological father.

In the story, where Kathryn understood her mother's feeling of being lost as the loss of her own safety, her violent behavior escalated, and she disregarded all boundaries and wasn't considerate.

In our practice, we encounter many cases where parents were very nice to their children before puberty, they raised them by avoiding conflicts, but then, in puberty, children suddenly manifested themselves as violent and completely apathetic.

Related Topics
Part 1 of the book | Where Are the Boundaries? | What to Do with Rules? |
Attitude to Authority | Autonomy and Individuality | Experience of Independence

Within the Scope of Awareness

Before puberty, children see their parents "from below," which signifies the idealization and glorification of their omnipotence and power. Teens see parents "from above," as worthy of criticism. When parents wonder what is going on, as their teen keeps criticizing them, that he feels contempt for everything, that nothing is good anymore, that there are no more values, it is important for us as parents to understand what is happening in the dynamics of development. After ten years of idolizing parents, a child needs to change that image. The image of parents who are perfect and can do it all, who have no flaws and never make mistakes, who were excellent students all the time, who are role models and ideal in all fields, who are morally pure, needs to be dropped. This process begins by criticizing what is largely misunderstood by parents as criticism of them as people and their past parenting endeavors. But a child can only wriggle out from subordination through awareness, which says that parents can indeed make mistakes, that they are sometimes wrong, that there are things they don't know and can't do, that there are things they don't understand, that they can be wrong in their decisions, thinking and actions. This is a developmental process of gaining independence and developing autonomy, which simply must happen for a teen. Therefore, parents are, in teens' words, *"pathetic, clueless, Neanderthals, thick."* Every family could give you its own vocabulary of degrading descriptions. It is important that parents understand that this isn't about our degradation. It is about the degradation and reshaping of the image our children have created about us, it is about their ability to make a developmental change in their awareness from the position and role of a child to that of an adult.

It is important in what way we allow and enable growing children to change the ideal image of their parents. This process can be carried out in a soft or hard way. Parents who have problems stepping out of their idealized role, because it has brought them great power in the past (which is related to their psychological economics and patterns) will experience the process as a painful removal from their position, and will fight it. Undeniably, this experience contributes to parents' collections of their experiences with life wisdom, as it means leaving the field of power, and seeking other forms of cooperative and more equal communication.

It isn't about teens assuming the position of their parents. The latter remain in their basic role.

One way for parents to help their teens is "self-ironization" or "self-descent." This means that parents show teens, in a humorous way, that sometimes teens know more than they do, or can do something they can't. Board games and joint chores are great options. A mother can say to her daughter: *"These flowers thrive if you care for them, you obviously know how to talk to them better than I do."* A father can compete against his son in basketball, where the son is more experienced. He can ask his son to help him get the bike ready for the new season. *"I can see that you've sorted out your bike like a pro, will you help me so I can catch up with you on our tours?"* This way, opportunities help strengthen competence and self-esteem. Opportunities for parents to compete with their teens, in playful and relaxed circumstances, strengthen mutual relationships, and are the most appropriate field for young power to compete. Playful wrestling between a father and a son is where masculine identification takes place.

The development of inner power, which is an important personal task and skill, is connected with the awareness that we can do something by ourselves, that we are stable inside, that we have an inner strength that helps us survive. Connections and experiences with power are developmental needs. Inner power is a need related to development of self-esteem; the awareness that we have the power to overcome hurdles in life. Teens test their power within a framework provided by their family.

Parents sometimes mix the perception of change and accompanying emotions with violence, mainly repeating their own experiences when they were growing up. So for many people, power is something they don't accept and something they need to fight.

Frequent setbacks which we encounter when providing counseling to parents refer to their children not being on the right path. Parents (mostly fathers) feel that they know what the right path is, as they walked it with great difficulty, and they won't let their children experiment and gain their own experiences. Prohibition or intrusiveness from parents results in rebellious children, and instantly starts a fight in the relationship.

When there is a setback in the relationship with the child, the use of power comes to mind first. When we are getting stuck with our teenager, it is a spontaneous thought that we can overcome the conflict by using the power – as a proven method from past experiences, when we were in more of a position of power than our child. And we accept it as a lifesaver, the best solution—reasserting power will "solve" the situation. But in the relationship with teens, when our actions are made with any eye toward exerting domination, then we can expect a counter move, similar to answering a call for battle. Stories where teens prove that no one can touch them, even at the cost of their health and, in extreme cases, self-destruction, are sad and tragic. Characteristic of them is the principle of gradual mirroring, where fighting between parents and teens escalates in every profound situation, then goes on and on, in a vicious circle.

Shocking stories of the loss of connection, and even sadder stories of eating disorders, bear witness to the extent teens are willing to go to show adults that they are more powerful than them. The story of a girl who wanted to convey the message stated below to her unsupportive and violent mother, by choosing failure at school: *"I'll destroy my life so that you can see, in my suffering, just how miserable you have made me."* Arguments are sometimes unbelievable and hard to understand.

Therefore, entering a power struggle with your teen is a battle lost in advance.

What do we need to distinguish? Power is not violence. Power is not defiance. Power is not fighting. Whenever a relationship turns towards the abuse of power, the parents' job is to step out of the vicious circle and think how they can provide a safer environment by providing a connection, being aware of connectedness and bonding, permitting autonomy, and by preserving boundaries and authority in a safe way.

This requires stability of our own inner strength. What were our experiences in this field when we were growing up? What messages do we carry in our belief and behavioral patterns?

If partners are separated, it is sensible to be aware of the following: aren't fights with or through children an extension of unfinished fights in a previous relationship with a partner?

Tips and Solutions

For most parents who are caught in the dance of power struggle, the heaviest question is how to step out of it. The first part of the answer lies in awareness of our inner emotional realm. What is under the surface of anger and the belief that we can achieve our goals by using power? In fact, we are powerless and despairing. Maybe we feel that we haven't a real connection, and that exploiting power is our last hope. Parents in **Story 40** needed first to realize how that dance was destructive to their influence, through bonding and consciously decided to step out of it. They presented the way out as the son's choice:

"We are completely estranged and there is no sense in repeating our prohibition and your rebellion. It's true, that you have more power than we do. And you can do a lot with this power. Either you can resist, continue your rebellion and harm to yourself and our family relationships. Or you use the power more constructively, to build yourself and your personality. We prefer to be parents who are relaxed, who trust in you, who don't control you like a helicopter, who don't prosecute, pursue and prohibit you all the time. Go to your room, take time and think about it, and then choose on your own. Come and tell us afterwards."

After two hours, the son returned from his room and announced that he'd chosen the friendly family relationships, and that he wants to make something out of himself. Then they commonly defined borders and rules, which the parents needed to feel safe. On the other hand, the boy expressed how important family relationships were to him, and that he would subordinate his principle of joy to maintain that value.

The other two stories include powerlessness and instability of the parents in the role of authority. Many times, such stories stem from the parenting style, which is based on a romantic belief: *"I'll never be violent against my child, I'll be friends with my child, we'll work out things nicely, I'll prevent conflicts in advance, I'll show him that he's everything to me and he'll return these feel-ings..."* [49] Instead of assuming a sound and safe position, with boundaries and authority, mothers complain: *"First he destroyed my computer, now he's calling me when he needs help to get him out of the mess at school."* And inside, they battle the dilemma: *"You're asking me and I'm in the position of power—if I don't indulge you, am I can only expect a new wave of uncontrolled rage and behavior which will exceed the boundaries?"*

A change towards good hope in the second story **(No. 41)** happened at our weekend workshop.

---

(43) Empathy with Own Childhood Story enables Empathy with Own Child's Situation

Vera emphasized that she would like to get rid of her anger in the relationship with her daughter, because she recognized it as a pattern she repeats after her mother. Then she chose the option to have an imaginary talk with her now-dead mother, dialing her-self back to the time when she was ten.

In a role play, we used guided dialogue to help Vera come in contact with her emotions, anger and pain, connected with her childhood story. Her pain surfaced, along with tears, in this story because her mother wouldn't let her play with other children, because she had given her the responsibility to care for the family, because she had pulled her hair and humiliated her, because she hadn't been interested in her, because she had never seen any of her ath-letic matches where she could have seen her qualities, because she had nev-er praised her. These were deep and painful yearnings related to very intense feelings. Vera remembered how she had cried on the balcony, gazing longingly towards other children playing in their carefree youth. Later, she had found a secret nook where she had felt safe and could read in peace.

With such intensive emotions, Vera connected her behavior and empa-thy with her daughter, who was probably experiencing the same with her behavior (a replica of Vera's mother's pattern). Vera was thinking, in silent

---

[49] The beliefs mentioned have their own logic of emergence and their own sense. Mothers were traumatized as children by being physically punished, with abuse of power, and in their own growing-up process, they couldn't safely replace the ideal image of their parents they had as children. Children's naivety continues in their parenting strategies, repeating this pattern.

thoughtfulness when she could still feel tears on her cheeks, that now she really understood how her daughter felt. Decisions on important internal changes were outlined in her silent rapture.

John was sitting opposite her, and through tears, he was experiencing the same. He experienced very strongly that Vera acted the same towards their daughter as her mother acted towards her. And he experienced first-hand how their daughter felt when her hair was being pulled and when the object of physical violence. He also recognized his powerlessness, when his daughter wouldn't do her homework. He explained this to himself that his daughter intentionally didn't want to do her homework, that she was rebelling, that she was deliberately provoking him. But inside, he believed that doing homework was the only way to learn responsibility, work habits, that this was the right thing to do, because they said so at school. They were called to school many times, where they listened to messages about their incompetence and bad parenting. This was how they interpreted what they had been told to themselves. Then one day, a social worker turned up and took their daughter to foster care.

They were both shocked when they learned of the suffering child's pain. This was the right time for questions.

Can they imagine what it will be like in twenty years' time? What is their relationship with their daughter like? Are they in touch? Does she come visit? Can they enjoy their grandchildren? Will their daughter have a profession and will she do something to support herself? Can they imagine asking their daughter in twenty years' if her homework in the sixth grade was really worth all the grief they're suffering? And what would the answer be?

In the next few days, they started arranging their daughter's enrollment at a school with an adjusted learning program, and she moved back home.

How can we avoid setbacks in power struggles and harmful consequences, both material and psychological consequences?

1. By consciously applying connective behavoiours *(See page 58)*. This is awareness we can choose in advance.
2. We need to be aware that teens' criticisms are not a personal attack against us.
3. We *mirror* the teens' messages conveyed in the cocktail of provocation, criticism, complaints, aggressive attitude, frustration *(See page 121ff)*. Mirroring is the best defense, as it reduces tension. When

teens are aware that we really heard them (without their own mental additions, interpretations and advice as to what is right and how), they calm down, and the enthusiasm with which they try to tell us something negative diminishes.

4. Empathic responses include the ability to see sense in what a teen is communicating or wishes to communicate.

5. We should choose tolerance with a condition, instead of "no" *(See page 83).*

"Mom, gimme money for the movies!"

"You'll get it when you've done what I told you: I'm waiting for you to put away the things you left around, and fix the damage you've done by slamming the door."

And then there is a story with several subjects. This story shows the traps into which we parents step when overwhelmed with intense emotions, that come to the fore based on a resonance with our past experiences. This case demonstrates how difficult the parental role can be, when we struggle with ourselves, spontaneous and emotionally overwhelmed on one side, and an awareness of intent on the other. And, also, how difficult it is sometimes to choose appropriate responses and behaviors.

---

(44) Mom Trapped in her Feelings

 A mother called. She was utterly shaken, and said that she needed help immediately. She had read, on Leonida's blog, about the need of parents to be aware of their role, and to remain adults.

"But I just can't do it, Sophia says something and I totally lose it. If she wasn't fifteen, I'd hit her, but now, we yell at each other and she's just hung up on me."

At first, I try to calm the mother down, hear her distress, recognize her emotions. I articulate all of the above. I try to see sense in her panic and anger. The mother's behavior hides her share of the reason for the conflict. I know this, even though I don't know the story yet. She got stuck in her own emotions, and Sophia only opened them up further. These are the mother's childhood emotions, emotions from the period when she was growing up. I know the mother well, she regularly comes in for counseling.

I listen to her attentively, seeking space to calm her down. As she pauses for a second, I tell her that I see sense in her feeling of powerlessness, because she doesn't have a clue how to say nicely to Sophia what she expects from her.

She immediately responds, saying: "I'd like to be nice, but I just don't know how, I'll never know how. I grew up in chaos, and now I'll destroy my own family with this chaos, too."

I ask her if she wants to learn about other ways, and she agrees. I ask her to tell me the story. After ten minutes, I still don't know what really happened. This proves that the content of a story isn't important, but our experience of the story is. I need the story to understand her experience.

"Sophia spent three weeks with her relatives abroad. She's coming home today, and she called me before she left for the airport. I'm at the seaside. A family of Sophia's best friend is here, too. She'd like to come down here first thing tomorrow, just to see her friend and be with her (the mother's interpretation), and she wants to go back home with this friend, so we wouldn't spend any time together. When I asked her how she imagined that panning out, and that she'd stay with us for at least four days, she flipped out and hung up on me. And you know, I won't allow the little brat to hang up on me!"

The mother's story has already moved away from its essence.

What is its essence? To stay connected. What is the goal? To spend a few days at the seaside.

Then she got a text from her daughter: "You've had no one to pick on for the last three weeks???? And the first chance you get you're on my back? You don't even want to know how I am, what I want...the only person you see is yourself...just so you know...you've killed any desire I had to see you!"

The mother answers (with help): "I'm really looking forward to seeing you, too." *The mother stops, drops everything destructive, and focuses on the essentials—that she is happy that she'll see her daughter after a long time apart.*

The daughter, tearful and about to snap, says that the problem is not what her mother says, but the way she says it.

Mother's thoughts: I really don't know, I was kind and happy, how can I be bossy then?

Mother to daughter (text): "I'm sorry you heard and experienced me that way, it makes sense if you're disappointed. My intention was to show you that I'm looking forward to seeing you, and that the two of us, and all of us, will be together for a while. Dad can hardly wait to see you, and we both want to spend some time together with you. Can we talk, more kindly and in peace, when you get back?"

The daughter answers: "Okay."

8 Responses in Communication (with a Selection of Potential Complications)

Communication is a reflection of the dynamics of relationships in a family. It reflects our connections, bonding, care, and also absence, distance, power games, ignoring games, unresponsiveness.

Rules of communication say that not communicating is not an option. Each response, even silence and ignoring, is a manner of communication we choose. This creates a pattern in which our mutual relationships take place. We inherited many of these patterns from the time when we were growing up, and we aren't even aware of many of them, or aren't in conscious contact with them.

Parents usually complain that it is very hard to communicate with teens. Some teens won't say anything, some shut off, some would argue all the time, other are unresponsive, they don't like anything we suggest.

---

(45) *Coming Home from School*

Mom: "Hello."

Teen: "Hey."

Mom: "How are you?"

Teen (mumbling): "Fine..."

Mom: "What have you been up to today?"

Teen: "Nothin.'"

Mom: "You seem strange, is anything wrong?"

Teen: "What the fuck, quit nagging. You've been picking on me since you saw me. I'm out."

During the conversation, the father arrives and observes the outburst.

Father: "Hi. What's up?"

Teen: "Oh c'mon, not you, too!"

Parents often turn to us, asking us how to functionally communicate with teens. How to communicate at all, since their children changed unnoticeably and withdrew in their own world that is off-limits to their parents. This can be written on the door to teens' rooms—sometimes literally.

In stories of relationships with teens, parents express lots of concerns:
- She slacked off at school.
- When you ask him how school was, the most you get is: *"Nothing special."* or *"Okay."*
- How do we get him away from the computer?
- He has no limits when it comes to his phone bill.
- He has no work habits and disregards all kinds of authority.
- He started talking back, he uses words we don't use in our family.
- He can hurt me and throw me off, as soon as we meet.
- The child brought tension even to the relationship with my partner.
- I feel like I failed as a father. I wonder where we went wrong. My wife thinks that she isn't a good mother.

Most frequent complaints from parents coming to our workshops are almost typical: *"He used to be quite manageable, now he does everything his way. I used to influence him, he listened to, and complied with, at least the basics. Now his computer, Facebook, and phone are all that matters. I don't even know what he does there. He isn't interested in anything, he hates school. He doesn't even do the basic stuff. I don't know what will become of him. No way will he help at home, he doesn't feel like studying, and there is no way to move him. None at all. He doesn't respond to any incentive."* Similar stories, with various additions, can also be heard about relationships between parents and their growing daughters.

What happened? How can we understand it? And how do we act?
What influences the possibility of having a better relationship with our growing children? And is it possible to change anything during this period?

Related Topics
Part 1 of the Book | Where Are the Boundaries? | What to Do with Rules? | Attitude to Authority

Within the Scope of Awareness

Perhaps parents are too violent, in the way we talk to our teens. Do we tell them stories from our everyday lives? Do we answer the problematic questions? Are we spontaneous in communication?

Spontaneity is connected with the way we respond when we don't consciously control our behavior. In spontaneous responses, parents tend to choose disconnecting behaviors, described by teens as yelling, brusqueness, criticism, constant nagging, picking on people. Since communication is a constituent part of our behavior, and this topic is dealt with throughout this book, this chapter focuses on certain characteristic ways parents respond.

As we respond to the presence of our children, we convey to them important messages about their value. Therefore, it is important that we are consciously present in our everyday responses. Feedback, as one of the key principles of systemic operation, is discussed in Part 1 of the book. Feedback is response. The principle says that we get from communication what we put into it. This is especially true for growing children. Particularly in respect to our beliefs and thoughts about them.

The story, when we come home and see the schoolbag and shoes on the floor at the doorstep is typical. The teen is on the computer. The water for pasta has just been turned on, even though we told him fifteen minutes ago to get it ready. It doesn't take much to see movies in our heads and give in to spontaneous behaviors in high frequencies.

This is our response, in which we can choose various behaviors when we come home. Can we stop responding spontaneously and choose a different behavior? What am I aware of? What do I want? Do I want to know how the child feels? Do I want to preserve the connection? Which of my child's behaviors do I want to prompt with my response? Do I want the child to withdraw and fall silent? As adults, we set our awareness in advance, and make a conscious decision to choose our behavior.

Some people will first say hi and make a connection with the children, check the mood in the house, and begin with a neutral subject. Then they will repeat their demands, and see to it that they are done immediately. Other people will give in to their spontaneous thoughts, and start yelling, offending, criticizing. These may be everyday patterns which recur and create a communication pattern. This pattern is imprinted in the "dances" we repeat in our relationships.

The rules of functional communication include some well-known conditions:

1. We need to have a **connection**. Without it, and without physical contact, we won't be able to send or receive messages in our relationships.
2. We need to clearly distinguish between the role of the **listener or recipient** of a message, and the role of the giver of a message. We have an advantage over teens, if we first secure the role of listener, provided that we are good listeners. This also contributes to maintaining our communication channel, through which we can send and receive information.
3. **Context** means that a message must refer to something the recipient understands. It often happens that we communicate in different contexts, and both participants in the communication process are under the impression that they are neither heard nor understood.
4. To use a **common code** means that we share the field of understanding, that we speak *the same language* with the person we speak to. This is sometimes most difficult with teens. It isn't about us using their terminology and addressing them as *"dude."* It also doesn't mean that we need to use their code, but to maintain and create a common code which is characteristic of us. This is a code with our rules, habits, boundaries, rituals, with our *"soul."*
5. A **goal** means that communication is headed in a certain direction. This is something we, as parents, are most often not aware of. Do we want to preserve the connection, do we want to criticize, do we want to change our behavior, or do we want our teen to hear us, and pay attention to us? We also have to admit that teens are masters of throwing us off the track, when we are focused on a clear goal.

Albert's experience:
"Before I focused on working in our counseling and psychotherapeutic practice, I dedicated fifteen years to the search for an answer to the above questions, by researching behavior and understanding the needs of young people. These were efforts to try to find answers to questions of what we can offer to young people,

for them to be more motivated, what young people really need and how society can provide it, especially in the field of informal activities, which forms of working with young people are most appropriate for them to respond creatively and enthusiastically.

Last but not least, first-hand experience with my own four children have shown me that the answer to successful and functional communication is not to focus on teens, but in the awareness of our own contributions, and in contact with our internal processes. Parents and guardians are closest to their children, and have the greatest influence on them. We also influence communication in a way we are usually not even aware of. To make matters more complicated, growing children push our most vulnerable buttons, and instead of understanding this as an opportunity to explore our emotional responses and personal growth, we place the understanding of the reasons for our unusual state on our growing child. These are processes which take place outside of our awareness, and are therefore difficult to detect and control. But if they are pointed out to us by our partner or any other person, we usually protect ourselves by denial, or another kind of defensive behavior."

Tips and Solutions

The First Complication: How Was School? Okay... (and silence).

This is the most common sentence parents exchange with their growing children when they first come home. And the most common one that makes communication stop. Stopping communication is actually among the best results. It can take a turn for the worse. A few options: *"Quit badgering me; don't you have any other ideas than school, school, school; did I have to be born into this family; did I have to be the one to get the lamest parents..."*

With these replies, usually the author of the innocent question strikes back at this unfair situation, and stands up for himself. Stands up for his authority, his parenting maxims headed by the principle of parenting for work and learning. Other parenting ideas join in as he proceeds.

The result is predictable and well-known. If it's just slamming the door, that's a good thing. The functionality of the described dialogue is—null. Our agitation—maximum. Effect towards our parenting intentions—null.

Atmosphere in the family—plummeting. Our equipment and motivation to keep trying for the closest persons in the family—at risk.

We usually also try to perk up our beliefs, most adequately expressed by a complaint of a mother: *"It's a disaster in our house with the teen. A short time ago, he was my little boy who could listen, he did well at school, he had a bunch of extracurricular activities, he helped out around the house. And I knew everything that was happening to him. But now, he talks back, he fights everything, his room looks like a bomb exploded in it. He stopped trying at school, he says that everything sucks, I get called to school for his inappropriate behavior. He quit sports and won't practice anymore. The only thing he'd like to do all the time is to be on his computer. And the hardest part for me is that he shut himself off, and I can't get anything out of him. On top of everything, my husband withdrew from parenting, and I'm on my own. I'm telling you, sometimes I'm going nuts. I have no idea how to influence him."*

Wise people advised: If something doesn't work, drop it and replace it.

Do we really need to start with the killer question *how was school,* when we meet our child? Does our partner or friend first ask us how work was? We usually say to each other: *"How are you? Have you had a nice day?"*

We have tried this at our house. A wife is preparing lunch, the withered creature that is our child, who used the last bit of energy to drag himself from the bus stop, comes into the kitchen. It's four in the afternoon, he left the house slightly before six in the morning, before that, he got dressed and prepared things, then he went to school by bus, which is normally late, then he had at least eight lessons, went back home, the bus was packed, perhaps he was left without a seat—and that's that.

"How are you?"

Silence... *"Lousy, do you have to ask?"*

"Has anything nice happened to you today?"

"Nothing, everything sucks."

"Would you like a peanut butter and jelly sandwich and a soda?" These are in his top 10 treats.

Silence again. After five minutes of calming down and tuning in to the world of familiarity and his favorite flavors, he talks.

217

On his own. What else is there to talk about, other than his life experiences? And they include the world at school and around it. Relationships with classmates and peers, professors at school with their typical designations; and of course, what they did, what was going on during classes, what the subject of oral exams was, what the test was about, if they got the test back, a few sarcastic remarks about illogical things in the curricula. Do we need more?

Those five minutes of our waiting and patience are crucial. Five minutes.

And also: allow children to tell stories. Stories contain all the events that are important to them, and are told through their perspective. Everything that matters and is vital to them. And we will get enough information from them that we need for ourselves.

Meaning of Responsiveness: What Does It Mean to Really Listen and to Really Hear?

Most important for our children is that they know that they matter to us. That we care about them. We communicate our care with behaviors and responses (not so much with what we think). Some parents think that they will show connectedness (and consequently parental influence) if they copy the fashion trends of their teens. But in fact, such behavior of parents shows that they aren't adults yet, and that they missed their own identification process. Children find it tacky. Parents will never again enter this world and experience it, but they can experience it by taking interest in it. We remember a statement a teen girl made: *"My parents are constantly on my back, asking me stuff, but I have a classmate whose parents never come to school, they don't care at all what is happening with him. That's the most horrible thing that can happen to you."*

On the basis of our personal, as well as our professional, experience, we deeply believe that a connection with growing children is the key to all our setbacks and dilemmas. A connection ensures that they respond, that we know their thoughts and intentions, that we know their world, including their friends, that we know all their worlds. A connection ensures that, with all the shocking events in our lives, we respond in a way in which preserving the connection is most important. A connection also leads to responsiveness and exceeds the power struggles in which teens are unyielding fighters, even at the price of harming themselves. Focusing on preserving the connection

218

in the long run is also the most reliable prevention of our worries about the threats we see in the world outside our family.

Teens always give us opportunities to respond.

(46) Encouraging Independence

Sixteen-year-old Dylan was physically less developed and less independent. When he was in elementary school, he never went on a multi-day field trip, and his mother is convinced that he is several years behind, in his personal development. "Mom, I'd like to go to an event, something like the Lollapalooza music festival."

First, let's take a look at a spontaneous response, when parents are worried and angry at the same time that their son is still not independent at his age. Fantasies they play in their heads: he won't know how to get there, he'll get lost on the way, he won't be able to stand up for himself, people will use or even abuse him, he'll get mugged, he won't know how to take care of himself if he's in danger or if he falls ill, he expects me to give him money.

But they will say to the child: "What are you whining about? Who's stopping you? Earn the money and you can go. First, do something by yourself, before expecting us to just bring everything to you. We've been waiting for ages for you to go somewhere on your own."

The teen's response is silence. He thinks that they don't trust him, that they don't believe in him, that they never help him, that he doesn't have the support he needs at home. And that it's best he stays at home.

Parents who are aware that they want to know what is in their teen's head will respond differently.

"Yes, I hear that you'd like to attend an event." (*Use mirroring as the starting point of our curiosity, and to get more information.*)
"They say this year's Lollapalooza was great."
"What was so great about it? / What do you like about it?"

The son told his mother that there are people there who accept different styles, that they would accept him being shorter. The mother got some important information about what worries her child. How he felt about his delayed physical development, when his peers tease him or make fun of his statements. And about the company of his peers, where he feels safe. When the mother knew the background and the meaning of her son's statement, she could continue towards the realization of the plan.

"Which event do you want to go to?"

"There's one in California next month."

"What are you willing to do to get there? What can you do and what do you expect from Dad and me?"

To recap: in functional communication with our teens, we allow them to have their own world and seek sense in it. A reflective response enables us to share the ownership and also responsibilities, for each side to accept its share, and for their share to remain on their side. Seeking sense in their world means working our way towards an empathic response.

Danger of Double Bind Messages

The story about the permission to go to a festival could continue differently.

The mother allows her son to attend the festival, provided he earns the money he needs by himself.

The boy tries and, in impossible conditions, he manages to find a job he dutifully carries out and saves the money. But in the meantime, the son broke some rules, for example he didn't stick to the agreement about the use of the computer, and about the time when he has to be home in the evening.

The mother then changes the initial rule: *"You can't go to the festival, because your broke the rules."*

This is an example of a double bind[50] message, where the parents' behavior in the second part demolishes the validity and value of the first part. Double bind messages destroy the trust and safety of children. Let's remember a mother who was grieving after she had divorced her husband, and she came

---

[50]The concept developed by **Gregory Bateson**. Cf. Dalos & Draper (2015).

home with a sad face every day. When her son asked her what made her so sad, she denied all her emotions and told him that everything was alright. The double bind message was that she denied with words something that was obviously contained in the expression on her face. Her son lost his sense of reality, and chose behaviors at school which were difficult to understand, and deviated significantly form the norms in that community.

Our relationships with our relatives can suffer dearly because of double bind messages or double standards. This creates the feeling of not knowing where we stand, the loss of safety and of the contact with reality. The child never knows whether what we agreed will happen, and so he completely disregards our agreements and begins overstepping boundaries. We get angrier and punish him whereas, in reality, our share in such a story is huge.

We need to be able to clearly plan our agreements, clearly define all constituents, and to keep our focus on what we agreed.

In their decisions about consequences inefficiently referred to as punishments, parents often mix various fields of consequences. In the story above, going to the festival is one story, and breaking the rules is another. The stories should be treated separately. It is clear, however, that the mother has no authority which she could use to impose consequences. In similar stories, this is usually the basis for shifting dynamics to a fight, where teens persist in their belief that injustice is being done and that they will disregard their parents because of their inconsistency.

I Messages

I messages[51] communicate that I am the owner of the message, that the message arises from me, and that I bear the responsibility for it. *I messages* are drawn up in the first person singular and sent from our own perspective. That means no pointing to the other person, saying *"it's you."*

Examples of *I messages:*

"I would really like you to say good morning to me without any nagging tomorrow."

"In such a situation, I felt left out and disregarded."

"When I have to put away other people's leftovers, I get the urge to stop cooking, and fantasize how I would teach you to respect my work."

---

[51] According to T. Gordon and his *Parent Effectiveness Training* (P.E.T.).

"The thing that throws me most off-track is when I don't have the feeling that you're listening to me."

In *I messages,* we generally encounter situations related to other people and their influence on our thinking or feeling. When mentioning and including other people, it is important to first place them into our own perception system (I see, I notice, I hear) and only then into our system of experiences and emotions (it makes me feel, I understand that as, something happens in me...).

"When I hear you talking to me like that, I feel sorry that I can't finish saying what I've started."

"When I see you looking down and not talking to me, when you mumble, I say to myself that you're hiding something."

I messages are used to prevent the person we talk to from feeling attacked and having to defend himself. *I messages* help us clearly define responsibility and delimit the ownership of statements.

We often encounter people with communication manners which are part of the family cultural tradition, and who make a clear delimitation of responsibility more difficult. Here are a few characteristic examples:

▸ **Using second or third person.** *"If you hear something like that from a teacher, you're bound to fly off the handle. / How can anyone leave such chaos behind?"*

▸ **Use of indefinite and impersonal description** which creates a cold and formal atmosphere in relationships. *"With such difficult adolescents, it is hard to stay kind. / Such actions are usually followed by consequences which people regret. / In such cases, you can't flip out over nothing. / It doesn't suit students to go to such places."*

▸ **Black and white (all or nothing) illustration.** *"If you could pay attention to what I tell you to do, for once in your life. / How can people who never finish their tasks expect anything good in life to happen to them? / If you continue with such an attitude towards work, no one will ever hire you."*

▸ **Generalization.** *"I've never seen someone at that age think so foolishly. / All ordinary teens go on vacation with their parents. / Don't even try to convince me, because I know what people with dreads look like. / Anybody would respond the way I did."*

▸ **Comparison.** *"When we were your age, we didn't even think that someone would come pick us up. / If I had the opportunities you do, my life would be completely different. / We created stuff from scratch, but you can't put anything together, even with all the stuff you have. / Why does Faith next door always go to the store with her mother, but you never go with me?"*

Exclusion

When parents can no longer control the tension, they may resort to excluding themselves or the child from their relationship. Exclusion is similar to the disqualification of a player from a match: the game can't go on. The only difference is that we can't be in a non-relationship in a family. Exclusion damages the awareness of safety, attachment and belonging. Exclusion from a relationship is like the death of a relationship. It jeopardizes integration, which is crucial for internal balance (between the brain and emotions), and for the balance in relationships with other people.[52]

Exclusion, denial and rejection arise from a view which only sees things in two colors, without other shades, in the "all or nothing" manner. These are beliefs which are expressed as: *"If you disregard me, I won't be your father anymore. / You've crushed my expectations and I won't be bothered by you anymore. / Since I can't get the rules in this house through to you, you'd better just leave."*

Exclusion may be also connected with double bind messages.

When someone unplugs himself from a relationship, irrespective of who triggered it, parents are, as adults, in the role of people who can and must be initiators for the preservation of the connection and for reconnection. Threatening children that we will abandon them or place them somewhere deteriorates attachment. Remaining offended and waiting for the child's apology signifies emotional blackmail. Persisting in the position of being excluded from the role of parents is a choice, and we are responsible for it and all its consequences.

Unplugging from a relationship occurs when adults are not aware and are thrown off their internal balance. That is when our defensive strategies prevail. That is when we think along the lines of: *"He offended me, now that he needs me, I'm okay again. / She should apologize to me first, then I'll be willing to*

---

[52]Cf. Siegel, 2013.

talk to her. / I'd never expect this from my child, I'm very offended. / If you don't listen to (consider, accept, respect, greet…) me, I won't listen to (consider, accept, respect, greet…) you." As long as we insist on holding a grudge, we lose our nerves, are offended and powerless at the same time, conspire, and fantasize revenge, we leave and come back powerless, are constantly in a bad mood because of our teens—all these are signs that we are in a defensive mode, which prevents us from assuming the role of adults.

In stories we know, teens more often exclude one of their parents, and sometimes both of them. They stop talking, they distance themselves, they don't share information, let alone emotions. These may be stories of lifelong exclusion.

The story of a mother from the previous chapter (**Power Struggle**, *see page 202*) shows opportunities when the mother excluded herself from the relationship. She denied her share, and when she allowed the question *"What is my share in the dynamic that is taking place?"* she immediately found the answer.

Denying one's share in a problem is perhaps one of the crucial hurdles in parents connecting to their awareness. In power struggles, a hodge-podge of stubborn influences occur, which fights any changes. The awareness of our family patterns, a contact with our needs, the understanding of our own attachment story, and empathy with the child's need for attachment may help loosen it.

Moralizing paves the way for exclusion in communication. *"I've been telling you long enough, now you finally see that I was right. / If you'd just put in a little bit of extra effort, so much more could become of you."*

Secrets and Hiding

Family secrets destroy mutual connection and are cut from the same material as exclusion. We are referring to secrets between partners (for example an affair, hiding contacts and relationships with members of our primary families or relatives our partner can't stand, secrets related to work or profession, addictions to alcohol, pornography, gambling, computers), and to topics which are important to us, but which we don't consciously share with other family members. These are topics not spoken about in the family, but everybody knows about them.

Secrets may be a family pattern which function to keep the distance between family members. Secrets have the power to create an atmosphere of entrapment, with no obvious way out.

We need to distinguish between secrets that cause disintegration, the loss of connection, and exclusion, and the fact that parents have the right to their privacy and intimacy, where we set our own boundaries about who to share with and how much to share.

We need to consider that teens have the right to their secrets, too, which is part of a healthy development of intimacy and autonomy, and of personal maturity.

---

(47) Secrets in the Family

"I know you'll ask me why I turned to you. I don't even know where to begin. I'm overwhelmed with the feeling of guilt, and I can't step out of the familiar circle.

I'm here because of my thirteen-year-old daughter. She had an eating disorder. My husband and I live in the same house, but we haven't slept in the same room for years. He works all the time. Whenever there's something wrong with the kids, he tells me that it's my fault, and to solve it any way I know how. So I don't tell him about those stories. I try to solve them alone, in secret. Hope started eating, but now she cuts herself. Her hands, stomach... I try talking to her alone, I had the feeling that we trusted each other, that she was honest about how she felt, until last time, when she took too many pills, and then she called her twin sister.

My husband denies that this was because of our relationship and estrangement, and he keeps repeating that Hope needs help, but he isn't willing to change anything. He won't accept any help, because he says that there's nothing wrong with him. He expects doctors and therapists to do something with Hope, to stop her suicidal thoughts and actions.

I'm tired of all these games, of appearing nice in front of others. I don't have the strength anymore, and I don't know how we can help Hope. Her twin sister is doing a bit better, but it's clear that they both want us to know that they are in severe distress.

I don't know if you can help me at all. I don't need consolation, but concrete guidelines on how to act."

There was only one answer: will you just turn a blind eye to your child's distress and sacrifice her, so you can keep maintaining your family secrets? The mother gave the father an ultimatum: accept help and participate in therapy, or withdraw from the relationship. The father chose the first option.

In therapy, it was clearly demonstrated that the relationship between the partners was full of secrets, insincerities, and long-running resentments. The distance that was so obvious in the relationship between the parents was in opposition to Hope's needs for safe attachment and bonding. Each parent was attentive and caring towards the children, but something didn't add up. There were too many double bind messages. And with her behavior, Hope was unconsciously trying to solve and balance the unbearable gap in emotional experiences, which emerged due to all those family secrets.

Couples' therapy enabled the partners to remove the secrets and resentments from their relationship, and to speak frankly about their disconnection with the children. They separated their partner disagreements from their role of parents, and relieved their children of the responsibility to save the relationship between them.

9 Trust

Teens need their parents' trust: the trust that they are capable, that they can do it, that they will remain on the right path, that they can make the right choice, that they will make it. As a gift in return for being given this, teens will trust parents more.

Children whose parents don't trust them don't trust themselves, or use extreme behavior to satisfy all their needs.

The parents' trust during puberty is a reflection of the trust in the power of past parenting. The trust from relationships with this quality will also spread to new relationships.

---

(48) She Threats with Suicide

We were sitting, in the midst of our evening routine, when our daughter came to sit with us. Our thirteen-year-old Paige, pretty introverted.

We wished she would talk more. It seemed that she suffered a great deal growing up, but couldn't share it. I was hoping she at least did so with her girlfriends. On the other hand, I was hurt because I felt she perhaps didn't trust me.

"What are you doing?" *she asked indifferently.*

"We're talking about what made us happy today, why we are grateful," *my husband replied.*

"I just want to kill myself and then I'd be grateful because I did," *she said.*

The feelings in my body accumulated, I was terrified of the sentence I had just heard. What is my child saying? Does she want to kill herself? What happened to her? Is anyone threatening her? I saw a thousand fantasies in my head, and I know that my husband played a thousand times more. The emotions were unbearable. I could just scream, tell her to stop, what is she doing, that she has everything, that..., that..., that...

I forced myself to take a deep breath, and grab my husband's hand, which meant that he should keep quiet. But in fact, I knew that it wasn't as bad as my overflowing emotions were telling me.

There was a long silence after she uttered that sentence. We were just sitting there and...nothing...

227

"School sucks, teachers are there cuz they have to be, we annoy them, they can't wait to get out of school, they humiliate us, tell us that we're losers, that we should just go home, what we are doing there anyway, that they know that we're there cuz we have to be, that they've never met lousier souls like us... I can't listen to that anymore. I'd just kill myself."

"I can see that you're really upset," *I say calmly.*

"Wouldn't you be? Do you think it's great listening to that shit? Do you think it's great going to a school where they don't wanna teach you any-thing? I don't know what's up with them, I guess they're afraid that we'll do better than them. They're all incompetent. These kind of people teach. Others who know stuff make their money in smarter ways."

"If I had been experiencing something like that, I'd have been even an-grier," *I say.*

"Nothing's good enough, they just criticize. I feel like shit. I should just kill myself."

I take a deep breath: "It really is hard to live with such feelings."

"I remember the time when I felt like that. When they...at work." *My husband tells his story.* "I fell to pieces then. I know how you feel. And you're a child, I was an adult. On the other hand, I wasn't ready for such responses. At my age, you'll just brush off such an experience."

"I can't wait to finish this friggin' school. Jesus, and I chose it myself." *(Note: She isn't killing herself anymore.)*

A very strong connection arose among us. Then she told us about her fri-ends and boyfriend. In the end, we were all laughing.

Related Topics
Part 1 of the Book | Emotional Development | Autonomy and Individuality | Attitude to Authority | Experience of Independence | Responses in Communication | Shaping Self-Esteem, Self-Image

Within the Scope of Awareness

When children are young, they trust us unconditionally: they tell us all about their thoughts, their intentions, their actions. Then they endure great changes which may cause fear, from emotions to understanding rules and behavior of other people. Teens are no longer trusting and open. They communicate their perception of the world in their own way, which may be completely different from the way in which they communicated before. This can confuse and scare their parents, and they respond to teens' messages accordingly—and this creates a vicious circle of misunderstanding and distrust.

Trust isn't created by disclosing intimacy. Trust is an effect, the conditions for which are created with our past behavior.

The first important thing is our attitude to trust in everyday life and in family patterns. What patterns and stories from our personal experience with trust do we carry inside? Are there secrets in our family? How do we trust our partners and relatives? Do we have friends we can confide in? Did our parents trust us when we were growing up?

Which fears prevent us from trusting? What do fears that prevent us from trusting convey? What do we need, to be able to trust?

Trust and mistrust act in a circular process of responsiveness, where the rule that one person's trust creates and strengthens trust in the response from the other person applies—the same applies to distrust.

Trust is related to connection and safe attachment.

For teens whose parents trust them, trust is their top value. Their attitude is that they wouldn't want to abuse their parents' trust, no matter what.

Tips and Solutions

What did the father and the mother from the story above do to create trust? First, they listened to their child all the way and didn't comment, they weren't "smart" about it, they weren't intolerant, and they were able to keep their scary fantasies to themselves (that she didn't work, that she didn't study, that she provoked her teacher's responses).

They were focused on listening and seeking the essence in the flood of unconnected words. What is the essence, in such cases? It is by no means in the content which you can't make head or tail of, and it isn't constant or realistic. Getting stuck in inconsistencies, in terms of content, means withdrawing from the essence. The essence is in feelings and emotions. Teens tend to express that openly. When they managed to reflect their emotions, they conveyed the message that they were taking their daughter seriously and understood her. It is important that they were able to keep quiet and keep their fears to themselves.

Trust is built with the feeling that the child is okay, that he has the right to all his emotions and to fantasies, even death, by not criticizing her experiences, behavior and thoughts.

Which behaviors strengthen trust?

Easiness and spontaneity are environments where trust thrives. We are at ease when we see no worries, no fears, have no secrets, when we trust in ourselves, when we are balanced within, where we can bear difficult topics and remain upbeat. Teens invite us, over and over again, to the atmosphere of easiness, witty jokes, a humorous outlook on the world. Our serious response may overlook and suppress such invitations. Suppressing a more relaxed atmosphere doesn't mean letting up on boundaries and rules, but our ability to color the monotonous atmosphere of life with more creative and playful spirit.

What kills trust in teens?

The first answer is general: *everything that threatens the teen's feeling of safety with us.* A lot of emotions are always involved in these stories.

One of the worst blows to trust is if we disclose secrets confided in us by our teens without their permission. (It is so exciting for mom to tell a friend: *"You know, our thirteen-year-old girl is in love for the first time."*)

We lose trust when we disregard what is really important to them, and what is their top value. This means that we need to know our teen's world and be sensible to their emotional responsiveness. If we overlook or even ignore pain they suffer when a friend loses her pet, we may fall into distrust for a long time.

Parents like to take away their teens' favorite experiences as punishment for their offenses. If we punish teens by taking away something which means a lot to them, we step on the side of their enemies, to whom they are willing to make a lifelong promise of distrust. A thirteen-year-old girl made a promise to herself that she would never again tell her parents what she liked most, what she liked doing most, and which her favorite things were. The reason? Her parents punished her by always taking away what she liked most. She concluded that if they don't know, they won't take it away. When she told us about that, she cried. She was aware of the loss of connection, but she couldn't help herself in any other way.

10 Attitude to Physical Development

Physical changes in teens are accompanied by intensive emotional experiences. These are changes related to sexual maturity which teens encounter for the first time in their lives.[53] They are also changes which are prone to moral judgments from society on the one hand, and related to dangerous behavior of teens on the other. This topic concerns the shaping of physical image, the danger of body abuse, dilemmas about attitude to health, and the shaping of sexual identity. These are important areas, since a healthy attitude to one's own body is one of the best preventives against deviations in this area, especially in addictions and eating disorders.

---

(49) Cruel Beginnings of Physical Changes

Every morning when we wake up, parents of teens wish for this day not to bring us any new conflicts, new challenges. We wish for a peaceful day, like days used to be.

But there are days when things get ahead of us. Days which come to life with all their power, before we even open our eyes.

We have a fifteen-year-old boy, and a thirteen-year-old and eleven-year-old girls. I won't pretend that everything is great. It is, but every day, there are new rebellions, new arguments about boundaries, school, food, clothes, computer, sleeping, outings, cleaning... Everything! Everything's upside down.

This morning, I wake up in peace, only quiet sounds can be heard, and I think I'm in for a beautiful day when a person comes into the room and says: "Bye."

My brain detects a person it doesn't recognize. I quickly open my eyes and shout: "Hey, you, come back!" And think: "Whoever you are."

The next moment, there's our thirteen-year-old in front of me, looking thirty-five. I look at her bemusedly, wondering how I can settle this in the most "non-conflict way." Let me cheer you up. I don't think that's doable.

So the image in front of me looks something like this: the hair is messy, fixed with tons of gel, the eyes... Where are the eyes? I try my hardest to find them. Something is wildly flashing where the eyes are supposed to be, and around it, black, black, black... and on top of it, lipstick.

---

[53] D. Siegel (2013) writes more on changes in the brain.

I look at my husband, who doesn't get too upset. He is lying next to me, peaceful like Buddha, watching us. I think to myself: "Look at him, all cool, he surely thinks I'll sort everything out." *Which, of course, raised the degree of rage in my body. In this powerlessness, the creature who mistook Mardi Gras for a normal school day speaks again:* "Well, bye, gotta run."

"Where are you going?" *I sigh, astounded.*

And she says cheerfully: "To school. Mom, you still sleepin' a little? I'm going to school, you know, like every day. Sucks."

I desperately try to connect with myself in my forcefully-woken body. I'd rather just stand up, smack her, stick her head under the shower, and pour huge quantities of water over it. Feeling like this shows signs of severe **powerlessness**.

The next moment, I get a grip on myself, jump up, and become a (lame) mother: "I'm glad you're going to school. But first, go to the bathroom and clean yourself up. School is a working environment, not a carnival. You won't go to school looking like that!"

The eyes opposite me stand slightly out from the blackness, and begin shining even more wildly: "Are you nuts? I'm dull as it is, this makes me just a little bit normal. All girls wear makeup, all of them, but I have such a moronic mother who doesn't understand that. I'm not going to school without it. Ever. I'd rather kill myself. Get it? I'd rather kill myself. You're so lame..."

I try to look her in the eye, so that her words don't hit me straight in the heart, I let her say what she has to say, and continue calmly: "You'll wash yourself before you leave the house. Otherwise, I'll go to school with you, count the girls who are made up and not made up, to understand what it means when you say *"all of them wear makeup,"* and I won't argue anymore. So you have a choice: Either you wash up now! Or we go to school together. And I'm dead serious."

She takes a deep breath. At that moment, my Buddha raises from the bed, mumbles a threat, and the only thing that can be heard from our little monster are shrieks of despair about the most pathetic folks in the world. She goes to the bathroom, cleans herself up, and leaves in protest.

I fell back to bed, tired, worn out, destroyed, as if the day had already gone by.

When she came home from school, we devoted some time to her. She could tell us how very important makeup was for her beauty. We reached a compromise. Only mascara is allowed at school—at least teachers must know who you are. In your free time, you can be the way you like. This way, we enabled her to take one step further towards independence and allowed her to have her own image. For teens, this is one of the most important things—to be the way they want to be and to be accepted as they are. This compromise still stands today. And the interesting part is that, without any overt agreement, my younger daughter respects it, too.

Related Topics

Part 1 of the Book | Where Are the Boundaries? | Power Struggle | Autonomy and Individuality | What to Do with Rules? | Taking Responsibility | Teen Love and Sexual Maturity | Emotional Development | Responses in Communication

Within the Scope of Awareness

The basic task of teens' parents is to reflect their physical changes in a way that conveys that physical development is part of life, that it is natural, that physical development makes a teen a person with integrity, dignity, respect, and that the teen, as a person, is just fine.

This is related to teens' odors, inconsistent growth of the body, and the appearance of all other signs of sexual maturity. The teen's body is like a container in which he experiences his own personality. Therefore, responses from parents have a decisive impact on the shaping of his beliefs. Beliefs are an area connected to the choice of behavior in relation to the body: its care, health, food. If we ignore, scorn, taboo, criticize, deny, shame the signs of physical development with our responses, we convey the message that there is a problem with their biologically-conditioned physical growth. This is a mixed message which puts growing children up against an unsolvable puzzle. If they have to solve it alone, they choose paths which worry us adults.

The story presented opens up a dilemma between two parenting tasks: a response to physical changes which the teen is aware of and expresses in her own way, and the setting of boundaries. What has priority in the story? A change which unlocks the awareness of physical changes also unlocks other parallel changes, through the recognition of new *"rights"* which haven't

234

been clearly defined yet. This is a trap which makes us overlook the crucial topic of development in messages which simultaneously happen on several levels. The way the teen communicates somehow self-evidently plants a new logic onto conclusions: now I'm a grown-up and have grown-up rights, I won't be restricted anymore, I'll set my own boundaries.

Parents' attempts to restrict her are accepted by the teen as a declaration of war. They have to be fended off by all means, as they are an attack on *"fundamental human rights."* Such a maneuver often pays off, and parents tend to give up at this point, and withdraw from the fight. The ultimately effective argument is: *"Everybody can, just I can't."* This is an argument known to us from the child's earlier periods.

At this point, we should mention something about responsiveness in a rather difficult situation: fighting with a teen in bed in the morning, when we are all still moody and not in top shape. When we really don't feel like it, and our idea of a beautiful start of the day includes everything but the scenario unfolding before our eyes. But precisely our responsiveness in such impossible circumstances is crucial—it is unbelievable how teens can pick impossible and even more impossible situations.

It is better to respond at least in some way than not to respond at all—ignoring is the worst thing you can do.

The parents in the story didn't overlook what was most important—the topic of physical development. They recognized it as the main topic and responded accordingly. They devoted time to the teen to talk with no time pressure, after school, in their kitchen, at the table. The parents gave the teen space to express her attitude towards makeup. It was her new need reflecting her attitude to her own physical changes. The daughter needed the parents' permission. And a safe response, a message that her physical development was okay. With their feedback toward a growing child, parents give meaning to teens' own physical development and answer teens' internal dilemmas: Am I normal? Am I developing like others? What if these unknown changes (zits, body hair, other signs of sexual maturity) are pathological?

The parents' job is to soothe teen fears and dilemmas about physical changes and development. Here are a few questions that may help parents do so:

Do we respond as if the children were still six years old?

Do we ignore or forbid the facts of physical development?

Can we accept the facts of our teen's physical development and mirror them with respect and curiosity?

The influence of feedback from parents also determine the value and paths for the development of the teens' physical identity. So it is all the more important to have a connection with our teen, to be safely bonded with him, and to have trust that our communication allows for differences and acknowledges the significance of difference. These are conditions for our teens to be willing to hear and respect our messages about physical changes, the (in)appropriateness of certain behaviors and experiments with the body, suitable body weight, suitable care of the body, and about the development and shaping of our body image. In this process, parents need to be internally stable, as their attitude to a certain question conveys the real value. Double bind messages, and contradiction between the beliefs expressed and the actual behavior of parents may also be encountered in this respect. Teens involuntarily (and unconsciously) identify with their parents, some by directly imitating them, others by being their opposites. This is most distinctly shown in imitations of posture, and attitude to one's own body and gender.

The acceptance of one's own body is an important part of the development of self-image. Research proves that a bad self-image is related to the onset of anorexia, obsessions, agoraphobia, frigidity and depression.

When, in the story above, the teen's attitude to changes in her own body, and the recognition that she was growing up, were given the right to exist, this created space for new definitions of boundaries and rules. It should be pointed out that the parents' responsiveness, which included permission for a new developmental need (along with physical changes), prevented space for fights and mutual intolerance from emerging.

The parents chose negotiations instead of orders, fights and the demonstration of power. They learned that they were always the weaker party in power struggles with their teen. Negotiation is a much more effective strategy.

Tips and Solutions

The introductory story takes into account important content of the parents' awareness, and is an example of an empathic response to an early physical change in the girl. Here is another confession story from a similar period of development, which describes the way parents overcame their embarrassment, which was the result of family patterns.

---

(50) First Bra

A mother suggested to a father to go with their daughter to buy her a bra. The father, raised in the spirit of ignoring physical changes, got scared and confused. He simply wasn't equipped with the necessary skills. His impulse was to continue the family pattern of ignoring: "Where did you find me, of all people, to do this?" *In reality, his wife's incentive provoked shame in him, on the one hand, whereas on the other, he found himself in a dilemma with the awareness of the role of a father he wanted to play. He wanted to be a responsive dad, to support his daughter in her development, to stay connected with her, and offer her firm support throughout this period. He couldn't imagine how to respond to the fact that his daughter was becoming a woman, which was related to talks about subjects which were taboo and left to vulgar explanations in the street, when he was growing up: zits, growth of breasts, how to treat hairy parts of the body, periods, safe sex talk.*

With the idea that he should swallow this bitter pill as soon as possible, he asked his wife which store to go to, and how to find a suitable product. He felt utterly ashamed and powerless, and had the urge to withdraw. He'd prefer to just run away and disappear into thin air. His wife replied jokingly: "Well, they don't sell bras at the butcher's. Just go to the X store in Y Street, park your car opposite, go to the first floor, turn left, and if you don't find them, a clerk will help you. The clerks there are very nice and give good advice. Just ask for a girls' bra, size Z, and that's it." *The daughter was hopping excitedly next to her father, who was embarking on one of the hardest roads in his life. Everything went as the mother predicted. The father and his daughter accomplished the mission, and they even had an ice cream on their way back. When they got home, the father collapsed into his armchair. His wife stroked his forehead understandingly, and congratulated him.*

The daughter rushed off to meet her girlfriends, and one of them accompanied her home. The father overheard her comment: "Man, your old man rocks. He bought you a bra, he's, like, the coolest."

The casualness of the mother's attitude was passed on to her from her family pattern. Her memory of her first period was connected with an important story. Her family and she were just about to go for a visit, when she called her mom from the toilet and told her that blood was coming from her vagina. Her mother put her mind at ease and explained to her that she got period. She was happy. Her father put the coat and hat down, called their relatives and told them that they would visit another time. The parents made a holiday of the event, they went for a festive lunch. Her mom and dad explained to her what hygiene was, what a healthy attitude to her body was, what a period meant in terms of sexual maturity, what safe sex was. They also shared with her their experiences and stories, conveying the message about the values in mutual relationships, and their impact on personal experience and evaluation of one's own body and bodily integrity. This experience marked her attitude to her body, and she passed it on when raising her own children as a pattern of healthy development.

11 Emotional Development

Each behavior is based on emotions. We are aware of some of them, but we aren't aware of most. In order for teens' brains to develop, they need to be in touch with emotional impulses.

The teen's emotional world is very dynamic. Their emotions shift from one intensity to another, and most often they are expressed in extremes. Therefore, the response of parents to these emotions is very important. What is so important about emotions?

Emotional connection with parents facilitates the feeling of safety and stability in life.

Managing emotions, which means recognizing an internal emotional world, being aware of emotional experience and being able to manage (refrain from) behaviors related to emotional experience is another important task when growing up. We need this skill to be able to cohabit with tolerance in mutual relationships, using social and emotional intelligence.[54] But it is even more necessary in relationships with our relatives and parents, especially in relationships between partners and family members.

How can adults survive with all these intense emotions? How can we understand all these reckless and fierce responses from teens? Most often, these are fits of uncontrollable rage. It seems as if some teens are angry with their parents all the time. Joining in yelling, slamming doors, expressions of disgust, utter sadness, despair—just because you ask her when she will do her daily chores. Then her friend calls her the next minute, and she becomes incredibly happy and thrilled with life, she is overjoyed with the tiniest details, and even grateful, and especially infinitely tolerant and kind. How can parents understand all this?

Teen years are a period of numerous intense and overflowing events in development. During this period, they become aware that they are the owners of their emotions for the first time in their lives, which comes together with their physical development, brain development and the awakening of their hormones. They also perceive all other aspects of life in a completely

---

[54]More information in Goleman, 2006.

new way. As their sexuality awakens, their awareness of the social dimensions of mutual relationships opens up. They begin experimenting with, and being curious about, what life is, what it means to be autonomous and independent. What do they do with the awareness of enormous power? A true eruption of self-awareness and the awareness of others they encounter for the first time in their lives, accompanied by intense emotional experience teens need to place somewhere and determine its meaning.

(51) Uncontrollable Teen

 Lisa brought her fourteen-year-old daughter Ruby in for counseling. Their relationship was cold and estranged. The mother complained that she had no authority with Ruby, that Ruby slacked off at school, hung out with older people, consumed prohibited substances, smoked weed, disregarded their agreements, came home whenever she felt like it. And that she didn't care at all. Ruby was completely indifferent to what her mother was saying, and didn't show any signs of emotional response.

Her answer to the question of who she was attached to was: nobody.

Since her parents divorced, she had been living with her mother and older brother, whom her mother always set as a role model. She didn't have any problems with him, only her with mother.

The mother kept repeating that she would like to connect with Ruby, but that Ruby made it impossible.

Ruby responded to the therapist, and he soon brought her into contact with her feelings about attachment. Somewhere under the numbness on the surface, there was endless loneliness. Through tears, Ruby managed to say that she missed her mother, and grieved for her father, who committed suicide a year ago.

Ruby's tears didn't make her mother respond.

What was holding her back?

In Ruby, she saw her ex-partner whom she'd hated, and couldn't tune in to Ruby's needs for attachment and bonding with both her parents. When the mother told them about this hurdle, Ruby and she hugged and cried their pain out. Instantly, there was a connection between them, and Ruby began respecting her mother's authority.

Related Topics
Part 1 of the Book | Power Struggle | Learning How to Be Responsible

Within the Scope of Awareness

The ability to recognize and express emotions, thoughts and bodily expressions, and to recognize and understand the expressions of emotions in others, is a skill called mentalization or mindsight.[55] These are crucial skills that determine the way we will survive in social relationships. They reflect the methods which were used to teach us these skills and, as parents, we pass them on to our children.

When a child is around fifteen, the development of the brain enters a decisive phase, reaching the function which enables teens to independently learn from emotions and use their mindsight to shape their experience, think strategically, and to manage their emotions.[56] This gives parents the opportunity to co-shape and support their development, and provide them with a safe environment for a healthy development.

Our responsiveness arises from how parents can be safe with our emotions. The basis for the management of emotions is that we allow all emotions to exist. What was our emotional development like when we were growing up? Which family patterns do we carry in our psychological functioning? Which emotions were allowed during our puberty and which ones weren't? Which emotions of other people are easier for us to tolerate and be in contact with? And which are more difficult?

Another important aspect is how we respond to emotions.

Do we let our teens know that emotions are allowed and can be safely expressed? Are only certain emotions allowed, while others aren't? Do we deny certain emotions? Do we ignore certain emotions?

To communicate with emotions, we need safety, permission and responsiveness. Somewhere deep inside, emotional messages trigger the need for bonding, connection and safe attachment.

---

[55]More information on mentalization is in **Fonagy,** 2007. Peter Fonagy's mentalization is comparable with Daniel Siegel's mindsight. Cf. **Siegel** (2011: 82), **Siegel,** 2013; **Siegel,** 2004.
[56]Draiby & Seidenfaden (2011a: 65).

How many emotional matters aren't permitted because we aren't connected with our child? Because he doesn't feel safe with us?

How many emotions are withheld because we don't find the words to express them?

How many emotions aren't expressed because we are convinced that they aren't appropriate?

When communicating with our teen, it is especially important for us to be aware of the two layers of emotions: the one on the surface, and the one underneath it.[57]

How to Understand and Respond to Anger?

Anger is always an emotion that hides something else. Underlying anger is usually the powerlessness to understand, to change things, perhaps even powerlessness because emotions don't have permission to be released. And during a period when power is very important, anger is the most suitable choice to show and express the search in an internal emotional labyrinth. The strength of the eruption is a message about the importance of underlying emotions.

In emotional situations, teens need a "safe haven" response by parents, and permission to be owners of their emotions—this makes them feel safe. Safe response means that their emotional world isn't forbidden, suppressed, criticized, scorned, humiliated, ignored, denied, compared (with adults, ourselves), or translated into a "correct" form. Responsiveness simply means that we hear what they are communicating, and return it, just like a mirror returns their images—without additions and changes. This way, we will give them permission to have their own emotional world, and the world where all the intensity of this period of development takes place, as well as permission to have emotions. We will let them know that they matter, just the way they are. The latter is a very important message they need to develop safely, and the condition for them to become the adults we wish for them to become—responsible, independent, autonomous.

---

[57]More on this is in Part 1 of the book.

(52) Response To Teen's Emotions

 A teen is screaming from the bathroom that she won't go to school because she looks terrible, her hair is messy, she is in a rush to catch the bus, and doesn't have time to fix herself up, and she isn't leaving the house looking like that. Parents can perceive that as responsibility and concern. We usually recognize in such behavior: a fit of rage, provocation, we wonder why she didn't think about that before, we worry about potential absence from school, we play horror movies about it in our heads, laziness, lack of sleep because of the computer—and we get lost in our worries. This constitutes our response to the child. Even in our fantasies, we have problems controlling difficult topics, and choosing a nice and calm way: "C'mon, you'll go to school, won't you?"

This is usually enough to receive a tougher blow from the opposite side. We will hear from the bathroom: "How can you be so pathetic, you grown-ups are all the same..." *This intensifies the emotions which appear with anger, which may further escalate into a fight, ending up with a power struggle about who is right, who the authority is, what the rules are, where the boundaries are... During all this, a leap to a more delicate subject usually happens, and the fight flares up. Such struggles are a sad and non-functional part of the environment, which doesn't provide safety for growing children and their safe transition to adulthood. Is there any other way?*

Another option is to use reflective function with empathy.
"I hear your hair's messy."
"Yeah, and looking like this, I'm not fit to go out."
"Hm, so you feel like you can't go out looking like that."
"Yeah, and I won't go to school like that."
"I understand, such a feeling always throws me off the track, too."
"C'mon, Mom, shut up."
*(The bathroom door opens, the teen comes out with her hair in a ponytail, she's rushing to get ready to catch the bus to school. The mother **keeps quiet and walks her out**.)*

Teens usually, and most easily, express their internal dilemmas with anger, complaints, nagging (be honest and think about where they learn this!).

We mean both parents and (especially) teachers, who spend more time with teens than their parents do.

We are normally not equipped with tools to respond to their fierce and shocking emotional outpours. Our spontaneous response is that we are overwhelmed with emotions, we treat them as our own, and deal with them by moralizing that this isn't appropriate, that we won't allow it, that it can be expressed in other ways, and by seeking solutions instead of the teens finding the solutions. This generally leads to complications.

Even if teens' messages are conveyed as provocation, the mechanism of the adults' response is the same. If we get personally involved, we miss our opportunity to show ourselves to them as a firm support.

A response which can carry difficult emotions and be heard as an attack on an adult is a response where we reflect and allow teenager's feelings:

"I can see that you're furious and I hear what you're saying... / Do I understand you correctly that you mean that ... / I hear that you're angry, but can you tell me what is really bothering you."

When teens get the feedback that says that we allow them to have their own world of experiences, that we hear their manner of expressing emotions that are important for them, that is when we can help them to take responsibility and accept the ownership of everything related to these emotions. This way, we also preserve the condition for them to regard us as an authority, and to take us seriously, and let them know that we care about them and they matter to us. This is the connection and the sense of a relationship in which we are equal, with all our differences.

Only at this point does a parenting addition with real effect kick in: seeking suitable solutions, determining responsibility, accepting consequences.

Independent seeking of solutions is fostered by experience and permission to learn from mistakes. Teens must get an opportunity to gain such experience, and permission in their everyday life, at home and at school. This requires adults to be mature, patient and tolerant.

Tips and Solutions

Denial, ignoring, and prohibition of emotions are parents' responses that contribute to the depletion of the child's emotional and personal development.

The following are statements which prohibit emotional expressions:

"You can't be so sad."

"Aggressive words aren't allowed in this house."

"Can't you be anything but angry?"

"Do you always have to exaggerate?"

"Calm down. Your screaming is getting on my nerves. Do you have to exaggerate?"

Prohibition and other strategies (beliefs, behavior, norms) which don't allow emotional expressions can also stem from the family pattern, which works without anyone ever saying it out loud.

We give permission to emotions by recognizing their expressions and meanings. For example:

"If I look at this through your eyes, it makes sense that it's driving you to despair."

"Yes, I hear that you're angry and there is probably a reason for it."

"It's really hard, and I understand why it makes you sad."

"I believe that you must be really afraid."

By noticing and articulating emotions, we give them permission to exist. Just think how many unarticulated emotional situations we survived when we were growing up: sadness after a loss (divorce, death of a friend or family member), fears when facing new situations in life, excitement when discovering new things, curiosity about physical development and sexuality, expectations of achievements, pride after success and disappointment after failure, joy after victories and achievements, excitement when new changes are in sight, impatient expectation, yearning, daydreaming about long-term goals...

Do we have the vocabulary to capture and encompass the description of events with emotional implications?

"I remember how excited I was when I went to the seaside with my friends for the first time. How happy I was to be on my own, and how scared I was about whether everything would be safe."

"When I was commended for participation at my culture club, I was so proud of myself, as if I had gotten a medal from the state."

"My story about how friends didn't accept me in their company is the same as yours. And I can imagine how you feel. I felt..."

"I remember the expectation before I went to teen dances. My cousin and I went to a disco by bike. For teens, it was open before night. We checked who liked who and that was the most exciting. Then we rushed home and didn't dare tell our parents where we'd been."

Telling one's own stories of growing up is a way to describe, and pass on to children, many emotional subjects, with a plot and a solution. Even though stories didn't end on an optimistic note, as far as our topic is concerned (failure at school, unrequited love, not making a team, rejected application for participation, failure at a public event, scorn because of naivety or clumsiness), they present stories of good hope for our children, because they see in us adults who survived these stories, whose value, in retrospect, is that they strengthen and teach about life wisdom.

For people who didn't have the chance to learn the emotional language in the communication with their parents, and are therefore not spontaneously equipped with the skills of emotional communication, the period when their own children are growing up is the opportunity to change their patterns.

Shame has a special place among emotions. Shame is an emotion that doesn't allow us to talk about it. It is like fear. Its effects are shutting off and withdrawal. Shame is the enemy of connectedness and sharing with others. Shame is very protected, in order not to be recognized: I'm ashamed of being ashamed. Telling about the circumstances which made us feel shame as teens may be a hint that we can help our child open a closed shell.[58]

Shame develops as a reply to responses of parents who deny, don't allow or degrade important emotional messages. When our responses convey the message to a teen that he isn't allowed to express his emotions (joy, pride), or that there is something wrong with his behavior, using *"Shame on you, how*

---

[58]Cf. Cyrulik.

could you do / say / think that; I'm very disappointed in you; I don't have time to listen to you...," we are on track to create shame.

In recurrent circumstances with recurrent messages of parents, teens (and also younger children) may develop shame as a personality trait, which becomes the prevailing manner in which a person experiences himself. The purpose is not to avoid conflicts, boundaries or expressing his own opinion, but we must avoid creating shame. This applies to both parents and teachers.

Shame hinders development. To avoid the traps of the hindering part of shame, a person should reestablish connections and bonding, which is again the job and responsibility of adults. Creating the possibility to reconnect and bond is an experience which heals a traumatic gap in the child's trust in others.

Everything that hurts relationships can be fixed. If adults cause harm with behavior and words, we can always apologize. Along with an apology, it is important to give meaning to what we have overlooked in the teen's mental processes.

A father who humiliates his teen can go to his room and say: *"What I said to you wasn't right and I'm sorry. I understand that it was important for you to tell me about your success at the match and that you were very proud. And it wasn't right that I didn't take the time and listen to you."*

Such messages open the way to gentler emotions, and children always give us another chance to fix things.

Teens can find great support in expressing their emotions in pets, who are their confidential listeners in situations when a suitable human being isn't available.

12 Shaping Self-Esteem, Self-Image

Both adults and teens frequently state that teens lack self-esteem. We all understand that self-esteem is an attribute and a virtue which opens opportunities for making and maintaining social connections, overcoming hurdles more easily, tackling stressful situations more easily, being more accepted in society, having more friends, being more productive, and having a more successful everyday life, in all areas. Self-esteem can be strengthened when we succeed at something, and gain belief in our own, our self-worth and our qualities. Adults with significant influence (parents, teachers, coaches) for teens (and children) build self-esteem with their responses in situations which include involve learning and testing the necessary competences. Inappropriate responses from parents have a decisive role in destroying self-esteem. Lacking self-esteem is one of the heaviest burdens when growing up, and on the way to independence. Self-esteem is a universal psychological and personal need, which helps us to find our way in the new and unpredictable situations life keeps tossing in our path.

The loss of faith in yourself, your internal soundness, and of the awareness of your value, which teens rely on in every situation in life, can occur in various manners and in various circumstances. What these stories have in common is that the children didn't get an appropriate response when they needed it, one which would have helped them maintain or restore their self-worth.

---

(53) Self-Esteem and Bad Grades

 School counselors encounter plenty of cases related to adverse responses from classmates. Any child can find himself in a situation when his classmates laugh at, or even scorn, him. Some children seem to be immune to such responses, while others decide never to expose themselves in front of others again, at any price.

The parents of a teen in the first year of high school describe this in the following way: "He's afraid of the teacher's response. He isn't strong and is very sensitive to humiliation. Every little comment or criticism on his account breaks him. It is also true that he is a magnet for situations in which he is humiliated or wrongly accused by teachers. He is the

youngest in the family, and he has always been weak, in terms of his self-esteem and standing up for himself. He has always seen himself as less competent, he gives up easily and never fights, instead he cries, he lags behind his older sisters, he has never suitably evaluated his accomplishments, because he sees that he is behind and will never catch up. At home, he understands any laughter or joke as shaming. He always shuts up at school, and never wants to expose himself, because he is afraid of being shamed. He never strengthened his immunity to criticism, and he completely fails in situations in which he could experience it. So he'd rather withdraw from oral and written tests. When we force him to go to school, because he has studied and knows things, he is never sure of his knowledge. If he is given an oral test, his grade is better, but his written tests are a disaster. He is never sure of himself."

---

(54) Fear of Company

 "Our daughter has been shy ever since kindergarten and has never pushed herself to the forefront. At school, other students have always been 'stronger,' they have always raised their hands before she did, they have always gotten on the teachers' good side before she did. So she is this quiet and shy adolescent. She says that she doesn't know how to fight with 'pushers' and so she just shuts up. She hangs around the house all day long, she doesn't hang out with friends, she says she has nothing to talk about. She is shutting herself off, and I'm really worried that she'll never find a boyfriend."

The soundness of self-worth during puberty is supported by the way teens see themselves when they compare themselves with others, and it sometimes looks like they are searching for ways to degrade themselves. In such constructions, their assessments of their physical characteristics are degrading: too tall, too short, too fat, too thin, red-haired, with zits, with bow legs, too large or too small breasts... On this basis, they develop shame, which hampers their opportunities to enter mutual relationships and socialize.

(55) Experiences with Love

A twenty-one-year-old man recounts: "I think I began lacking self-esteem at twelve, when I got a brother, and my mother said to me to be careful at school, so I don't bring home any infections or diseases. I explained this to myself my own way. I began avoiding my classmates, they began teasing and avoiding me. I walked behind them, but they pushed me away. I was rather tiny and I interpreted their behavior as doing that because I looked younger and undeveloped, and I told myself that I was ugly. So I didn't even think about getting close to a girl in high school. Now I'm a sophomore at uni, and I feel inferior because I have no experience with girls, while all my peers do. This affects my ability to learn and concentrate, I'm grumpy and hot-tempered at home, and I'm totally dissatisfied with myself and my life in general."

Related Topics

Firm Support from Parents | Responses in Communication | Attitude to Physical Development | Autonomy and Individuality | Experience of Independence | Emotional Development | Where Are the Boundaries? | Taking Responsibility | Part 1 of the Book

Within the Scope of Awareness

In literature on psychology, the topic is discussed in sections on self-image, self-worth, self-awareness.

Self-esteem is a cluster of beliefs about ourselves which enable us to rely on ourselves in relationships with other people. These beliefs may be passed on from family patterns, or arise from personal experience in relationships with parents, at first, with close family at home, and then with persons outside our home who influence us. The cluster which creates beliefs about ourselves is a combination of many perceptions, both conscious and unconscious: experiences with self-worth in relationships with other people, the sense of one's own body and the processing of experiences, opinions of parents, the awareness of one's own competences, the awareness of weak spots, the use of defensive strategies.

Beliefs about ourselves, which we can rely on, are beliefs about our own physical appearance, our connections with other people, especially about acceptance and desirability, about the significance of family and social belonging, skills and abilities, social skills, intellectual and emotional capacities, physical skills, talents and other skills we carry inside, about situations in which we do well for ourselves.

All beliefs which help us have faith in ourselves as people worthy of entering social relationships and able to do so, act with different strengths: they may be beliefs which signify security in all situations, they may be beliefs which speak about doubts related to past experiences, in which there was no safety point on which we could rely.

According to research on adolescence, the lack of the awareness of self-worth and low self-esteem are related to many problems during this period: loneliness, depression, risk of abuse, susceptibility to stressful events, suicide, intoxicating substance abuse, early pregnancy, poor results at school, eating disorders, dropping out of school, and criminal behavior.

How many beliefs that we recognize in our children are ours? How many beliefs about self-esteem have we passed on through behavioral patterns, without even being aware of it? Are these messages that build or destroy self-esteem?

Beliefs that build:
- Dad will fix this, there's not a thing in the house he can't fix.
- My mom is very resourceful, money-wise.
- We'll trust mom with this, she really knows how to cheer people up.
- You always buy me a gift that makes me happy.
- This situation appears difficult, but I believe that we will solve it successfully.
- I can always rely on your resourcefulness and orientation, so it's not difficult for me, if I get lost.
- Our food at home is always tasty.
- I'm so glad that our apartment is furnished with style.
- You get your tidiness, and the fact that you always know where things are, from me.
- You like to read as much as your grandma did.
- Mom can really see to it that our family is healthy.

- I'm so proud of you, when I see that you're never ashamed in front of anyone.
- If you need a draft of a written piece, dad is the person to help you.

Beliefs that destroy:
- I'm ugly, I don't belong in photos.
- Don't trouble me with this speech, you know I'm not able to speak in public.
- Other people are better, because they are more educated (have more money, belong to high society), we're just retarded failures.
- I've never had any luck in my life, and now I have what I have.
- Why would you hang out with these guys, they just gossip and wish the worst for you?
- Don't expose yourself and don't push yourself to the fore.
- It's better not to wish for anything, at least you aren't disappointed.
- Why are you being so pushy, you know you don't stand a chance.
- Where is this world going, it's getting worse by the year?
- This isn't right for our family, we are total sports anti-talents.

On the basis of past responses and experiences, growing children create their own beliefs about the soundness and resilience of their mental strength, and about how they see themselves in their relationships with other people. The period of puberty is also a period when beliefs of one's weakness and inabilities, arising from the child's experience in the world of adults, are transformed. The teen's job is to shape new beliefs which support the creation and development of self-esteem. They seek the right balance, as in everything they learn.

Crucial in all elements of self-image, from accepting yourself and your body, setting goals, standing up for yourself, positive mindset, dealing with hurdles and stress, responsible actions, being aware of your uniqueness and emotions, is that all these qualities are shaped by adolescents through responses of their parents and guardians.

Growing children need adults they can rely on. Especially important are responses from adults, which direct development in two possible ways—destructive/hampering or connecting/encouraging.[59]

Encouraging and supportive responses give teens an opportunity to learn how to stand up for themselves.[60] And parents are the first role models they imitate. This brings us again to the questions about family patterns imprinted in our everyday behavior through generations, and passed on to our children.

A few prompts to understand the stories described above:

(Example 53) As far as the youngest child is concerned, parents often overlook the way "hidden altercations" are carried out among siblings. The significant bit in this story was that the youngest child was protected by his older siblings, and he never had to bear any responsibility for the consequences of his insufficient schoolwork. Therefore, he didn't develop a suitable attitude to learning, by accepting mistakes as a constituent of this process. It is about the child's misunderstanding of power relations.

(Example 54) In the second story, it is also obvious that the girl didn't have enough inner strength (assertiveness) to protect her needs in social interactions, and to be able to claim her share. Her mother's patterns and attitude to power were decisive for her understanding.

(Example 55) When a person is twenty-one years old, it makes sense to work on changing non-functional past beliefs and to learn new models of behavior, which support responsiveness by confirmation and awareness of personal qualities.

Tips and Solutions

The way parents respond to everyday situations is crucial in building self-esteem in teens.

The ways to convey criticism, praise *(see page 87)*, choose destructive or connective habits *(see page 58)*, about the meaning and effects

---

[59]See Table 3 in Part 1, *page 91*.

[60]A quality professionals call assertiveness, which can be learned.

of our responses *(see page 60)*, and functional and less functional manners of communication were extensively discussed in the previous chapter. All these significantly influence the shaping of self-esteem, and could be deemed fundamental.

One of the most effective manners to strengthen self-confidence and self-esteem is empathic responsiveness. It is crucial that our response enables our children to remain the owners of their own experiences.

---

(56) Owner of His Achievement

A son proudly comes home from school, saying he 'only' made five mistakes in a dictation in English, which isn't his strongest subject, but also barely passed the line for grade B.

His mother responds: "I see that you're proud of yourself and satisfied because you passed."

This enabled her son to stop, and realize the fact that he was the reason for his success and to be aware of his self-worth. [61]

Possible responses which would have a destructive effect on the development of the teen's self-esteem (in the example above):

- Our disappointment and question: *"Why couldn't you do it better?"* The message of this question is: you aren't good enough. This question ignores the child's message and emotions. We appoint ourselves a judge, and rob the child of the ownership of his achievement.
- Our joy: *"Oh, great, I was so afraid, but now you've made me so happy."* This response says that the parent is taking over and carrying the child's emotional world. His achievements aren't his own, but are a way to put us in a good or bad mood.
- Comparison: *"Oh, that's too bad. Which grade did Jon next door get?"* We let the teen know that he is worth something only in comparison with others, that other may always be better than him.
- Ignoring messages, no response. We let the teen know that we don't care about his achievements. The child's conclusion: there's no point in trying.

---

[61]*See* chapter on taking responsibility, *page 181.*

We can help children in early teen years by enabling them to be in connection with us when doing everyday chores. To see us stand up for ourselves, tackle a certain job, face complicated matters and setbacks, overcome hurdles, and correct our own mistakes. To set boundaries when other people try to invade our space. These are specific behaviors in everyday situations through which we pass on influence, and which speak for themselves.

Have we taught our children (in younger times) to say hi to other people? Do we say hi? Do we look the person we speak to in the eye? Can I clearly express my needs and positions in the form of an *"I message"*?[62] Do we persevere in, and are we focused on, a clearly set goal? Can people reach us on our work phone during family meals? Do we allow the person we speak with to finish his thought? Can we get our space when other people don't let us speak? Do we let other people speak? Can we be respectfully curious? Can we, decisively and without violence, stand up for our rights, if anyone tries to cheat us? Do we stick to the agreed time? Do we respect other people's time? Do we allow and respect emotions which occur in mutual relationships? Can we respond empathically by seeking sense in the person we speak to?[63]

---

(57) Connected Father

 A father decided to spend time with his son playing, having fun and working. They went fishing together. He invited his son to a gym. They made a dog house together in their workshop. The son could observe his father's behavior and acquire a model of how to act when meeting friends who share the same hobby. How to ask someone for help? Doing things together creates a bond that facilitates connection and brings out spontaneous courage to speak. When we speak to other people, we are aware of ourselves and of the permission to be. When doing certain things, the son could watch his father enter a place, speak to the receptionist, manage money, ask about changing rooms, speak to an instructor, ask a craftsman about wood processing, solve the embarrassment because of forgotten material by going back to the store. The father's behavior

---

[62]*See page 221*

[63]Siegel (2013), Siegel & Bryson (2011), Slade (2005), Slade (2006).

in specific situations is an exemplary pattern through which the son realized what self-esteem was.

Being included in organized spending of free time, which requires public performances, may be an external aid to enhance self-esteem (music school, sport skills practice, other activities where children need to perform, theater groups, improvisation sessions for secondary school students). The same opportunities are provided in the informal environment: offering help to peers with schoolwork or to assist elderly people with small everyday errands, babysitting, an important role in shows to which many people are invited.

The best ways to strengthen self-esteem are opportunities in which we act calmly and spontaneously. How much calm is there in our family life? Direct experiences are those related to everyday life, reality, people with spontaneous permission to make mistakes which can always be fixed. Another important message is how we can bear consequences, and that even unfavorable consequences aren't a disaster.

13 Friends (and Fun)

The behavior of teens makes it seem as if their friends and peers are the most important people to them. Friends influence their lifestyle, mindset, teens compare themselves to them, share their thoughts and other achievements with them, hang out and have fun with them.

In their relationships with peers, teens satisfy their need for socialization and fun and, at the same time, develop their vital social competences, learn to assert themselves among their peers, acquire experience in distinguishing between what a teen imagines and how he realizes what he has imagined. Friends and peers are a circle where the socialization of a child becoming an adult takes place. Friends are also the first bridge to more intimate attachments, and the door to the world of teen love and first experiences in relationships with partners. Such an environment enables them to test patterns for becoming adults and all related skills.

For teens, peers are a safer system in which to learn by trial and error, because they are more tolerant than their parents, especially when it comes to encouraging trials and tolerating errors. Friends and peers are companions in the story of changing and witnesses of events for which teens don't have suitable words or reflection.

Another part of the story of growing up takes place among peers, where teens satisfy their need for fun, whether with personal contacts or via virtual media.

---

(58) Night Outings

My fourteen-year-old daughter is blackmailing me into letting her go out at night with her friends. I trust her, but all her friends are older. We live alone in a small apartment. Recently, I went away for a couple of days, and I told my daughter that she would be staying with relatives, and that she had to observe the rules we had about her outings and schoolwork. On the first day of my absence, she called me and said that she'd prefer to be home alone. I had a strange feeling, so I went home a day early. My daughter was at home, in her room. When she heard me come to the house, she was reluctant to say hi, she didn't come out of her room for

quite a while, and I felt this strange tension. When she finally unlocked the door of her room, I went in and found someone on the other side of the window. This is how I met her boyfriend.

I haven't heard anything good about this boy. He is seventeen, doesn't go to school, he is into some strange business. And my daughter is head over heels in love, enchanted by him. Even though he already broke off with her a few times and went off with another girl, she always forgave him and rekindled their relationship. Now I'm worried that he'll influence her, that she won't finish school because she started missing days, and she says that she doesn't see any sense in learning. Another thing I'm even more worried about is that I've heard that this boy is a drug dealer.

I know that if I forbid her from seeing him—I know a story when my acquaintance did this—, it'll only get worse. She'd rebel completely and will totally disregard my authority. Now at least we have a connection and trust each other. She also respects the time I set and tells me where she'll be when she goes out. I also know that her company means a lot to her, that she needs to relax, but I'm not sure if I should let her go out with these friends.

(59) Rude Behavior

My son is in the seventh grade of elementary school. So far, he's been manageable and obedient, but now he's completely changed. He is rude at home, he rebels and uses words we haven't used before. He began slacking off at school, but my wife and I were most surprised about his absences. In the end, a counselor helped us find out that he had joined a group of behaviorally difficult students who go, from time to time, to abandoned shacks near school during classes. They smoke there, and we've heard that they also use weed. We are worried about the influence of this company, as their values are completely distorted. No one controls them at home, and they spend most of their time playing computer games and checking adult websites. School sucks, it isn't worth working and struggling in life, money can be earned the easy way. Also their view of people is twisted, they advocate fraud, pushing, lies. Everything's upside down. What should we do?

Related Topics
Where Are the Boundaries? | *What to Do with Rules?* | *Attitude to Authority* | *Trust* | *Part 1 of the Book* | *Shaping Self-Esteem, Self-Image* | *Experience of Independence* | *Addiction, Dependence*

Within the Scope of Awareness

The company of peers our teens hang out with suddenly becomes part of our family's wider relationship. This is a culture influencing the mindset, the choice of trends in music, fashion, sports, interesting activities, socializing... As parents, we can develop different attitudes toward these influences. These are youngsters who have different roles in the company of peers: they are friends, influential leaders of the group, interesting and attractive subjects, with power in certain circles... When we are attracted to a certain quality in a person, this means that our unsatisfied need or longing is related to this quality. Therefore, it is sensible to meet and be in contact with friends who mean something to our children, because of their certain attractive qualities or skills. This way, it will be easier for us to understand and *"familiarize"* this influence, and to connect it with our understanding of the world of our teen needs. But we can also use the other two options—to not know and ignore them, or to not allow them. Each choice of our behavior leading away from connection may result in expected responses of teens. Ignoring opens the door to experimenting without boundaries, while prohibition adds fuel to the wish and courage to rebel, most often by overstepping the boundaries set.

Company is important for teens to develop social skills, especially for those teens who shut themselves in the world of electronic communication. Entering a social group may be made easier by independence skills a teen has acquired beforehand. Parents of numerous teens notice that they avoid personal contact. When we researched such cases during counseling sessions, we often stumbled upon unsuitable experiences in learning how to be independent and responsible, in the setting of boundaries, in autonomy, feelings that they were inadequate, the lack of perseverance, high sensitivity, and the evasion of experiences in which they might fail. Parents, in these cases, were overprotective, they tried to protect their children from unpleasant consequences and unfavorable experiences in their relationships with peers, or they didn't allow their children to have suitable experiences. In this context, everyday chores at home provide a myriad of opportunities.

Researchers have found that teens who say that they are happy accept challenges within safe boundaries.[64] Parents are afraid of risky behavior related to alcohol abuse, smoking, drugs, sex, and reckless driving. Neuroscientists speak about the role and meaning of dopamine, the need to experience exciting things, increased need to experience comfort, and greater susceptibility to dependencies. Teens may encounter all this in risky behavior which is reinforced, without any rational limits, in the presence of peers. But risky behavior for teens also includes sleeping under the stars with friends, traveling abroad alone, decorating one's own room, assembling a bike from disused parts, leading a small group as part of youth work, managing one's own money without parental supervision (in the amount determined by parents), organizing a trip, discussing and organizing a New Year's Eve party... There are many risky challenges in peer groups, which may be acted out in a playful way, for example *"If you lose the bet, you'll have to sit in the street in front of school and sing for half an hour."* Risky situations enable teens to develop faith in themselves through practical experience, and to strengthen management and learning in unpredictable situations.

Many parents are affected by the realization that their teens devote more time and attention to their peers than to their primary family. For teens, what their friends say is more important than what their family says. At least, so they claim, although they don't really mean, and much less feel, that. Parents' fears consist of questions: *"What if he falls into bad company? He's so insecure and unstable, what if he is tricked into drugs? Will she be able to resist the influence of her girlfriends, who overstep all boundaries with their behavior? He's blackmailing me, saying that all his peers have their own cars. I'm afraid he'll want to assert himself in front of them and do something inappropriate, which he wouldn't otherwise. Do we insist on him coming with us to family visits?"*

Fears standing in the parents' way of trusting and letting their teens socialize are related to the dilemma of supervision and safety. When a child goes out alone for the first time, parents no longer directly control him. That

---

[64]Cf. Marilyn Price-Mitchell, *What Happy Teenagers Do Differently.*

is when we can only rely on the values and skills passed on to the child beforehand. Do we have a connection? Do we know that the child respects boundaries? Have we set safe boundaries in relation to pleasure in general? Can we rely on our child's trust? Do we trust his independence? Has the child had enough opportunities at home to learn from risks and mistakes? Were we there for the child, when his learning attempts failed? Can we share an emotional world with him?

When parents think that we no longer matter to our children, and listen to their statements that support this concern,[65] the way we respond is really important. Statements about our ineptness are part of the child's strategy when gaining independence, which we have already described. Therefore, the awareness of our connection is a safety area for parents. Based on this awareness, parents dare take risks and are able to wait for life events to unfold with their own logic.

Hanging out with peers enables teens to get vital experience in social skills. Situations that occur in peer groups open up completely new chapters in their experiences in mutual relationships: trust and betrayal of trust, deceptions, lies, unreliability, sneaky plots and loyalty abuse, breaking agreements, disappointment, different images about friends they have created and believed in and real life experiences, abandonment and exclusion, unreliability and double bind messages, inconsistency. These are stories parents may only enter through listening, reflectivity, and empathic responses. We can contribute our experiences from the time when we were learning to survive, and perhaps went through the same distress. Each story of ours, no matter how sadly it ended, is a story of good hope for our children, as we are proof that we survived the situation and can view it in retrospect, from a distance.

Parents often wonder if their teen can be independent and think with his own head, when he is with friends. The question of how to become autonomous in a group of friends, among peers, arises in this respect. It is about skills teens use in new circumstances, if they had the chance to acquire them beforehand.

---

[65] "Where did I get such lame parents? Mom, dinosaurs were obviously still alive when you were a kid. What have I done to anyone to have been born into this family? As soon as I'm 18, I'll leave you forever. How can all my friends have normal parents?" The list of statements could be refreshed every day.

The parents in the second story decided that they couldn't forbid their son's company, and that he would have to see for himself whether that was the right company for him. But they didn't slacken their boundaries and rules or values. At the same time, they had to trust in the power of attachment to the family and its values, in order to risk their child having an unpleasant experience. They didn't have to wait long before their son came home crying because his friends had betrayed him. They were together in a violation of school rules. Teachers caught them and took them to the principal's office, where they had well-deserved consequences waiting for them. The leader of the group suddenly transformed into a well-behaved "mama's boy," denied his involvement and framed the others. All of them went with the same strategy and, in the end, the son remained the only guilty party in the story. This experience left him completely devastated. In his opinion, he was wrongfully punished. His parents didn't worry over it, as their son no longer hung out with this crowd, which hadn't seemed reliable and safe to the parents.

What about relationships with siblings who argue and fight? Leave them or intervene? As parents, we face a dilemma. If we leave them, we convey the message that we tolerate the behavior which may be violent, humiliating, that we tolerate the manner of communication which is in no way part of our family culture. If we intervene, we need to take sides, which is even worse, because we never really know the background. Parents who try to intervene generally become part of the game, and take their children's responsibilities on themselves. Forbidding children to insult each other may result in forbidding expressions of emotion. A mother solved such a dilemma the following way: *"I understand that you argue. I also understand that you have to solve certain issues by yourselves. But I don't have to listen and put up with this. Deal with it in your room or outside the house. The only thing I need to take care of is to prevent violence."*

Tips and Solutions

We collected a few testimonies from parents describing stories in which parents have contact with their children's friends. But first, the question of whether it is allowed in your house to bring friends over.

(60) Youth Club at Our House

"I often hear parents complain that their child's company is weird. When I ask them if they are in contact with these "weird" friends, if they talk to them, let them into their house they, appalled, reply that they don't. So what is the basis for their judgment that the company is weird? Looks? Posture? Parents? Nationality or another denomination?

Our house is always open to friends. This means that sometimes we need to buy an extra treat, but that's alright. I know our children's friend's names, I know where they live, I know what they do, I sometimes even know about their problems. I know what color their eyes are, and it has already happened that I've asked them for help. These friends sometimes make an interesting first impression, because of their unusual looks. They wear dreads, piercings, tattoos, some of them smoke... What I want to say is that they may look "weird," but in fact they are nice, interesting, and witty young people. My principle is: every person who has the guts to walk into our home, offer his hand to me and my husband, and look us in the eye, is welcome.

But I do agree that, many times, this comes at the price of peace and tidiness. This is the point where we have to choose. Do we really want to know our child's friends, or would we rather have peace and order? I choose the first option. I choose a vibrant life in our household, because I know where my children are, and with whom."

How do you respond when friends act in circumstances which exceed the boundaries set?

(61) Teen and Alcohol

My son celebrated his seventeenth birthday. He told us where and with whom he was going. We agreed on the time, but even before midnight, someone called me from his phone.

"Ma'am, are you Max's mother? This is Nick, his friend, could you come pick him up?"

"Can't Max call me himself?"

"I'm afraid not."

"Oh. Where are you?"

(He lets her know where they are, the mother comes and sees her son sitting bent on the pavement, barely conscious, vomit all around. The mother insists on giving Nick a ride home, too, although he first resists.)

In the car, Nick apologizes: "Ma'am, I'm really sorry I called you in the middle of the night, but I couldn't carry him myself."

Mother: "Nick, I appreciate what you have done, it was very noble of you. For me, a true friend doesn't leave his friend alone, in danger or unhappy. And I know you had to overcome your fear of my reaction. You know, I'm really grateful for your concern, and I can see that you're a good guy."

I'm in touch with my children's friends' parents, we take each other's children to concerts and evening events, we have a chat here and then, we share our concerns, just so that we feel safe.

How do we respond when our teen's friends are in trouble and our child wants to help?

---

(62) We Are Best Friends

 Monica has been rather quiet these days. I've been inviting her to spend some more time with me, but she spends hours staring at the ceiling in that typical teenage way.

She isn't interested in friends, she doesn't answer her phone. If I say anything, she isn't very nice and she rejects me. I know something's bugging her, and because it's been so long, I become rather powerless in my actions. My husband and I are pretty concerted, but she pushes him away even more. As I'm a panicky sort of a mother, I convinced my husband to get us some professional help, which strengthened our parental functionality and gave us the message that it was okay if we let Monica know, every once in a while, that we can see that she is in distress. Despite her rejecting us.

Yesterday, I told Monica that I was going shopping and that she had to come with me to help me. I thought I'd seen enough, and didn't want to give her a choice. I also saw that it was high time for her to move into a social environment.

In the car, she said to me that she knew she was being impossible, but that she had promised not to tell certain stuff to anyone.

"Who did you promise?" I asked her.

At first, she was tightlipped. Then I said: "Okay, I understand you don't want to betray anyone or get anyone punished. But let me tell you that you're a victim of a promise, and I wouldn't want anything to be so wrong that you'll feel guilty and responsible in the end."

"Holly does stuff I don't approve. She's been throwing up for a while, sometimes she even cuts herself. I had to promise her that I wouldn't tell anyone. She's just texted me that she's grounded and can't go out for three weeks, because she got a C on her math test. I don't understand what's wrong with her parents. They haven't even noticed what's been going on with her, and then she can't go out cause of a C??? Helloooo?? Are they sick or what??? And her mom and dad walk past each other, as if they were neighbors." *(She is crying.)*

I simply turned the car around and we went back home, where I could hug Monica, and we discussed the boundaries she will have to set on this friendship. Especially after she had told me that she felt like she wasn't normal, because she didn't do any of that stuff.

We stopped here. We haven't yet discussed how Monica will set boundaries for Holly. She seemed too vulnerable and emotional. And I know that she has to think, and that she will come to me and ask, because I gave her the experience that it was safe to tell me. I didn't make a scene, I didn't call Holly's mother... I don't even know myself how I will solve this. I will speak to my husband first, and then perhaps also to other people.

14 Teen Love and Sexual Maturity

Most people connect the awareness of puberty with the onset of sexuality.

The awakening of the sex drive in teens cause different emotional and other internal sensations, from anxiety and fear to fascination and confusion and also to the loss of the feeling of self-control. They usually don't share it with anyone, perhaps girls share it with their girlfriends, more than boys with their peers. Sex drive is a new sensation which is, for teens, a new area to build identity.

Over a century ago, Freud described how, during puberty, individual fragments of the sexual development mature mentally which, from the biological aspect, are shaped through experiences of pleasure from birth on.[66] So the subject of sexuality is one of the most diverse subjects in the functioning of our psychic apparatus. It is connected with our stories of safe or insecure attachment to, and bonding with, parents, stories of attitude towards pleasure, with learning about the attitude towards ourselves and experiences in relationships with others. Sexuality develops in the area of intimacy, where we need safe experiences with bonding and trust, and permission for playfulness, trust, dedication, exploration and curiosity. The area of intimacy begins in ourselves and how we view ourselves, especially in terms of the acceptance of physical changes. During puberty, it gradually becomes an experience of expansion and sharing of the intimate space with another person who isn't a relative. The experience with attachment to peers is an important basis for the shaping of skills for subsequent relationships with partners.

In this process, we as parents and adults have an important opportunity to accompany growing children on this path, providing information and messages, which will create a realistic picture of life, and a safe intimate space.

In the period of growing up, regarding our connection with the child, we reap what we sowed in the past, about curiosity about physical development, trust in distress, emotional bonding, and physical closeness. If, in these fields, our child received safe responses from us, he will also ask us questions in

---

[66]Freud (1905).

puberty, and he will want to know our opinion about his first intercourse, masturbation, etc… Our response will, naturally, be based on our beliefs and patterns, which we draw our responses from our own experiences.

Here are some questions we should ask ourselves, and answer:

How are we equipped to safely respond to the topics of sexual awakening in our teens? Do certain behaviors and explorations of our children embarrass us? Are we afraid of sexual experiments beyond certain boundaries? Are we afraid of early sexuality in our children? What are our stories, our own experiences? Are we relaxed about the topic of sexuality, do we feel safe, inside ourselves, about it? Are we anxious, perhaps have a negative attitude?

We believe that this topic is related to great differences, which depend on culture and world views.

Perhaps the European context, with a moral cultural influence in this topic, is something that distinguishes us from other cultural environments? Are we ignorant, like in the Victorian period, covertly repressive, having no words and discourse about this topic? Are we free of the taboos of past generations, and can we easily talk about all aspects of sexuality with our children?

---

(63) When Is The Right Time To Talk About Sex?

We watched a movie with our thirteen-year-old daughter. In it, there was a couple who had sex on their first date.

A few questions were intensely spinning in my head:

What kind of a message does this convey to children at the beginning of puberty?

How should my wife and I show to our daughter that physical closeness needs an emotional basis? Are these beliefs justified?

How and when should we start a conversation about the beginning of sexual activity, without being moralistic and without prohibitions? How should we convey our beliefs and life stories to her?

We wouldn't want to be intrusive. And how should we maintain discretion in the field intimacy?

Nevertheless, we wonder if sexuality is something young people engage in without prior emotional attachment. Just like that, out of curiosity, for pleasure? What does our daughter think about that?

Then there are also our fears. How should we talk about the possibility of contracting an STD (sexually transmitted disease), and how should they protect themselves?

---

(64) Caught Son Masturbating

"So...briefly. Yesterday, I came home from work early, thinking I was home alone, that my son was with friends or at our neighbor's house. I opened the door and everything was as usual until I came to the living room...I wasn't particularly loud and there I saw...my twelve-year-old masturbating on our sofa...the reaction was... typical I guess...the boy jumped up, turned red, swore, and ran off to his room...I shouted after him: to the bathroom, and hid myself in the kitchen for a few minutes. I didn't know how to solve this mess... so I went to see him...that it's normal for boys to do that, but I'm mad that he does it in the living room, not in the bathroom...not to mention porn videos playing on his laptop when I went back to the living room after a few minutes. So yesterday, we avoided each other...soon after this, his dad took him to practice. They came back late, then he quickly ate something and went, for the first time, to his room until he went to sleep. But today, I'd really like to talk because I don't know what to do... was my reaction inadequate? What experience do other parents have...my coworkers' children are younger. Or should I tell my husband to talk to him? Oh boy, I knew that we'd have to talk about this sooner or later, but when it comes to it, even I feel embarrassed."

---

(65) Between Ignoring And Parent's Concern

My child is on the threshold of puberty and, as a parent, I have a plethora of questions:

How to talk about sexuality with a boy at the beginning of puberty? What information should he have that is most important?

How to talk about sexuality with a girl at the beginning of puberty? What information is important for her?

How to talk with a boy in mature puberty who is interested in sexuality?

How to talk with a girl in mature puberty who is interested in sexuality?

How should I resolve my fears about early sexuality and all its potential unintended consequences?

How should I prevent my daughter from seducing men with provocative clothes or publishing steamy photos online? How should I protect my child from abuse and other traumatic experiences when meeting and contacting strangers online?

Who can help me, because I am ashamed to talk about sexuality and protection?

Dances we get into: prohibition, ignoring, tabooing, intrusiveness, anxiety, withdrawal, etc.

Related Topics

Attitude to physical development | Emotional development | Part 1 of the Book | Where are the boundaries? | Autonomy and individuality | Shaping self-esteem, self-image | Learning how to be responsible | Friends | Responses in communication | Trust

Within the Scope of Awareness

Interest in the opposite sex, longing for love, and thoughts about sex are things that occupy teens' mind most. The excitement of this subject is all the greater because of its newness, intimate nature, latency, and their lack of experience. Teens explore this subject intensively in their conversations with peers, which is part of the acquisition of experiences which will later shape their sexual behavior and behavior in relationships with partners. The awakening of sex drive and the awareness of libidinal energy are psychological parallels to hormonal changes in the body. The exploration of reactions of the body to impulses of sexual arousal during masturbation is one of the first opportunities to acquire experience and learn how our own body function. In this area, the history of mentalities hasn't changed for centuries. Therefore, parents and adults can understand this part of development through memories of our own story.

269

Parents are convinced that children are very well informed about sex and pass them by even before they find an opportunity to introduce a new subject in communication. But in everyday information and culture, sex is reduced to attitude to body. This creates the mentality of the attitude to sexuality which creates myths about two separate worlds of notions. One is the boys' or men's view, and the other is the women's view. There are huge differences perceived by teens, but they aren't equipped to talk about them. This is accompanied by pornography industry which needs customers. People can't talk about what sex is because it is an intimate relationship with another person, which is based on bonding emotions, and the physical contact is an addition.

All these subjects develop in their own way, and during puberty, merge into a specific image. Underlying such development is our confidentiality with our child. If we have never discussed personal subjects with him and we only ask him questions about grades and school, the child didn't shape his experience about trust and learn how to share personal subjects, so he doesn't feel safe. Another issue is the pattern from our primary family. People have problems because they are simply not equipped with words. We can encounter various attitudes to this subject: easiness (safety), pursuing (forcing), and withdrawal (ignoring). Some people prefer to avoid the subject of love, intimacy, and sexuality. They try to find the right moment, but they find it hard, they stammer and feel foolish.

People tend to run out of words, and we don't recognize the moment in our child's development which is crucial to start such a conversation. It isn't just about the sexual intercourse, sexual practices, but also about the attitude to ourselves, our bodies, dignity, connections, patterns of attachment to parents from the primary family, and other subjects.

As parents, we may be equipped with various responses to the topic of sexuality from our own experiences. Our parents might have responded in a safe way, and we are at ease about it, we have the vocabulary to address the content of sexual maturity and activity when we encounter it.

But we can also be uncomfortable with the topic, we are not relaxed, we are embarrassed, we avoid, ignore, we are at a loss for words, we don't know how and when to put a certain thing into a suitable thought. Also questions we encounter in online forums in Slovenia show that parents today are rather lost in terms of how to respond. Perhaps the situation is similar in some other countries? If parents respond with shame and great embarrassment in communication, when they see their teen sexually maturing, questions arise about what is normal at a certain age. But underlying it all is huge embarrassment when facing obvious signs of sexual maturity which require mirroring with a message which will allow developmental needs to go their own way and enable our children to safely enter the world of sex.

Physical development and the awakening of sex drive is part of biological development. Girls are affected a little sooner, around ten years of age, and boys about two years later.

Growing children are in distress about the changes happening to their bodies if they don't have suitable information on the physical signs of sexual maturity. With girls, the latter comes with their first period, and with boys, with their first night ejaculation. This comes with various physical signs, spots, body hair in intimate areas, growth of breasts, desire to look good, and the significance of appearance as dictated by fashion trends, which means desire to wear make-up, change cloths, color hair, remove body hair... In addition to spots in boys, new odors can be detected, especially when friends come to visit and there are a few pairs of boys' shoes outside the front door. All these are biological characteristics which are part of development. They are associated with experience in which parents' responses create the meaning of this experience for the child.

Our responsiveness outlines our understanding of the teen's internal world—we give or don't give permission to physical changes. Safe responsiveness means that we accept physical changes which are part of growing up. This means that our responses should normalize them, not pathologize them. Parallel to physical changes and sexual hormones starting to ramp up, our teens experience intensive emotional processes. Our responses will determine whether the emotional experience of physical development will be safe, or teens will be tormented by fears and internal dilemmas and rebelliously dive into their sexual experiments.

We live in a time when sex seems to no longer be a taboo. It is widely spoken and written about, pornography is available to everyone. But when we mention sex as intimacy, we see that only few families have a relaxed attitude to discussion about such subjects. This especially applies to puberty.

When we held preventive programs for thirteen-year-olds in elementary schools a few years ago, they were most distinctly interested in physical development and sexuality.[67] It was interesting that most of them had already seen pornography on the Internet. But when we asked them what period was, no one knew the answer.

The questions that give thirteen-year-olds a hard time are sometimes funny, but very serious for them, and related to the development of their attitude to self-esteem and important beliefs that build and balance their first experiences in relationships with partners.

- How long is a penis normally?
- When can we have the first intercourse?
- Is masturbation a sin?
- Why do we have body hair?
- What happens when you go to a gynecologist?
- Why does period hurt?
- What is period?
- When and how the first ejaculation occurs?
- What is an abortion?
- Do our parents have intercourse?
- Until which age do we have intercourse?
- Why do boys become "annoying" during this period?

These and many other questions are very simple. Why don't children ask them at home? One or two raised their hands in class when we asked how many of them spoke to their parents about this subject. This subject brings secrecy and withdrawal in relationships. Parents complain that children shut off, and children carry numerous questions related to shame and prohibition.

As with all subjects, parents are the ones who should find the right moment to articulate the topics related to sexual maturity and practices. Sexuality is an important subject about bonding, love, and relationships between partners. If we let our child make up his own fantasy explanations, we take away the opportunity for him to loosen up and commit to an intimate relationship. We also feel the duty to explain to our children who, without a

---

[67]The same is reported by European child helplines.

doubt, have contact with pornography, which is unreal, misleading, and promotes myths.

There is no recipe as to how to address the topic of sexuality with our child. Parents need to be aware that this is a subject teens will never bring up on their own. Adults are the responsible party here. The conversation can't take place by parents sitting their child at the table telling him to ask everything he has to ask about sexuality. We need to find gentle, safe, and intimate ways to start such a conversation.

Do we feel that our teen is in distress, due to physical changes? Are we a safe haven for our child, so he can share his distress with us? Such distress may be related to acne, worries about the emergence of first pubic hair (and when), about the growth of breasts, and about periods in girls. Do boys tell us when they have night ejaculations? Are we able to talk to them, when we see traces on the bedding? Do our children feel safe with us to talk about it? Do we feel safe to talk about it?

Do we have the skills to use the stories our child encounters in everyday life (a peer who got pregnant unintentionally, the distress of a friend cheated on by her boyfriend because another friend seduced him under the influence of alcohol). Perhaps we can use our own stories? ("When I was your age, I was wondering what intercourse looked like. I remember having my first ejaculation when I spent my holidays away at my aunt's house, and I didn't know what to say.")

Ever since kindergarten, children give us opportunities to include the subject of sexuality into our everyday communication when they come home with the question *"What is a condom?"* or similar questions about sexuality. Already then, our responses may vary from ignoring or denial to facing the issue.

What consequences can a disruption (forcing or avoiding) when discussing sexuality have?

Since we are social beings, we need contacts and feedback. If we don't get them from the most important persons in our life in a suitable way, we will search for them elsewhere. Of course, there are endless other possibilities to learn about sexuality, which tell another story about the attractiveness of bodily pleasures in a twisted way. Especially free access to pornography on web portals and TV programs creates notions and beliefs which aren't realistic, and prevent people from experiencing mutual intimate pleasure in real

273

relationships. In our therapeutic work, we often come across people who believed strongly in these stories, and later had serious problems in their relationships with partners, especially in terms of intimacy.

Emotions involved are important when conveying messages about sexuality. If we speak through fear, shame or moralistic persuasion, we will convey that we are the weak link in the dialogue.

In any case, the behavior of our teens when they are in love needs boundaries, rules, defined relationships, responsibilities, and tests of independence, just like other areas of their lives. Our role as authority and the right to be worried remain unchanged too. But the most important thing is to remain connected and provide safe attachment.

Attitude to sexuality is a value passed on through family patterns and our ways in everyday life. We comment sexuality on everyday occasions when we speak about events that happened to other people, about deceptions, abortion, and early pregnancies. The message that an intercourse doesn't happen with the first kiss should be conveyed before our teen has his first serious relationship. Attitude to loyalty and commitment is shown in everyday responses among relatives. Fondness, affection, and loving body language corroborate the relationship with our partner.

Part of this chapter is also the issue of parents' responses when they face the information that their child is a homosexual. In most cultures, homosexuality is still more of a prejudice than an accepted circumstance, which stems from the right of every person to choose . It can be a very suitable subject for teens battling with their parents to lure the latter to the area of uncertainty, powerlessness, and despair. The notions of homosexual experiences may be one of the thrills of exploring their sexual identity for teens, especially where their home environment doesn't provide them with a stable notion of a relationship with a partner. Usually, the family story, which is a model for the shaping of a notion of a relationship with a partner, is full of chaos and lack of value. These notions are also a fashion trend of certain style groups of young people. The parents' response in cases of provocations follows the feedback principle: every attention will give more power to provocation.

Another option concerns a real homosexual choice. In such cases, teens face numerous internal dilemmas related to the shaping of their identity, and the experience of themselves and their value. This is when the true value of the safe connection with parents is manifested, which enables teens to share their distress with them. An important message from parents to their child: *"Even though it is hard for us to accept your choice, we are still your parents, and this changes nothing in our attachment and bonding. We still love you the same."*

Tips and Solutions

The subject of sexuality is, first and foremost, a test of personal stability for parents. Initially, in ourselves: What are the messages and beliefs in our relationship in our own story of sexual development? Perhaps everything from Part 1 of the book is especially important in relation to this subject. If, in situation when we need to speak about love and sexuality openly to our children, we are overwhelmed with discomfort or shame, this is a hint to take a step forward in our personal development and an invitation to conclude our own stories. Another question concerns the manner of communication when talking about sexuality between parents, which is about the functionality of the relationship between partners and the sensitive subject of sexuality. We need to distinguish several different areas: infatuation, love, sex, intercourse, intimacy.

Parents' responses depend a great deal on the integration of all areas in ourselves.

Can I safely share my embarrassments with my partner? Is my partner a person I can trust and be intimate with? Do I see myself in the role of parent as a person whose developmental needs were satisfied during puberty or do I still feel the excitement of unrealized adolescent yearnings? The answer to this question largely determines our stability and adulthood as parents when we face subjects related to sexuality and intimacy.

Let the stories related to this subject speak for themselves.

(66) Embarrassed Father

 A wife to her husband: "I can smell sperm in our boy's room (he is thirteen). C'mon, talk to him about masturbation and hygiene."

Husband (blushes, wishing the ground would swallow him up): "I can't imagine that. How do I talk about it to him? What do I say?"

The wife took the matter into her own hands. She told her husband to sit next to her and she would do the talking. At the first opportunity when they were alone together, she said: "Look, my dear son. You're thirteen, and we can see that your body is changing, your hormones are maturing, and that changes are going on inside you. It's completely normal for the sex drive to be waking in you and that you're interested in sex, that the thought of naked women arouses you. Masturbation is part of that. We both know this, dad can tell you that it was the same when he was growing up, and that times haven't changed in this respect. Perhaps the only difference is that we couldn't talk about this with our parents because we were all ashamed. We understand that you have your secrets and intimacy. I just want you to know that, and to put away the handkerchiefs you used to clean up the sperm or put the clothes or PJs in the laundry basket if you have a wet dream."

We need to be aware that children talk more about this topic with their peers, and seek answers online. Therefore, a conversation about who to believe, what such information can convey or bring into the child's imagination is also important. At this point, we are back at the beginning: We can have this conversation only if we have a connection with our child, not by inviting him to the table, ordering him or trying to persuade him that something isn't okay or true, but in a "softer" situation, when we feel we are connected or close (during a walk, in the car, while cooking together, etc.), somewhere where our teen feels good with us.

Perhaps, he will respond by saying that he isn't interested in our opinion, or that he doesn't want to talk to us about it. We can respect that. The important thing is that he heard our opinion, because it will make him think about it.

Here is a tip for parents who catch their sons watching pornography and masturbating. This is a topic which addresses the question about how to talk about the excitement of sexual curiosity.

The response which needs permission refers to the permission to be curious (I understand that you're curious about sex) and to the permission to be aroused (I understand that seeing naked women or sexual practice arouses you). But teens need an addition to their understanding which is lacking in the pornography industry—the value and significance of a relationship between two people engaging in intercourse. There is an important difference between sex as a manner of physical activity of stimulating erogenous zones and seeking satisfaction of arousal, and sex which is based on closeness and connection between partners, and the quality of the relationship between them. And of course, about all the myths and unrealistic perceptions of how to arouse and seduce, the capabilities to assume sexual positions, the duration of erection, and other myths depicted in pornographic materials. This is an area which includes subjects for parents to discuss and co-create suitable answers for growing children.

(67) Contraception

 A seventeen-year-old girl comes home from school, leaves her satchel open on the table, and runs from the kitchen, asking what is for lunch. By coincidence, her mother notices condoms in her daughter's satchel. The daughter has been in a serious relationship with a guy for a few months.

Mother: "I've seen condoms in your satchel."

Daughter: "Yeah, we got them at a party the other day."

Mother: "I want to talk to you about seeing a gynecologist and suitable protection."

Daughter (upset): "I won't talk to you about that." *(She storms out of the kitchen.)*

When she gets back, her mother looks her decisively in the eye and says: "I just want you to listen to me. You said that you won't talk to me about seeing a gynecologist and suitable protection. That's your choice and your business. It's important for me as your mother to be at peace with

277

your protection. And what I need to be at peace with is a confirmation that you've seen a gynecologist. And that's all."

Daughter (upset again and embarrassed, on her way out of the kitchen): "But that's none of your business."

When the daughter returned again, her mother said: "I'll tell you another story I know which happened because of unprotected sex at your age. I also know the consequences which ruined the youth and opportunities for development of a girl your age. *(Tells her the story.)* What I want for you is to take responsibility for your actions."

Daughter (still upset): "But I can't go to a gynecologist with you."

Mother: "You have girlfriends, they've probably experienced this, ask them about a gynecologist they trust. You don't have to see mine."

Daughter: "Can a daughter and a mother have the same gynecologist? I'd like to see yours."

Mother: "Sure. Call her and make an appointment."

Daughter: "What do I say?"

Mother: "Tell her who you are and that you'd like to make an appointment for an examination."

Daughter: "What's it like there?"

The mother gets a chance to share her experience with her daughter and tells her the story of her first protection. At the same time, this is an experience which strengthened the bond between the mother and her daughter. They agreed to see a gynecologist together, and then they treated themselves to a girls day out at a mall.

---

(68) Daughter Embarrasses Her Father

Daughter (to her father): "Dad, what's masturbation, what's erection, and what's ejaculation?"

The father tries to explain about libido and arousal, and the need to relax. And about the physiology of erection and about what is ejaculation in a man's world. And about what orgasm is. What he told her was too complicated for an inexperienced twelve-year-old.

"Dad, I don't understand any of this. Can you show me?"

The point where the father could get confused and stop communication by withdrawing, denying, and making it a taboo. This would have stopped and

prohibited his daughter's curiosity about development, and impeded the con-
nection and openness as well as her trust. But fortunately, the father was ma-
ture and had a good head on his shoulders.

Father: "Unfortunately, I can't show you that. You know, there are things only partners share. I think that when you have a boyfriend, he can show you that, and when you know that the bond you share is strong and you feel it as love, trust, and devotion. The fact is that we mature sexually much earlier than personally. And I can tell you that it's worth waiting for the right person to share the beauty and pleasure sex gives us with."

Parents first encounter the subjects of crushes and infatuation. For teens, choosing a partner is an experience where they have the opportunity and cultural support to assert their autonomy and independence. First, they ask themselves how their family will accept the partner they have chosen. How and when to tell that they are in a serious relationship? What if parents don't like my choice? What if they disapprove of my choice?

For parents, it is a challenge and a dilemma if the partner their child has chosen triggers reservations that the choice is inappropriate. Perhaps their age gap is too big (for example a sixteen-year-old daughter falls head over heels in love with a thirty-two-year-old man) or they come from different cultural and religious backgrounds (an eighteen-year-old daughter of Catholic parents has been in a relationship with a radical Muslim who demands that she accepts all religious rules of behavior, including covering her face) or parents recognize in the partner influences of family patterns which worry them (infidelity, addiction, violence) or parents recognize in the partner personal and behavioral characteristics which worry them (irresponsibility, immaturity about professional ambitions) or parents recognize in the partner values which are in contrast with their family values (the son's ambition is to finish his studies, his girlfriend without education says that education is the least important in life because you can get money in much easier ways).

It is hard for parents if they can't bear the fact that the autonomous choice of a partner is the right young people won long ago. If anywhere, it is true in this area that open and hidden opposition strengthens the power of the teen's choice. The only sensible role of parents is to offer their child a stable support as he acquires independent experiences in his relationship with a partner. The techniques of conscious and empathic response described in

Part 1 are the safest haven in dilemmas in numerous situations. Parents can be a safe support when their child is disappointed, afraid, when he comes to unpleasant realizations, when he learns about the principles of relationships with partners. With all experiences that give young people distress, the only way to support them is through trust and connection. Otherwise, teens will live through these stories in silence and withdrawal from family life.

---

(69) Huge Age Gap

Brooke is our eldest. We have three kids. I know that the most difficult part of parenting fell on her. But I can say that she's a responsible girl, and my husband and I trust her.

I remember that she was head over heels in love. With a boy who was nine years older than her. She was fifteen, and I thought it was a huge gap. My husband and I were aware that we couldn't stop it, and that it was important to preserve our connection with her. At least we knew what was going on. But it was hard for us. We used to talk about this for hours on end, when she was with him and we were at home.

One evening, we were sitting in the garden, and I asked her:

"Doesn't it bother you that David is so much older?" *I noticed that the question was borderline, but she refrained and said:* "Mom, what kind of a stupid question is that? Does it bother you?" *She caught me off guard. I was quiet for a bit. After all, I provoked such response. I decided to be honest.*

"I really don't know if it bothers me. But I am scared," *I replied. Brooke was growing impatient, but it was still tolerable. My husband joined in and said that he felt the same way as me and that he liked us talking about it. He said to her calmly:* "We don't want to take anything away from you. I know how great such love is..." *(Brooke interrupted him:* "He is the love of my life. I'm gonna marry him!"*). My husband continued:* "Well, if you're gonna marry him, it is essential we talk." *(That was an expression of permission instead of prohibition or scorn or ignoring.)*

At the moment, Brooke calmed down and said: "Well, Mom, what are you scared of?"

Then I could say: "I'm afraid you're gonna have sex too soon. I don't know if you're ready. I don't want you to be disappointed. For me, my first boyfriend I was intimate with was very important. I'm worried that you won't protect yourself."

Brooke stared at me with her big eyes and was slightly angry: "Mom, how can you perceive me that way. I'm in love with David, he's the man of my dreams. I talked to him about this. He doesn't pressure me. He said he'd wait for me to grow up, to want it, and we'll go to a gynecologist together. I'm not as dumb as Tess. She and her boyfriend were the same age, and he convinced her. Then she got pregnant and had an abortion in secret cause he demanded it from her. I know the psychological torment she went through after this experience. You think I'm stupid and don't know how these things work? Sometimes older guys are a lot more patient, you know."

Of course, the story ended. In a few months, David met another girl and Brooke cried for days on end. We bore those tears together. We did or said nothing that could let her know that it was better this way. He was her "husband", the one she chose. This didn't change and she had to mourn it.

Now she's nineteen, she has a steady boyfriend, she laughs at this story, we're still connected. Naturally, we are deeply aware of the fact that the time when we knew everything has passed. We are proud that Brooke is a grown and independent girl.

15 Teens' Doubts and Fears

Changes brought by maturing affect teens physically and mentally. They can emerge fiercely, and cause surprise, embarrassment, fear and anxiety. When changes occur, teens find themselves in situations they haven't encountered before. Facing changes opens questions and dilemmas in them: "Is this normal? Am I normal? What if there's something wrong with me?" These are expected responses to the circumstances in development, which are accompanied by the feelings of unreliability. Therefore, it is all the more important that teens have a basic sense of security. If there are other circumstances which reduce the sense of security, doubts and fears may spread beyond control. Fears are usually a reflection of distress experienced by teens in other areas, in cases of uncertainty about their own image, responses of other people, and they can also be related to distress in relationships with relatives.

The development which makes teens face independent tasks in their life also brings risks, which require young people to develop resilience, and the ability to include and use the skills they have already acquired. When new challenges burden teens too much, doubts and fears arise.

---

(70) Fifteen-Year-Old Girl fears High School

I'm afraid ... I'm afraid that no one will accept me, that no one will like me, that I'll flunk, go from good to bad grades (even though I know that I only need to study hard, but I think I'll freeze up during tests) I'm determined to say no to everything that I can see isn't good for me. And now I'm left with this huge, hopeless fear that's getting closer, and this darkness, I think it'll just suck me in ... I dream that I'm wandering around school, but everyone ignores me, I can't find the right classroom, I get lost. I'm anxious ... then there's the fact that my parents are divorced ... my mother is on her own in everything. I used to help her, what about now? Dad won't see me or have any contact with me and my sister.

---

(71) Irrational Intensive Fears

 Amber is seventeen years-old. She is in the third year of high school. She has no problems at school. As the first child, she is the most popular of all kids, among our relatives. She comes in for counseling with her mother. She says that she is overwhelmed with irrational fears. If something doesn't happen the way she imagined it, she is thrown completely off balance, gets headaches and stomach aches. Her fear may be triggered even if a girlfriend of hers doesn't show up in time at the agreed place in front of the cinema, or something happens differently than what she expected. Her mother says that she is difficult and hard to bear when this happens. She hasn't been sleeping in her own bedroom since she was little. Three years ago, she was treated for a serious disease which she beat. She has always been protected by all the people around her, wrapped up in cotton wool. She isn't ready for unexpected changes happening in life.

(72) Mother's Letter

I don't know where to start. I'm dealing with the feelings and emotions of our sixteen-year-old. I got divorced when Nathan was five, and I think he's never forgiven me for that. My partner and I set up a home, and Nathan got a sister.

In his first year of elementary school, he was denoted a "socially immature child," which was difficult for me to bear. He didn't have many friends, most of them were family friends, and he eventually stopped hanging out with them, too. I think Nathan spent a lot of time thinking about his father, even though my new husband completely assumed the role of a father. Unfortunately, Nathan didn't see it like that. He always wanted to do stuff with his biological father.

Then the teen years came. Nathan didn't have any friends he could talk to, share his joy with, his sadness, distress... He began shutting himself off, he said things we wanted to hear, he lied, anger was accumulating in him.

I'm probably largely responsible for that, because I did things instead of him. My husband said many times that I was putting him in a bubble.

We often argued before he went to school, as he intentionally did something wrong just to make me mad. And before he closed the door, he threatened suicide. I was going crazy, but everyone said that most teens just say that. What if they don't? What if he doesn't come home one day? It's hard to live like that.

283

After talking to him, it's clear that he misses his friends, wonders why his biological father doesn't like him, why he doesn't have a girlfriend. When will he have one? Isn't he handsome enough? Why does he have zits? He hangs out with elementary school students, because he doesn't hit it off with his peers. He's afraid of the world around him, he's a very unstable person, without his own opinion.

I accept the guilt, I didn't know any other way, I did the best I could. But I'm afraid that he'll find inappropriate company, just to be accepted by someone.

Related Topics
Experience of Independence | Shaping Self-Esteem, Self-Image | Attitude to Physical Development | Autonomy and Individuality | Taking Responsibility | Emotional Development | Trust | Friends | Lonely and Socially-Isolated Teens | Part 1 of the Book | Effect of Relationship between Partners on Parenting

Within the Scope of Awareness

The subject of fears and doubts is related to the awareness of safety and the experience of safe attachment. Think about a scene during early development of the awareness of safety when a child plays in the park alone, while one of the parents sits nearby. The child explores his world, and every now and then, runs to the safe haven of his parent to exchange a few touches, thoughts, to show what he has discovered, and then goes back to his world of play. Meanwhile, the parent can read or tends to his own things, the important thing is that he is present and available to mirror the child's impulses. This way, the child shapes the awareness of safety, and develops his own independence and awareness of his power, which he can rely on.

The role of present and available adults remains the same during the period of maturing. The only difference is that the circle of the child's independent exploration expands. If the adult doesn't allow the child to have independent experience, the child doesn't have the opportunity to develop faith in himself. Because of that, the child also doesn't dare take risks and develops fear of unknown low-risk situations. The path to independence is paved with new experiences, in which we need to be equipped with inner strength and resilience to a certain level of risk.

In their notions, many teens develop fears of unknown and new situations where they will have to act independently. They imagine a certain unknown or new social situation in their own way, and produce horrible fantasies about them. These may be situations which require more independent actions, more power when standing up for yourself, more determination, more of a fight for self-worth and own recognition. Each situation we tackle also requires the ability to overcome discomfort, to be able to enter an area of risk and uncertainty. When we overcome this, the experience strengthens the awareness that we will tackle similar situations more easily and with more self-confidence in the future.

We should also think about how we responded to situations in which our child had the opportunity to enhance his resilience, self-esteem and self-confidence. Did we allow mistakes to happen, so he could learn from them? Did we allow the child to have experiences in which we trusted him to manage on his own? (The first such experience is when we move the child from the parents' bedroom to his own room.) Did we only demand results, and were uninterested in the ways they were achieved? What responses did we use to tell the child that we trusted him and believed in him?

The second important area which may be the basis for fears to develop is the teen's acceptance of his physical and mental development. Responses to embarrassments about the physical development may be shaped in the teen's awareness through questions: What is normal? Am I normal? This is so weird, I'm embarrassed to speak about it. Teens compare their signs of sexual maturity with those of their peers, and if they deviate from what is thought to be average, they may soon develop fears. If we encourage conversations and speak about a subject, we can tear down barriers. Teens adore people without reservations, who allow themselves to speak openly about all subjects.

The third subject that needs to be checked if fears appear is our beliefs and patterns. How many of our children's fears are really our projections? What are our fears about our child in puberty? How often is fear our way of problem-solving in life? What is the ratio between fear and the courage to overcome hurdles in our life? How did we use to rise above situations which could bring out fear in us? Is the motivational force in our life fear or courage, faith in ourselves and optimism?

Do teens' fears stem from their lack of life experiences? Did we allow them to have such experiences, or is it about our belief that they can't tackle a certain situation, aren't independent enough, old enough, responsible enough?

There are also fears which are real and related to experience we don't want teens to have, and which aren't related to the development of independence—and we need to distinguish them from other fears. (Being alone in desolate parts of a city, exposed to all kinds of assaults; going alone and inexperienced to dangerous areas; driving unprotected and insufficiently equipped; being a passenger with an inexperienced driver.) We need to prepare safety measures for these fears and pass them on to our children by teaching them about safety and the setting of boundaries.

Tips and Solutions

The fear that had settled into the girl six months before she began high school may be related to the experience of independence and trust in her abilities. Such fears occur before specific experiences, and disappear after the experience has been acquired. Certain things must simply be experienced and survived, including starting high school and independence: independent orientation in a new environment, making connections with new peers, asking for help, seeking help, and showing weakness occasionally. Fears are soothed by experiences of peers who empathically communicate that they understand fear, because they have had a similar experience. However, they have also experienced overcoming fears and now function without fear.

Research into the story of a girl with irrational fears has shown that she was protected and at the center of attention, ever since she was tiny. There was always an adult who made sure that Amber was in no danger. She developed a pattern of creating safety in the presence of an adult, which was further reinforced by the habit of sleeping in her parents' bed. The second part

286

of the story is connected with her beliefs about ensuring bonding, and her agreements with herself. There was no permission for choice and change in these agreements. Then there was her emotional world which, on the one hand, included embarrassment about the awareness and expression of own emotions, and problems accepting other people's emotions, on the other. When the notions about others and about herself were put into a suitable emotional frame, her fears subsided.

Also important in the story is the discovery of fantasies and notions the girl created about situations which should include her. She wanted to join a dance group, but when she thought about the first meeting, she produced an image of being there alone, no one talking to her, all other people knowing each other and no one speaking to her, being an outcast.... Only images of not being able to overcome her distress. What she needed were new opportunities and positive experiences to prove to herself that she could do it, what specifically she would do to be noticed, how she would make contact with new schoolmates, which behavior she would use to overcome her distress.

The third story stems from the mother's internal dilemmas and pain related to safety. The mother's internal insecurity arose when she didn't feel safe in the relationship with her partner. The teen's fears were a mere reflection of the mother's experience. Naturally, fear is part of when teens are faced with developmental changes and internal dilemmas, as they acquire skills in all important areas of development.

Parents can reduce fears by preserving a safe space, including safety in family relationships, open communication, and giving them true information. Let's check if our expectations about children are realistic. If our expectations are realistic, the teen develops the awareness of his self-worth and competence. Otherwise, he feels like he isn't good or smart or hardworking enough, like he will never be able to meet our expectations. Each experience with the real world strengthens the teen's awareness that he can do it.

Equally important are responses of parents when teens are ashamed of something, especially how to create conditions, with our responses, for teens to develop an experience in their own way, and in line with their needs. The onset of fears in teens often provokes parents to respond intrusively when they, involuntarily, but out of worry, try to mend the child's distress by themselves (without listening, with denial or ignoring the teen's world): if they hear their daughter say that she doesn't like herself, her mother buys her beautiful clothes; if someone says that he is too fat, we put him on a diet and tell him that it isn't true.

Here are a few questions we can use to remain respectful and unobtrusive:

- ► Is it enough that we just listen to, and hear, the distress?
- ► Does the child need help, and in what way?
- ► Has the distress occurred when hanging out with peers and is it part of the social learning process?
- ► Does the distress require external help?
- ► Does the teen expect anything from us? What specifically?

When teens face distress they have to overcome (for example, nerves before a school test, insecurity in new situations, where it is important how they prove themselves), reflective responsiveness, with which we acknowledge and allow their feelings, is the first step to support them. Empathic response sees anxiety as a joint experience. In this context, our stories, which we survived in a similar fashion, are stories of good hope with the greatest healing power.

If the teen's panic before recurring events doesn't subside, we should observe whether our responses strengthen or reduce fears. Have we become part of the game which strengthens fears and panic?

We can get out of such dances.

"I can see that you're getting the jitters before tomorrow's presentation. I understand that this presents a great distress for you. But you'll have to learn to manage such distress. If you need my help, I'm always here for you, but I'll wait until you ask for it. Otherwise, please go to your room and solve it on your own. I don't think we have to put up with the drama for you."

16 Learning Life Skills and Career Development

Can parents influence the development of skills which will enable our child to be more successful and effective when planning his career? The decision about education and the area of work, or way our teen will ensure independent existence, depends on the teen.

There are no clear and predetermined paths to choosing his field of interest and work. Therefore, certain personality traits, preferences, and skills take part in the process.

Although different cultures and countries have different education systems, and young people acquire their qualifications to enter the labor market in different ways, common characteristics are becoming more relevant for each area of work: the ability to acquire knowledge through life—attitude to learning and knowledge orientation, which requires the awareness that knowledge changes fast, and its development needs to be followed.

The second characteristic is quick changes in work methods, technology development, communication methods and means, location changes. We need to constantly adjust to that. This means that we need certain personality traits and skills: adaptability and plasticity, flexibility, curiosity, mobility.

And also knowledge, adaptability, creativity, independent thinking, and life-long learning capabilities.

Along with this, they will have to have sufficient inner strength,[68] meaning that they will have to be self-confident, and trust in their abilities, skills, talents, dreams. They will have to be equipped with the awareness that they can overcome hurdles that will inevitably be encountered on a daily basis, in whatever we do. There are also certain specific characteristics each area of work requires.

How do children understand themselves? What is their attitude to setting goals, achieving results? Are they aware that they are the owners of their achievements, do they appreciate their achievements, are they proud of them, and are they happy about their progress?

---

[68]See chapter on power struggle, *page 199.*

As we choose a certain area of work or role in it, experiences, skills, abilities, attitudes, interests, achievements, knowledge, personal style, learning style, work values, and lifestyle needs carry a large share.

Today, the planning of a career is viewed holistically, as a combination of several fields of life: attitude to learning, setting life goals, trust in mutual relationships, functioning during work hours and beyond—leisure activities, amateur activities.

So when we, as parents, think about our children's professional career, we can anticipate that the labor market will require highly competent, flexible, and self-confident people who will be able to keep up with changes and be open to lifelong learning. In this context, we can help our children acquire skills which are not aimed at a certain professional path, but which will follow the guidelines described.

---

(73) Letter From A Desperate Father

We are a family of four with two children. The oldest is just about to turn twelve. We have a problem with him because we can't make him study. He simply doesn't hear when we ask him to study. It has come so far that he completely ignores my wife and me, he flips out and leaves the apartment. He even threatens to jump from the balcony. When he is in such a state, I try to be tolerant when communicating with him, but he doesn't understand that. He just wants to emphasize his ego. He replies: "I know." When we check his knowledge, it's negative. He gets help at school, and he's been seeing a specialist in defectology for three years. I personally don't see a lot of progress. So my wife and I work with him all afternoons, sometimes even in the morning before school. We also go to a counseling center. They said that there was nothing wrong with our son, he just needs to work. He was given additional tasks, but he avoids them. When he starts, he literally loses control, and then we're back to square one. I admit that I wasn't as engaged in my son's first years at school as I would be now. And problems weren't as big as now. Let me say that he had an accident at practice a few years ago. Perhaps it was then that he lost some self-esteem and gained some fear. My wife and I don't know what else we can do because the situation is very serious. He gets Es and Fs at school, we fight at home, and this is affecting our younger daughter, which is not okay. Let me mention

that my wife and I weren't brilliant at school, but we also weren't violent and offensive to our parents.

---

(75) I Do it Myself—It's Easier, Quicker and More Accurate

The parents of an eighteen-year-old boy and a sixteen-year-old girl came in for counseling.

"We don't know where to start. We think we went completely wrong with our parenting. We have two bored bums without any self-esteem. They don't do anything, anything at all. And they slacked off at school. Probably none of them will pass the year. Only computer and TV. They have never had to work. They only had school and extracurricular activities. That's it. Now they've dropped everything and don't even put their plates away from the table."

The children spent their childhood with toys and walks. Their mother took over most household chores, but did everything in the evening or sent her children to play with toys so that she could do it in peace. She says that it was faster this way. But that they acted indifferently even when they were younger, and that she had problems persuading them to put things away— shoes for example.

Now they don't even do the smallest things. If she tells them to take out the trash, they ignore her demand and go to their rooms where they each have their own computer. When the demand to do what they have to do is a little harsher, they usually yell back, become aggressive, slam the door. Their reaction is the same if their father wants to make them do something. When they are home alone, they can only prepare frozen food. The food you take from the freezer and put it in the microwave.

The parents are exhausted. The children are almost adults. They show no desire to be independent. They don't cooperate, they want the house rules to adjust to them. They take the fact that their parents do everything for granted.

Related Topics
Part 1 of the book | Emotional development | Where are the boundaries? | What to do with rules? | Autonomy and individuality | Taking responsibility | Power struggle | Evasion, lies | Learning problems | Lack of motivation, slacking off at school and dropping out of school

Within the Scope of Awareness

Whenever we, as parents, are under the impression that our children aren't motivated toward their future careers, we should remember what we discussed about the circle of safe responsiveness in Part 1 of the book.[69] The secret to a child's lack of motivation is in his safe connection with us, and in allowing children to feel responsible for their achievements—both encouraging and challenging. Our support means that we are there for them, and not doing things for them. It is very important for teens that we allow them to do tasks independently, in their own way, and remain connected throughout. We addressed the principles of connection in **Part 1** of the book, and we referred to the atmosphere of our relationships reflected in little everyday chores. In connection with our teen, we give meaning to work and provide motivation to do work which, in itself, has no meaning for teens.

Work habits help us achieve goals we might have, or even make our dreams come true. They help us shape self-esteem, overcome hurdles more easily, finish what we have started.

Parents sometimes link work habits to specific work, most often with schoolwork, thinking if our obligation is our job, your obligation is school. But the dwindling enthusiasm for schoolwork is usually not related to the lack of work habits, quite the contrary: it is related to the inability to express and function in any other area than school.

Work habits encompass the attitude to work in general, which means useful and vital skills. Remember that our role as parents is that our responses create the quality of the experience for our child. Above all, attitude to work requires internal discipline, perseverance, focus, respect of rules and order, attitude to own competences, self-esteem, and the awareness of self-worth, and also the ability and skill to assert our competences in relation to other people. To prove ourselves in certain problem situations. How did (didn't) teens develop the elements described in previous periods of development? What is our attitude to solving practical problems?

The influence of behavioral patterns in the family comes to light here. How do we tackle unexpected situations? Do we keep the balance and awareness

---

[69]*See* Figure 1, *page 35.*

that we will be able to solve the problem or do we fall into the catastrophic game in which our disorientation and powerless need to be solved first?

What are our beliefs about work?

Is work torture, something which we need to force ourselves to do, where we are serious, where everything is tense and strict, in relation to which we speak about responsibility and necessity? Is work something we enjoy, look forward to, and have fun with?

To invite children to participate in work, we need to be connected with them, and they need to see sense in work. Work may be an opportunity to talk to the child spontaneously and in passage as shown in the second story.

When children don't develop schoolwork habits, we usually find that they have no duties and obligations at home. That parents couldn't prevent them from avoiding household chores, tidying up the room, cleaning the apartment or its surroundings, helping with major work. That parents protected them from major strain just so the children could rest before school.

Work is an experience bringing satisfaction when completed, an experience which, in retrospective, rationalizes the strain and perseverance we put in. Work is attitude to our everyday activities. Therefore, work habits reflect our previous attitude to work acquired through experience. If work is something where we always fight, which involves tensions, criticism, messages about incompetence and laziness, children won't see any sense in working and will avoid work—not because of laziness or a negative attitude to work, but because of unfavorable mutual relationships.

It is true that attitude to work, in addition to family patterns, is also affected by beliefs in certain cultures and prejudices, such as that boys are lazy, or that girls are hard-working. It is also true that some popular activities of our teens, such as killing time on the computer or aimless channel surfing, increase their passivity in general. It is also true that we focus more easily on some work, while in other work, we need to concentrate more and have more control over disruptive factors.

So pleasant experiences with a successful ending are more suitable for teens to acquire work experience based on which they can shape an stimulating attitude to work. They may be minor projects in which we participate in a relaxed way, focus on organization and preparation, don't get upset because unavailable tools, and tolerate unexpected setbacks. And the end of which we celebrate suitably. They can comprise everything from painting the teen's room, washing the car, baking cookies, making a special lunch, going on a trip to helping with party invitations and similar.

If we imagine the requirements of certain work in relation to specific skills, we will find a range of possibilities for our child to learn from everyday household chores: communication skills, resourcefulness, creativity, self-initiative, the ability to deduct from specific to general, the ability to minimize the material used, the ability to be practical, the ability to find simple and quick solutions, the aesthetic feeling, the ability to persist when solving difficult situations, the ability to remain optimistic in problem situations, the ability to self-promote and be aware of self-worth, the ability to persist and be accurate at work, the ability to be loyal to the employer, the ability to take care of your rights...

Parents who can provide their children with flexible work experience outside the domestic environment contribute the most to their children's experience in various areas of work.

Tips and Solutions

(75) Work can be Play and Cooperation

 A mother with five children. She had one after another and she also kept her job. She wasn't a stay-at-home mom. She used to say to me: "When I spend too much time with the kids, I forget how to think and speak as an adult. I need company." *Because she didn't have an abundance of time, she simplified her life considerably. When her kids came from the kindergarten, she didn't jump into the toys with them, as parents usually do. Actually, there weren't even a lot of toys in the house. Legos, cars and babies. And a dog and three cats.* "Kids need animals, you know. When I have a bad day, when I'm jumpy, they cuddle with the dog or a cat, and tell him how terrible I am. That seems great to me. At least they dump it somewhere." *Their household was a game. When they got home in the afternoon, she sat them at the table, gave them utensils, and they peeled, cut, chopped... vegetables. All of them. The youngest one threw the chopped vegetables into a bowl. She didn't get upset when something fell to the floor, she didn't get upset if pieces of vegetables weren't the same size. They made a soup or sauce or salad...and the atmosphere at the table was full*

of laughter and curiosity. They set the table together, and they cleaned it up together. When her husband was at home, he joined in too or he worked with them in the garden, around the house.

"Everything goes more slowly and it's not done according to standards, but we're together and we enjoy it."

These children are almost grown up now and completely independent. They cook. They clean. They work in the garden. They take care of the animals. They find opportunities to work part-time. Everyday chores are no drama.

Their parents taught them to cooperate, tackle unknown things, are curious. For them, everyday chores, a nightmare for some people, were a game, socialization and cooperation.

There is a fine line between independent schoolwork and the manner which creates the atmosphere of forced labor, and shoves the teen into the recurring dance of rebellion.

This refers to cases when a child, a straight-A student in elementary school, starts high school. His school performance drastically deteriorates, he doesn't want to talk at home, he skips school, he hangs out with a crowd prone to drug use. When his parents come to school for the first time, the cruel reality suddenly kicks in. If parents show their disappointment by losing their nerves, getting mad at the children, yelling at them, this open us new opportunities for problems.

What happens? The connection is broken, the child shuts himself off even more, parents watch powerlessly and don't know where and how. If as parents we can't bear the feeling of powerlessness and remain adults, we need help. At our workshops, we often discuss how parents can see such a story in a different way.

A father thought long and hard when he realized that there must be some sense in his child's behavior, that, with all son's failures, something must be going on in his son's world. There are probably reasons he and his wife didn't even think about. They only saw their own disappointment, and were aware of the intensity of emotions that overwhelmed them. Once out in the open, when the circumstances were clarified to the point where they were willing to discuss the manner of permission for, and interest in, their son's world, they dropped their intrusiveness, they were able to understand each other, and the son began miraculously learning by himself.

Children don't learn for themselves, but for the relationships they have with persons important to them, especially with their parents. The child's school performance means a lot to parents. Some children are more aware of this, others less. Underlying it all is the quality of relationships. Parents can't make their child learn more effectively with all tricks and motivation techniques they can think of. But they can make that happen by being aware that they care about the child, and by being persistent and patient, using proven approaches we have already discussed: dialogue, clearly set rules, distribution of roles and work (with the possibility to choose), parents' determination and persistence to attain their goals regardless of the child's behavior. In any case, if you miss certain opportunities, the principle applies that starting with small steps and seemingly tiny tasks (for example removing the plate from the table) is, in this case, significant (and better than nothing).

---

(76) Connection Through An Emotional Experience

 A father and his son had problems with connection. Each conversation, no matter how simple, ended with increased mutual tension, the escalation of intolerance, and damage to their mutual connection. They went for a canoe ride on the Shenandoah River. They were together in one canoe, and had to agree on how to paddle, who will sit in the front and who in the back, and they had to respect each other's input and rules. Otherwise, they wouldn't have moved anywhere or would have had an accident. There were a few dangerous rapids. They capsized in one of them. Parker was afraid for his dad, and his dad looked on in panic what was happening to Parker. When they saw each other, they laughed with relief and hugged (physical contact). All these values, respect, cooperation, respect and all emotions from pleasure to fear created a strong connection between them. After this experience, they cooperated and connected even more. Of course, nothing lasts forever. We still need to work on the relationship.

Are you wondering what this story has to do with work habits? This is a story about a joint experience of connection. When the father told Parker to do some household chores the next day, Parker acted from the feeling of connection. He wanted his dad to be happy. He no longer felt that he didn't care about the old man who was terrible anyway." Children often mirror us so that we can see ourselves. We often don't recognize the repercussions, when we treat them like we don't care about them.

---

(77) Joint Work

 A mother will do something together with her daughter which may interest her: bake pastry.

Everything begins with a mother's enthusiastic invitation: "Oh, it's gonna be a fine day today. I'd love you to join me in baking something really tasty."

They will also have to clean up, go to the store, do the dishes. People always chat when doing work like this. Mothers try to encourage and not criticize.

On the other hand, fathers and sons do technical stuff, with tools, in a similar way. Slowly and patiently. The effects will be miraculous. Parents often need help with this because they didn't bring the pattern of cooperation and encouragement from their childhood. If this is too difficult, a joint experience, which includes pleasant emotional satisfaction, enthusiasm, playfulness, calmness, joy, laughter, is also useful—a trip to an adrenaline park, rafting, contact with animals, a visit to an amusement park...

The manner in which we invite our children to join us is very important. Do we order them to do so, and demand that they have to do a certain job they try to evade? Or do we choose to invite them to cooperate with us? *"I'd feel great if you helped me do this,"* or *"Come, we'll have a great time."*

Joint work may also be a requirement to which the teen doesn't respond with enthusiasm. The response depends on the type of dance in which the communication took place. If it happens during a problem period, you must reread **Part 1** of the book.

---

(78) Summer Job

A seventeen-year-old son got a summer job at a garage. He came home saying that he had been doing ancillary works, he had to sweep the floor and wash two cars. After he had finishing washing the cars, the boss told him off for not doing the job properly.

As his father was listening to the story, it occurred to him that this was the moment he had been waiting for since elementary school. He wanted his son to know how important it was to be thorough, to follow instructions consistently, to do work in a suitable sequence, not to jump and leave out anything. He saw the opportunity to reaffirm his belief that he would have had it easier at school had he been more consistent, respected instructions, and done things one by one. And if he hears criticism about a job done poorly, he knows that its purpose is not to make him feel sorry for himself, but to change, learn something from it, consider the comments, and improve the quality of his work. His wife guessed what he intended to do and stopped him before he could utter a word.

This could be an invitation to a fight between partners because the father would say that his wife was protecting the child and wrapping him up in cotton wool, while she would be something between offended and angry. Now the father listened to her opinion: "What else do you need when you see him learning from life? He just doesn't listen and hear what you've been telling him for years. Now you can see that something's touched him, leave it to take effect. We can be glad that he has the opportunity to learn."

As our teens acquire the ownership of their own experiences, the hardest thing for parents is to remain at a distance, and patiently wait for them to learn in their own way. Particularly because we have the wisdom, and our own easier, more effective manners.

---

(79) Embarking on Own Path, Without Schools

The success story of a famous musician seems simple. In the second year of high school, he let his single mother know decisively that would no longer go to school because he would live off his music. And that she shouldn't even try to contradict, because he would fight her all the way. His mother gave him a year to prove himself. And he did. The solution looks simple, but it involves several skills: a clear awareness of career path, work habits, communication skills, respect of the boundaries set, the mother's faith in her son, autonomy, independence...

All stories which, at first sight, seem simple, speak about connection, safe responses, trust, responsibility, and about ways that parents could teach their children to experience their achievements as their own. This also includes responsibility to the teen himself, his future, his career, and care for relatives. Independence, in this case, means an autonomous walk along the path of one's own inner callings, and a safe attitude to responsible contact with reality.

17 Teens in Blended and Foster Families

Parents who live with children from their previous marriages while in new partnerships often describe similar stories about dramatic changes in their child's behavior, when they reach their teenage years. Parents recognize an increase in impulsive acting out, particularly with their close relatives. If children were once cooperative, they are now refusing to behave and almost fighting. If before they were open, now they are closed. All those changes are accompanied by intense emotions, where anger, rebellion and rejecting play the leading role. It is similar with teenagers in foster families. Though the details differ, the same principle lurks underneath, manifested with different intensities and dynamics.

Teenagers seem that they will use all their energy to get what they want. This particularly includes violating rules and agreements and crossing the limits. From an outside perspective, it is like an eruption of intense resentment, which has been on the burner for a long time and finally boils over.

Parents, step and foster parents, and all other family members express difficultly understanding this behavior, and take it personally, often with feelings of guilt and a search for personal reasons in the past to explain it, or to blame for it. Some parents try to stop this behavior by using power, which opens new, and intensifies existing, power dances, as is described in the **Chapter 7.**

Below, there are two stories from two different worlds, with two different emotional dynamics. In such stories, you can clearly see what is on the surface very dramatic, but underneath is something completely different—it is connected with soft and vulnerable emotions.

---

(80) Mother's Story

Hi,

I need your help because we have horrible problems with our daughter. She's eighteen. She is my daughter from my previous relationship, which fell apart when she was born, or rather it had never really existed. I met a new partner, now my husband, whom my daughter accepted very nicely, and vice versa. I may say that their relationship had been beautiful and warm, until her puberty kicked in. I also have a son from my new marriage, he's nine. What hurts and worries me the most is that my son sees what is going on in our relationships with my daughter.

I admit, I'm largely to blame. When my daughter was young, I always protected and defended her. And she was really spoiled. In my new family, she had a special protected status. When her puberty started, she began rebelling, especially against the rules of my new partner, whom she called dad. She told him that he had no right to tell her what to do, that he had nothing to do with her, and the like. She was very determined and rude. This affected our relationship as partners very much, and we were solving it by attending your **"Blue Key"** workshop on effective partnership. We connected, and decided to act as a team, and so my daughter backed down from her power struggles.

In between, she endured an anorexia episode, which we successfully overcame. I really supported my daughter through that, my partner talked to her too, and we found out that it had been more of an experiment, she had stopped eating just for fun, but all the same, we barely saved her. She was really grateful to me for my support when she had problems with eating.

The whole time, we fought in court with her biological father, who did everything imaginable to take my child away from me, even though he ignores her and doesn't care about her.

But in the last two years, something has changed. She is rude, brusque, ignores all agreements and rules, she doesn't do anything around the house, she only lives for her interests, she tries to show us that we're superfluous, she ignores us, we're trash to her. This is just heartbreaking for me.

What caused our relationship to break down were her comments about me. Whenever she sees me and my husband cuddling, she goes haywire. She calls me a whore, a bitch and other words I don't want to repeat. She also does that in front of her friends, when they come to visit. She is totally rebellious and I can't bear it. If I say anything, it just gets worse.

It reached a point where we were even physically violent to each other. I feel completely powerless and degraded. My husband says that he won't get involved in our stuff, although he's on my side. One day, she lost her temper, she knocked down the furniture and destroyed things, I packed all her stuff in her suitcases and put them out in front of the door.

We took her to her grandparents' house, where she stayed during her vacation. I was sending her messages that I loved her for two months. I had sent her *such messages before. During this period, she cut us off even more, and there's no communication between us at all.*

Now she wants to live elsewhere, and we don't have the patience to bear her hatred of us. She blackmails us, she isn't willing to negotiate anything, she disregards all agreements, and I don't know how we can ever agree on anything. What should I do?

---

(81) Emily's Story

 I was born as an average child, or at least I was supposed to be one. Even though I was young, and I wasn't supposed to understand everything around me, I found out very early on that my family was different, special. I had a father and a mother who didn't live together, and I never felt any love between them. I accepted this as normal, and I thought it was cool, at least at first. But, there were a lot of moments when I wanted to have a family other children had.

And then one day, mom came and introduced Harry to me. Of course, I knew that something wasn't like it was supposed to be, but I didn't fret over it, because I still had her and my father then. After a while, the moment I feared most came. I was aware that my parents would never be together again, and that Harry was someone my mother wanted in her life and she was happy with him. What hurt me the most was that my mom wasn't just mine anymore, but I knew that she was happy. And that made me happy, even though I was unhappy. After they got married, I began calling Harry dad, and the reason for this was the happiness I saw in my mom. I had nothing to complain about, I had everything, but I never had the feeling that I belonged there.

My life came crashing down on me after a year and a half. We moved to B. where my biological father came to pick me up and took me to his home—these were arranged contacts. That Friday, I didn't want to go with him, but he was determined that I would go and wanted to take me by force. I started screaming and crying, but he was still determined to take me. I managed to fight him off, but he wouldn't give up and chased me around the kindergarten. I got hold of a phone, but he tried to pull it out my hands. Then I called Harry, who came to pick me up. Things were only settled when the police arrived. That day left great emptiness, disappointment, hatred, and fear in me. I needed professional help, because I didn't have the courage to be alone in the house, and I couldn't even think of my biological father. I felt bad, but that disappointment made me stronger. I never whined to my mother about how bad it was, because I didn't want to burden her with that, and I thought that she wouldn't understand it, anyway. School started, and my classmates were thrilled with my super dad Harry who was cool, but something was still missing in my life. I always envied my girlfriends who had fathers, but I never articulated that. The more time we lived together, the greater was my feeling that I can treat Harry, and my mom, too, without authority. But the feeling of not belonging remained, and even grew. My mom, whom I've been calling by her first name since then, was happy, and I didn't want to mention anything to her, so as not to spoil things. After that, Brian was born, and the gap was getting wider. My mom and Harry's world changed when Brian was born, and made an addition to their family. Sometimes, it was difficult to watch Brian have everything, while I didn't have anything, but I was happy for him and wanted him to be happy. I did everything for them to be happy, I took care of Brian to make it easier on them, but I was still blamed for everything. They blamed me for everything that ever happened, but I often just swallowed it and moved on. The older I got, the more I noticed what I had done for them to be happy, but it was never enough—my reaction was to keep quiet.

I didn't dare say anything out loud, I had to pluck up the courage to speak. But the response was—what else can you wish for, you have a little brother, a stepdad and a mom. But that didn't mean anything to me, because that wasn't the part I sought and desired. I gave up on explaining my wishes and needs, I simply lived the way they wanted me to.

My biggest dream was to have a dad, even though I'd have to give up my mom. It's hard for me to look at my biological father even today, but deep down, I still want a father, not him, but someone with whom I'll feel what you're supposed to feel, when you belong to a family.

I meticulously protected, and mulled over, all my problems, illusions, and fears, by myself. Since the incident with my biological father in kindergarten, I've seen things differently, and found that it was best if I kept things to myself. I also told myself not to trust people too much, because I didn't want to end up hurt. I chose a life like this, because I'm convinced that if I hadn't been like that, I wouldn't have survived. I could judge, and see through people very well. It was probably a defense system I'd created. I've heard many times that I'm cold and difficult to reach—but I've been building this wall all those years, and

I'll never be able to tear it down. I think that a person who will be able to climb over it must enter my life, and that I won't be the one to tear it down.

Related Topics
Emotional Development | Part 1 of the Book | Where Are the Boundaries? | What to Do with Rules? | Autonomy and Individuality |

Within the Scope of Awareness

The daughter's story focuses on the beginnings of the blended family. There are two stories, the mother's and the child's, in which time goes by differently. In each story, there is a surface and under-surface space. We can recognize a typical setting of the "parental dance" we described in **Part 1** of the book. The mother's story was dominant and was running on the surface, the child's story took place in silence, in quiet suffering and emotional distress.

When children experience the divorce of their parents, they long for family atmosphere and both parents. Children of divorced parents fantasize about how they could get their parents back together.

Her mother's new relationship made the daughter feel that a person was imposed on her whom she wouldn't (and didn't) choose. Her mother's new partner is a person she has to share her mother with. In the daughter's perception he is a person who takes up part of her mother's love. She was suddenly competing with him for space in her mother's heart. She was justifiably angry with, and dismissive to, him. But these emotions had no space or permission to express themselves. At first, in her, because everyone tried to convince her—and she believed that herself—that the new partner was a great replacement for her father, that her family was complete again, and that she should be more than satisfied with that. Other people also focused on "integration" and everything good around it.

Emily was split inside (without even realizing it): between the affection for her mom and the hostile emotions, which didn't have permission to exist and be expressed. Intensive emotional processes in Emily could only exist by being suppressed. In retrospect, we think that Emily lived, and was connected with, her mother at two levels. At the level of the awareness of her mother's happiness, because she had a family she had wanted for so long, and at the level of emotions, which weren't accepted and welcome by the world from the first level. The most important emotions were missing her mother and grieving for her idea of family. All this was taking place unconsciously, and without options to discuss or share it. That is a perfect base for developing different kinds of symptoms.

The mother struggled to preserve the connection by pampering, indulging, and protecting Emily's wishes. And by mixing wants and developmental needs.

A new child in the relationship gave rise to all the conditions for Emily to create two camps, and exclude herself from the system of belonging. At first, the partners experienced this as Emily's attempt to break their connection, so they enhanced their coalition, which worked only for their relationship, but not for the understanding of the child's emotional processes underneath.

Another setback and "power dance" in the relationship between the mother and the daughter occurred with the onset of puberty, and of developmental needs for power, autonomy, safe belonging, support from parents, emotional mirroring, and permission to be special. We can assume that setback happened, and the tension in the relationship grew on a daily basis.

On the one hand, the mother perceived Emily as becoming stubborn, while on the other, Emily put every disagreement on the scales of proof that the family wasn't accepting her. That was her inner feeling and she acted out of that, however it was all unconscious.

The key expression among Emily's needs was permission for emotional needs which, in her world, appeared in a strange form, so for her as for others, too. But for Emily's mental functioning, it was important to allow her to be in contact with the world of emotional distress, to articulate it and express it. Let's name the child's experience. The divorce was, for her, a traumatic experience, and inside her remain unfolded emotions sparked by that event.

The mother was focused on completely different things, related to ensuring comfortable conditions for her daughter to grow up in.

Children who live in foster families are even more in contact with the consequences of traumatized primary emotions. Foster parents are frequently unaware of these dimensions.

(82) Robert

 I met him when I was working at a residential care institution. He was a friendly and communicative fifteen-year-old. He lived with his foster family, but they could no longer manage him, once his puberty kicked in. He became instantly attached to me, because I created calmness and playfulness with music, when working with the group. He had a beautiful voice and was multitalented. He longed infinitely to meet his parents. He was an orphan, abandoned soon after he was born, and without any information about his mother or father. He was told that his mother was a bar dancer and a sex worker, and his father was a sailor. Then a social worker found his mother, and arranged for them to meet. Robert felt on the top of the world, like he was going to his salvation, and all his past yearnings would become a reality, and his pain would heal. But the story didn't go as expected, his mother rejected him, and Robert became a teen with a severe behavioral disorder. His life went steeply downwards, he was put into a series of care and re-educational institutions. He ended up addicted to heroin and was placed in a rehab.

I met him again when he came out. He was slightly over twenty. He was so happy to see me, as if I were his last haven on Earth. I brought him home, where he was generously welcomed by everyone. He told us about his fear of people, about being unequipped to live independently outside institutions. A social work center arranged temporary accommodation for him. He came to our house to clean up, and I helped him enroll in school for adults. He had a bath full of hot water and bath foam, for the first time in his life. He learned a few craft skills and helped us with painting the house. He was very handy in the kitchen. But he also played with children, had long talks with us, had warm meals, we went on trips together, and when he could sleep over, he was happy like a little kid. He enjoyed spending time with us, he was joyful. But he wasn't happy. All the time, he was longing and waiting to get all that from his parents.

But with our support, and the support from three other people, he had enough hope to stand on his own two feet. He found himself a job, and saw it as his salvation. He applied for a social apartment, and was put on the list. He was constantly speaking about his mother, he appreciated her and sometimes visited her, even though she was still rejecting him. Whatever she did to me, she is still my mother, he said decisively. He wanted to find his father really badly.

He searched for him in Italy and southern parts of the former Yugoslavia, but his efforts were futile. He wanted to look him in the eye just once.

Then the company went bankrupt, he lost his job, and in the environment where he lived, he came into contact with drugs again. At first, he stole to get drugs, and ended up hitting rock bottom, completely unresponsive and apathetic. One summer day, we got a note that Robert had been found dead. An overdose.

The story still deeply moves me. Perhaps this story marked my career path. I followed the development of a young person with endless potential and talent, but wounded in his basic attachment. I was flabbergasted by the fierceness of the need to reestablish the broken connections. As if he had believed, somewhere deep inside, that it would be enough to just meet a person who would give him a safe haven. This is related to profound yearnings and fantasies about bonding and connection, built on unrealistic and mostly illusory expectations of other people, of parents. In many stories, teens lose their interest in all things that motivate them, with rejections, unresponsiveness, harsh breaks of connections with those they attached their emotional yearnings and needs to. This results in radical changes in behavior, the dropping of activities and interests, the disregard for rules and boundaries, behavioral offenses, addictions, crimes. We have encountered such dynamics in some other stories, which will be described in our next book, on more difficult cases.

Emotional wounds of abandoned children require special professional treatment. People who take over the role of guardians of children who were hurt also need special understanding. Guardians and foster parents still don't get enough support to be able to provide a stable and safe support for children who were emotionally wounded.

Tips and Solutions

What could the mother have done differently to preserve the connection with her partner, and include Emily in the family?

The mother didn't have the strength to distance herself slightly from Harry, and ask herself what Emily was conveying with her behavior. She focused on setting boundaries for Emily, which was indeed necessary. However, she overlooked that she had to preserve the connection and attachment. And she didn't know Emily's emotional world. What could she have done differently, but didn't know how to? She could focus on meaning in Emilie's messages. If she talked to her alone and in name of their connection addressed the question, how Emily needs from her as mother to hear and understand her messages. And after giving permission for daughter's emotional realm, there is another step, to set boundaries to way Emily conveys her messages.

---

*(83) **The Reply to The Mother** (see story No. 80)*

My understanding of Emily's behavior is based on her deep emotional experience during her childhood. Those feelings comes from her deep inside and have nothing with actual interpersonal dynamic in the family. But it is about deep emotions which remained in her, and she wasn't able, to bring them to awareness, work them through and share them with a person where she feels save.

Her current behavior arises from this intrapsychic dynamic. I understand it as the search for a balance in comparison with how she saw herself in relationships before. I know that she is determined to pursue her goals, and focused on that, with everything she has. This is her survival strategy, which she can't let go (yet).

So my advice is that you and your husband don't give her a reason to fight, and don't respond in a way which could reinforce her provocations to fight.

What you can do is to adopt caring habits, which means behavior that connects. It is obvious that she doesn't want to live with you, and I believe that it is important for Emily to get permission for her emotions, thoughts, her difference. Permission for what is going on inside her. This doesn't mean that this has to be realized, or that you need to give in to her. No.

It is just about a permission best carried out by mirroring. For example: "I've heard that you don't want to stay at the boarding school, because of its rules. Do I understand you correctly? Are you thinking about commuting or to go to school in B. Do I understand you correctly?"

And try to evaluate the sense in her world—"I can imagine this poses a dilemma. You're attached to the town of A. and your classmates, but rules hinder your need for freedom. (Yes, the need for freedom is something that needs permission in her world.) Is there anything else?"

And let her be—you should preserve the boundaries and rules you set, regarding financial support and other things, you will articulate them when it is time for that.

First, give her the permission for her world, space for her own experience, evaluate her sense to give her the feeling that you can bear that she is different, and still preserve the connection. I think this is the way to make Emily cooperate, as long as she feels safe.

Indeed, Emily began responding.

The next step was a therapeutic dialogue with the family, based on the Emotionally Focused Therapy approach, where every member gets an opportunity to share their views, feelings and emotions. The first condition for this dialogue is a safe base feeling, which is part of the professional technique.

We first enabled that every family member could express his or her own way of perception, feeling and reasoning. Then we helped other members to understand and see the meaning of it without blame, criticism, rejection or taking offense. This opened up new opportunities for them to connect emotionally. We continued our discussion about their emotional experiences, about how they saw and experienced each other. That brought to all family members a lot of emotions, which among them hadn't had any space before. They reconnected and realized how they had misunderstood one another.

We will briefly illustrate some of the most crucial sequences from the family dialogue, which were the catalysts for reconnection.

---

(84) Mother, I Miss You

 Teenage Emily sat opposite her mother, and we could see how the teen was completely emotionally disconnected from her familial bond. It was reflected in their communication: blaming, complaining, attacking back and forth, in an endless vicious circle.

I helped to "translate" the words spoken on the surface into emotions that were hidden somewhere deep down.

I asked Emily if we could hear under her complaining some voice saying, "Mother, in fact, I miss you so much."

Emily nod and started to cry.

Her mother started to cry.

I encouraged her mother to express her emotions toward her daughter.

She said in tears, "I miss you very much, too. I miss our moments, when we were connected."

Mother came closer to her daughter and hugged her.

They stood for a long time in this healing hug, where they cried out all the pain of lost connection and longing, where they had been unable to be emotionally closer. Now it was safe enough to express it.

Between mother and daughter, something happened that was most important in the field of emotional bonding and belonging.

After the discussion, Emily had no reason anymore to hold grudges, as she had been doing throughout her life in the blended family. The mother figured out what it meant to give space to her daughter's needs, and she also gained a role her daughter had been waiting for all that time: the role of a mother, an authority and an adult who can bear the process of their child gaining independence.

18 How Children Who Are Different Growing up

Children who develop in a different way, and are denoted as children with special needs, also encounter puberty. They may be children with movement disorders, physical disabilities, with autism, with special needs in emotional and behavioral fields, with cerebral dysfunction, with Down's syndrome, with mental disorders.

Teenage years and developmental changes also affect growing children with various disorders. Most of them have the status of a child with special needs declared due to a long-term disease. The latter comprise long-term and incurable diseases, or curable diseases which require long-term treatment (for example diabetes, renal, colon and heart diseases, cancer and other serious diseases). They rarely include mental illnesses. Parents used to be focused on teaching their child to live with his diseases in all environments. Each case is its own story which requires specific adjustments. It is important to integrate teens' developmental needs in the parents' awareness, as in their concern for the sick child, they forget about the important areas of independence, responsibility and other skills important for life within a community.

If all attention before puberty is paid to life with a disorder or disease, it is equally important that, during puberty, parents pay attention also to the areas of development discussed in this book. The subjects of taking responsibility, setting boundaries, independence where possible, autonomy, emotional communication, respecting authority, attitude to power, were perhaps sidetracked, as most attention was paid to adjusted development and to compensation of deprivation. The aforementioned subjects are also part of a healthy development, and parents can treat them equally.

Related Topics

Where Are the Boundaries? | *What to Do with Rules?* | *Taking Responsibility* | *Part 1 of the Book* | *Shaping Self-Esteem, Self-Image* | *Effect of Relationship Between Partners on Parenting* | *Responses in Communication* | *Emotional Development* | *Learning How to Be Independent* | *Autonomy and Individuality*

Within the Scope of Awareness

Each disorder or disease completely changes the parent-child relationship, as parents need to adjust to special needs and to a special course of development. In many cases, parents commit themselves to the area of special needs so intensively that the disorder or disease consumes all areas of development. Thus parents also adjust learning skills not affected by the disorder or disease. This usually makes children less equipped for independent and autonomous actions, and overcoming hurdles which require more inner strength, eloquence, independence, self-confidence.

Let's take a look at how all this evolved, in some different cases.

---

(85) Child With Autism

It was strange that mother Judy was referred to therapy for depression by her twenty-four-year-old son Patrick. Other family members were, her husband Frank, seventeen-year-old sister Tracy, a teen with autism, and the family also included the elderly mother's father. It soon turned out that something wasn't working right in the family system. At a meeting, Patrick pointed out that there is no order and structure in the family. And that he was becoming intolerant of no one setting boundaries for his sister. He also noticed the lack of communication between his mother and father.

Frank saw the family's problem in their father-in-law and grandfather, who had no feeling when dealing with a child with special needs, and was very intolerant of her different behavior. His wife silently agreed with her father, while Frank withdrew and tried to have a relationship with his daughter by understanding her disorder outside the chaos at home. His manner of understanding meant indulging, without setting any boundaries.

Judy, who was extremely tight-lipped, managed to say that the problem was in communication, because she couldn't express her feelings and she swept things under the rug. If she was silent, at least there was no tension and conflict.

Tracy, the daughter with autism, had the entire functioning and life of the family adjusted to her. At first, this came with plenty of tolerance and understanding for her overstepping the boundaries in her everyday behavior. She could do whatever she wanted. Tracy's behavior was accepted by her parents, believing that it was the reflection of her disorder, and they burdened

themselves with living with a problem which they had to be completely toler-
ant of. If they so much as hinted at certain boundaries, Tracy started scream-
ing with non-articulated sounds, showing her disapproval with angry gestures
and destructive hints, in which she was stronger than the perseverance of her
parents. Thus the disorder without any boundaries became the focal point that
organized their family life. At first, all family members were very tolerant of it.
At home, Tracy could afford throwing the cutlery or whatever was on the table
around at lunch for no reason, scream uncontrollably when they had visitors,
and when they required her attention, she interrupted them and had her own
show. So they started avoiding visits and preferred to stay at home. Avoiding
complications became the strategy of life in the family with autism, which re-
quired more and more giving up, and unhealthy adjustments. The functioning
of the whole system suffered, and the meeting of the needs of other family
members was inferior to the tolerance for autism. The first to cave in on tol-
erance was the father-in-law, Judy's father, who wasn't considerate about it,
and then the son, Patrick, who wanted to respectfully discuss his needs and
preserve the connection.

But the most interesting thing was that Tracy was completely different
in the institution, and other environments where the rules and boundaries
were clear. She respected the boundaries and authority without any pro-
blems and tantrums.

Within the Scope of Awareness on Story 85

There are no functioning boundaries in the family, especially in the relationship between partners. This is linked to the roles not being clearly defined, and to dilemmas regarding who is loyal to whom, and when. It seems
that the partners in a joint household with the father-in-law failed to set
clear boundaries as to what their family was, and where and which rules
apply in the family. Also the boundary between what autism is and what
respect of rules means, and boundaries in their everyday life, weren't clearly
defined. This resulted in the vagueness of the roles and authority. The father-in-law wanted to be the authority, which was supposed to be Frank's
role, while Judy was torn between loyalty to her husband and to her father.

As for authority, all adults conveyed double bind messages, meaning there was no stability and safety. Because there was no authority or the authority was chaotic, the hierarchy was vague, too. In such a setup, their best bet was avoidance, disconnection, and exits. Frank found his way out in work, Judy in depression, Patrick in studying, and the father-in-law in alcohol.

The relationship between partners truly needed the help of psycho-therapy.

Tips and Solutions on Story 85

Judy and Frank attended our workshop on *Effective Partner-ship,* where they had the opportunity to reestablish the bond in their relationship as partners. When Judy got the opportunity to express her deep feelings of sadness, powerlessness, guilt, and anger, while accepting a child who was different, and Frank got the opportunity to speak about being pushed away in the family, the depression withdrew, and the partners started communicating more, and sharing their emotions. By doing so, they increased their power and began setting boundaries for Tracy's behavior. They accepted that autism meant a problem with under-standing one's own and other people's psychological processes, but not indefinite tolerance of the child breaking rules and boundaries which ap-ply in the family and in society. Frank assumed the role of authority in the family, and Judy supported him. Within daily functioning, and by respecting certain limitations, they approached Tracy with joint and uniform demands they defended consistently, and persisted until they were met.

Here are a few simple solutions we introduced into the family: while eat-ing, they were focused on food, and they turned off the radio and the TV; Tra-cy's job and duty was to set and clear the table, which she happily accepted, and the grandfather ate separately, and his comments no longer demolished the rules set by Judy and Frank.

After a few years, we met with the family again. Tracy lived an indepen-dent life at an institution for persons with special needs, where she was hap-py. She visited her family on weekends. Judy and Frank looked clearly rejuve-nated, carefree and connected.

(86) Child With a Movement Disorder

Jacob is sixteen years-old, he has a movement disorder, he's overweight, he still wets his bed. He's integrated into a high school. His parents complain that he disregards all food and computer time boundaries. We can establish that bedwetting is connected with the lack of discipline when it comes to drinking in the evening. The mother, who protected him from experiencing exclusion because of his difference all the time when he was growing up, has established that the father and she are completely powerless, in terms of setting boundaries.

Jacob's movement disorder is the least of their problems; everything else is an unsolvable dilemma for the parents. First, the story about breaches of food boundaries. Jacob lives in an institution and is addicted to candy. And he is willing to steal for it. He always snatches things from his younger brother, when he is at home. If and when he gets his allowance, he spends it on excessive quantities of chocolate. When he talks to his mother, he promises and ensures her that he sticks to his boundaries while, in fact, he secretly consumes food in impossible quantities and at impossible times, preferably in the evening and at night.

The second problem is bedwetting, which has been going on, with a negligible break, almost all his life. His parents have tried all existing methods to prevent this. He has undergone all imaginable tests. No clear conclusions and no changes.

The third problem is being accepted by peers. During his development, he always found support in his parents, and never improved his social skills. Throughout, he kept a posture of self-sufficiency. For a long time, he didn't show any shame. His peers isolated him because of the self-sufficiency he expressed on the outside. He tried to attract his classmates' attention by participating in activities teachers don't tolerate, but that, within a group, signify belonging and loyalty. Consequently, his school performance deteriorated. His parents say that he is a few years behind in emotional development.

Within the Scope of Awareness on Story 86

When Jacob's puberty kicked in, his parents endured a relationship crisis which jeopardized their joint parenting. The mother and the father withdrew, each in his own way. Jacob was a child protected by his mother from being hurt too much by comments about his difference from his peers, which she achieved by shifting him to a fairytale mindset. As a result, Jacob was convinced that boundaries don't exist in relationships, and that you don't have to give up comfort to meet your needs. Jacob's parents motivated him using conditions, and the game of obtaining pleasures through rewards became his way of functioning.

He simply wasn't motivated to try and give up instant satisfaction of his needs. Having everything, he created a safe world for himself, and this feeling was part of his addiction, and couldn't be replaced by any substitute. This way, he also wasn't ready to give up on drinking in the evening, which led to wetting his bed, because he was a sound sleeper. Only when his family set firm boundaries and promised him to fulfill his wish, as a reward, was he willing to make an effort and postpone the satisfaction of his wish. After years of medical research and research related to child psychiatry, this was the first tip that wetting the bed, in his case, had nothing to do with the principles of emotional disorders.

Tips and Solutions on Story 86

 After Jacob's mother and father reconnected, they attended group coaching, and they began developing trust in safety and stability, on which they based their authority to Jacob. After the family discussion, when Jacob expressed his fear of his parents getting a divorce and him losing them, they distinguished emotional needs, developmental needs, boundaries and rules, and defined Jacob's attitude to his own body. They divided areas which used to be designated "a child with special needs, handle with utmost care." This gave rise to new areas parents paid special attention to, and in which they redefined their parental role. Schoolwork became Jacob's job, and his parents expected him to be independent and responsible. The mother met Jacob's teachers less frequently, she let Jacob arrange his obligations and take the responsibility when he didn't fulfill them. The parents were less worried when Jacob went to events organized by the school, and demanded from him to care for himself, by himself. So Jacob was given the opportunity to make different contacts with his classmates, in an informal environment. Attitude to discipline when eating was a special chapter. The parents set boundaries, enabling Jacob to choose between more and less pleasant consequences. They were convinced that Jacob's bedwetting was a behavior Jacob chose, and that he was responsible for the consequences. This meant that they no longer woke him at night and cleaned up his bed for him—this became Jacob's responsibility. The father gave Jacob a choice: a dry bed for one week and he gets to visit his dream sports event, or he chooses indiscipline when drinking, carefree sleep, and remains without his sports treat. Jacob was dry at night for one week, but when the external motivation was no longer on offer, he went back to his old ways.

---

(87) Sick Teen

Nora went to a high school in a large town, where she had moved from her hometown. She lived in a boarding school. During school years, she got leukemia, which was successfully treated. She also finished high school and enrolled in university.

At the beginning of her studies, she encountered some problems. Nora lost the will for an active life. She lived in a dorm. Her older sister lived nearby, where Nora hung out with a few of her friends. Otherwise, she didn't approach anyone. Her mother was very worried about her, called her every day, and checked whether she attended the lectures, whether she was studying for midterm exams, whether she would go to sports practice, whether she carried out her daily work plan... Nora was a prospective athlete, but because she lacked self-esteem and communication skills, she didn't make any progress. Gradually, she didn't see any sense in school or her interests or hanging out with friends. She wasn't even interested in guys, even though she was very attractive. She decided to go home and think about what made her happy.

Within the Scope of Awareness on Story 87

A serious disease in a child brings concern for survival and related fears to the forefront of family relationships. These experiences are characterized as traumas. In similar experiences, actions related to treatment, the expectation of the results, the course of the disease, accompanying the child to treatment, and care are usually at the center of attention. These are actions which highlight the connection and build a safe attachment.

But when concern is focused on survival, into which parents or other family members put enormous efforts, those same people usually push the awareness of, and contact with, the emotional processes aside. Much of it is pushed aside so as "not to put any extra burden on ourselves." This way emotions, which are part of every more or less difficult story, remain in a lonely place.

On the one hand, partners can't share all the intensive emotions they are in contact with, from fear and concern to hope and relief. This particularly applies to men. On the other hand, parents don't share their emotions with children. There are stronger reasons for the latter, because parents see that their children need firm support.

When traumatic circumstances subside, and when life seems to be back to normal, the most intensive emotions remain somewhere deep inside. In our case, parents are aware that the growing child needs his space to develop autonomy and individuality, and learn how to be responsible and independent, but the relationship with him is still balanced by emotions from the past traumatic experience—fear and concern. This way, parents sort out things instead of the child, preventing him from gaining the necessary experience, and the child feels like he is trapped in a bubble, with no possibility to act autonomously or learn by trial and error.

Tips and Solutions on Story 87

 The work with the parents was based on creating safety in their emotional worlds, and on seeking areas that would be safe enough for their daughter to act independently. The parents also needed help with the setting of rules and boundaries: on which conditions they were going to support Nora with her studies, what they expected from her, what Nora's obligations to her parents were, what Nora had to take care of on her own.

When working with Nora, we focused on specific help with learning the skills for independent life, for planning her life, setting realistic work goals, overcoming fear in communication with other people, strengthening contacts with her peers, to subjects related to attitude to the opposite sex. When Nora began living her life, when every day had structure and sense, when she succeeded and was aware of her satisfaction with her results, she gradually got rid of fears and insecurities. Her days had a predefined sense. After less than a month, she reported that she had accepted a former class-mate's invitation to go on a date. She completed the first year of her studies, and was excited about the profession she was to have.

For parents with a sick child, groups where they can share their experi-ences with other parents in similar distress can be very helpful. They enable them to experience that the carrying of a load is usually reduced, if carried by several people.

Epilogue

I adore teens.

I adore their perseverance and courage. I adore their creativity and power. What they are willing to do to grow up. Give up their sweet safety, bonding, comfort...

But we see how they storm recklessly into the abyss, searching for who they are and walking the rocky road. The road we have cleaned up for them, which they don't want to see.

I adore parents.

I adore their hard work for their children and their endless love, which overcomes all hurdles.

The things we could do with that. Does that even go together?

As I watch my crazy teen on one side and me, the crazy mother, on the other, I wonder: *"Who's the adult here?"*

Simple answer: *"No one."*

Who should be the adult?

A simple answer is: *"Me, Mom (and Dad)."*

I remember those days. The beginning of puberty. I know today that it doesn't come slowly, but instantly.

Parents want results. And our teens have power over this.

This is what happened:

"Did you get your math test back?"

"No."

"Doesn't she give your test back in a week?"

"Stop badgering me, ask her, she's just lazy, she doesn't feel like correcting them."

The teacher has been perfect, also for my child. I look bemusedly. I don't get it, the behavior or the words. The only thing I do get is that they got their math tests back.

And again:

"Did you get your math test back?"

"Ooooohhhhh... Well, we did, but it'll put you in a bad mood and it's all your fault, you should've stopped harassing me."

"And?"

"You're pathetic! Where did you come from?"

My stomach hurts, I have problems breathing. I wonder where my precious, hard-working boy has gone. I don't have the energy to say anything. I just stand there, watching him, probably with an astounded gaze.

"I got a D."

He gets up, takes his skateboard and...

Then his father's famous speech starts:

"Well, I told you so. That's from his pants sagging. Can you see the way he's dressed? Why doesn't he just put his pants over his jeans to show all of them? And skaters. I'll show him skating. I'll nail his skateboard to the wall, and he'll just be watching it, from today on. And that weird crowd. A bunch of losers. One look at them and you know. Those pants below the ass and tees... That's it, I'll lock him up, and all he'll have will be his notebooks, books, water, and bread."

Me: *"Those guys seem okay, they're growing up."*

"Now you're defending them. I knew it, you just don't care. Then you see to it that he does something with his life. We'll see, well, I know, it'll happen the way you..."

You know the story. Can you see where it is going? From Ds at school to chaos in relationships with partners. In the end, the teen and his responsibility are nowhere to be found.

Can we make the teen remain at the table, so we can talk to him, and preserve the connection?

How can we talk so that our child knows that we care about him, and not just about his results? How can we make our child break the ties, grow up, get experience, without us getting sick with worry and horror?

The fact is, we all know that the child must grow up.

We also know that to do that, he needs the experience of independent actions, decisions, problem-solving.

We know that teens have immense power, and that our weapons are elsewhere. In connection and safety.

Do you know what the teen is thinking, as he lies in bed, stares at the ceiling angrily, and doesn't talk to us because we *"don't understand him?"*

He is scared. And he hides this fear by showing anger. It isn't easy growing up, and finally—aren't adults meant to help him? And children are meant to help us adults grow up.

We have already learned that, and we are still learning. Today, this kid is a grown-up and responsible child. We learned a lot during our studies, but we have learned the most from our own children. With their help, we became more and more grown up, more responsible, more of a mother, more of a father, more of a wife, and more of a husband. There's nothing simple about it, but it is worth every ounce of effort.

But we know a story about your child ...

Do you remember?

Do you remember the first time you held him?
How tiny he was.
Helpless.
Do you remember how he smelled? Mmmm, he smelled so good.
You counted his tiny fingers, checked his arms, legs. How beautiful he was...
How is it possible that this child, this miracle, is yours?
The most beautiful child was yours.
Do you remember the moment he looked you in the eye for the first time?
Do you remember this moment, when you could see into his soul, into his heart? When he was completely yours, and safe in your hands?
Do you remember the first time he smiled at you?
He has the most wonderful smile in the world, and he is yours.
Do you remember the first time he called to you? Mom ... Dad ... Took his first steps ...
The smartest child, and he is yours.

Now this child is a teen. No longer so obedient and devoted. He needs his own experience. He no longer trusts blindly everything you tell him.

But you will close this book now, and the next time you see him, you will know that he is still the same child.
Your little miracle, the most beautiful and the smartest. Your child.

"You have all the tools you need. Now it's up to you to implement them."

After reading this book

Parenting can be a challenging experience. As years go by we tend to forget some of those important moments, memories fade away and the perception of those experiences change in time. Here you can write them down and let them speak (to your ex-teenager and soon-to-be-parent) in the future.

What did you learn about yourself?

_____

_____

_____

_____

_____

What did you learn about your teen?

_____

_____

_____

_____

_____

What changes do you want to make in your relationships with your teen?

_____

_____

_____

_____

_____

_____

_____

_____

_____

_____

_____

_____

_____

_____

_____

_____

What change in your behavior would you find easiest to make, that you feel might help improve your relationship with your teen? Do it.

_____

_____

_____

_____

_____

_____

_____

_____

_____

_____

_____

_____

_____

What is your notion of a connected relationship with your teen?

References

Allen, J., & Fonagy, P. (2006). Eds., *Handbook of mentalization-based treatment.* Hoboken, New York: WILEY.

Arnett Jensen, L., & Chen, X. (2013). Adolescent Development in a Diverse and Changing World: Introduction. *Journal of Research on Adolescence, 23*(2), 197–200.

Bluestein, J. (1993), *Parents, Teens and Boundaries: How to Draw the Line,* Deerfield Beach, Florida: HEALTH COMMUNICATIONS, INC.

Bowlby, J. (1969). *Attachment and loss, Vol. 1: Attachment.* New York: BASIC BOOKS.

Bowlby, J. (1973). *Attachment and loss, Vol. 2: Separation Anxiety and Anger.* New York: BASIC BOOKS.

Bowlby, J. (1988). *A secure base: Parent-child attachment and healthy human development.* New York: BASIC BOOKS.

Carr, A. (2005). *The Handbook of Child and Adolescent Clinical Psychology: A Contextual Approach.* TAYLOR & FRANCIS e-LIBRARY.

Cooper, A.; Redfern, S. (2016). *Reflective Parenting: A guide to understanding what's going on in your child's mind.* London: ROUTLEDGE.

Cyrulnik, B. (2010). *Mourir de Dire.* - Slov. transl. (2012). *Sram: če povem, bom umrl.* Ljubljana: MODRIJAN.

Dallos, R. (2004). *Attachment narrative therapy: integrating ideas from narrative and attachment theory in systemic family therapy with eating disorders.* JOURNAL OF FAMILY THERAPY 26, 40–65.

Dallos, R. (2007). *Attachment Narrative Therapy: Integrating attachment, systemic and narrative therapies.* Maidenhead: OPEN UNIVERSITY PRESS/McGRAW HILL.

Dallos, R., & Draper, R. (2015). *An Introduction to Family Therapy: Systems theory and practice* (4th ed.). Maidenhead: OPEN UNIVERSITY PRESS.

Dallos, R., Denman, K., Stedmon, J., & Smart, C. (2012). *The Construction of ADHD: Family Dynamics, Conversations and Attachment Patterns, Human Systems: The Journal of Therapy, Consultation & Training, Volume No 23, Issue 1,* pp. 5-26.

Davidson, R. J. & Begley S. (2012). *The Emotional Life of Your Brain.* New York: HUDSON STREET PRESS.

Draiby, P., & Seidenfaden, K. (2011a). *The vibrant family.* London: KARNAC.

Draiby, P., & Seidenfaden, K. (2011b). *The vibrant relationship.* London: KARNAC.

Duncan, L. G., Coatsworth, D. J., Greenberg, M. T. (2009). *A Model of Mindful Parenting: Implications for Parent–Child Relationships and Prevention Research, Clinical Child and Family Psychology Review,* 12:255–270.

Duncan L. G.; Coatsworth J. D. &, Greenberg M. T.(2009). *Pilot Study to Gauge Acceptability of a Mindfulness-Based, Family-Focused Preventive Intervention, The Journal of Primary Prevention,* 30:605–618.

Fonagy, P., & Target, M., (1997). *Attachment and reflective function: their role in self-organization, Development and Psychopathology, 9,* 679 -700.

Fonagy, P., Gergely, G. & Elliot, L. J. (2004). *Affect regulation, mentalization, and the development of the self.* London: KARNAC.

Freud, S. (1953). *Three essays on the theory of sexuality.* In J. Strachey (Ed. and Trans.), *The standard edition of the complete psychological works of Sigmund Freud* (Vol. 7, pp. 125-245). London: HOGARTH PRESS. (Original work published 1905).

Glasser, W. (2002). *Unhappy Teenagers: A Way for Parents and Teachers to Reach Them.* New York: HARPER COLLINS PUBLISHERS INC.

Glasser, W. (2010a). *Choice Theory: A New Psychology of Personal Freedom.* HARPER COLLINS e-BOOKS.

Glasser, W. (2010b). *Choice Theory in the Classroom.* HARPER COLLINS e-BOOKS.

Goleman, D. (2006). *Social Intelligence: The New Science of Human Relationships*. New York: BANTAM BOOKS.

Greene, R.W. (2010), *The Explosive Child: A New Approach for Understanding and Parenting Easily Frustrated, Chronically Inflexible Children* (Revised Updated edition), New York: HARPER COLLINS PUBLISHER.

Grienenberger, J., Kelly, K., Slade, A. (2005). *Maternal reflective functioning, mother-infant affective communication and infant attachment: Exploring the link between mental states and observed caregiving behavior in the intergenerational transmission of attachment. Attachment and Human Development 7(3), 299-311.*

Hart, S. (2008). *Brain, Attachment, Personality: An Introduction to Neuroaffective Development*. London: KARNAC.

Holland, S., Dallos, R., & Olver, L. (2011). *An exploration of young women's experiences of living with excess weight, Clinical Child Psychology and Psychiatry, 0(0) 1–15.*

Hooper, A., & Dallos, R. (2012). *Fathers and Daughters: Their Relationship and Attachment Themes in the Shadow of an Eating Disorder, Contemporary Family Therapy, 34: 452–467.*

Hoover-Dempsey, K.V., Ice, C.L., & Whitaker, M.W. (2009). *"We're way past reading together:" Why and how parental involvement in adolescence makes sense.* In N.E. Hill & R. K. Chao (Eds.), *Families, schools and the adolescent: Connecting families, schools, and the adolescent* (pp. 19-36). New York: TEACHERS COLLEGE PRESS.

Hughes, Daniel A. (2004). *Building the Bonds of Attachment: Awakening Love in Deeply Troubled Children*. New York: THE ROWMAN & LITLLEFIELD PUBLISHER INC.

Hughes, Daniel A. (2009). *Attachment-Focused Parenting: Effective Strategies to Care for Children,* New York, London: W.W. NORTON & COMPANY.

Hughes, D. A., Baylin, J. (2012). *Brain - based Parenting. The neuroscience of caregiving for healthy attachment.* New York, London: W.W. NORTON & COMPANY.

Johnson, S. (2004). *The Practice of Emotionally Focused Marital Therapy. Creating Connection.* New York: BRUNNER/MAZEL.

Johnson, S. (2008). *Hold me tight: Seven conversations for a lifetime of love.* New York: LITTLE, BROWN AND COMPANY.

Johnson, S. (2013). *Love Sense: The Revolutionary New Science of Romantic Relationships.* New York: LITTLE, BROWN AND COMPANY.

Johnson, S. M., & Whiffen, E. V. (ed.) (2006) *Attachment Processes in Couple and Family Therapy.* New York, London: GUILFORD.

Jones, E. (2000). *Family Systems Therapy. Developments in the Milan-systemic therapies,* New York: JOHN WILEY & SONS.

Kabat-Zinn, M., & Kabat-Zinn, J. (1997). *Everyday blessings: The inner work of mindful parenting.* New York: HYPERION.

Kabat-Zinn, J. (2005). *Wherever You Go, There You Are: Mindfulness Meditation in Everyday Life.* New York: HYPERION.

Kabat-Zinn, J. (2013). *Full Catastrophe Living (Revised Edition): Using the Wisdom of Your Body and Mind to Face Stress, Pain, and Illness.* New York: BANTAM BOOKS.

Kahneman, D. (2012). *Thinking, Fast and Slow,* New York, London: PENGUIN.

Lerner, R. M., & Steinberg L. (2004), *Handbook of Adolescent Psychology* (2nd ed.), Hoboken: JOHN WILEY & SONS, INC.

Levine, P. (2010). *In an Unspoken Voice: How the Body Releases Trauma and Restores Goodness,* Berkeley: NORTH ATLANTIC BOOKS.

Meins, E. (1997). *Security of attachment and the social development of cognition.* Hove, UK: PSYCHOLOGY PRESS.

Meins, E., Fernyhough, C., Russell, J., Clark-Carter, D. (1998). *Security of Attachment as a Predictor of Symbolic and Mentalising Abilities: A Longitudinal Study. Social development, 7, 1 - 24.*

Meins, E., Fernyhough, C., Wainwright, R., Das Gupta, M., Fradley, E., & Tuckey, M. (2002). *Maternal mind-mindedness and attachment security as predictors of theory of mind understanding. Child Development, 73, 1715-1726.*

Miller, A. (2003). *Banished Knowledge: Facing Childhood Injuries.* London: Virago Press.

Miller, A. (2004). *The Drama of Being a Child: The Search for the True Self.* London: Virago Press.

Mikulincer, M., Shaver, P., & Pereg, D. (2003). *Attachment Theory and Affect Regulation: The Dynamics, Development, and Cognitive Consequences of Attachment-Related Strategies. Motivation and Emotion, 27(2): 77-102.*

Mikulincer M.; Shaver P.R. (2007). *Attachment in Adulthood. Structure, Dynamics, and Change.* New York: Guilford Press.

Moretti, MM.; Peled, M. (2004). *Adolescent-parent attachment: Bonds that support healthy development. Paediatr Child Health 2004;9(8): 551-555.*

Ogden P., Minton K., & Pain C. (2006). *Trauma and the Body: A Sensorimotor Approach to Psychotherapy,* New York: Norton.

Price-Mitchell, M. (Posted July, 15, 2013). *What Happy Teenagers do Differently.* Psychology Today. (http://www.psychologytoday.com/blog/the-moment-youth/201307/what-happy-teenagers-do-differently)

Race, K. (2014). *Mindful Parenting: Simple and Powerful Solutions for Raising Creative, Engaged, Happy Kids in Today's Hectic World,* New York: St. Martin's Griffin.

Schofield, G.; Beek, M. (2005), *Providing a secure base: Parenting children in long-term foster family care, Attachment & Human Development, 7(1): 3 - 25.*

Siegel, J. D. (2001). *Toward an interpersonal neurobiology of the developing mind: attachment relationships, 'mindsight,' and neural integration. Infant Mental Health Journal, Vol. 22 (1–2), 67–94.*

Siegel, J. D. (2011). *Mindsight, The new science of personal transformation.* New York: Bantam Books.

Siegel, J. D. (2013). *Brainstorm: The Power and Purpose of the Teenage Brain.* New York: Jeremy P. Tarcher/ Penguin.

Siegel, D., & Solomon, M. (2003). *Healing Trauma: Attachment, Mind, Body and Brain,* New York: W.W. Norton & Company Inc.

Siegel, J. D., & Hartzell, M. (2004). *Parenting from the inside out.* New York: Penguin.

Siegel, J. D., & Bryson, T. P. (2011). *The Whole-Brain Child: 12 Revolutionary Strategies to Nurture Your Child's Developing Mind.* New York: Bantam Books.

Slade, A. (2005). *Parental reflective functioning: An introduction. Attachment and Human development, 7(3), 269-281.*

Slade, A. (2006). *Reflective Parenting Programs: Theory and Development. Psychoanalytic Inquiry 26, 640-657.*

Steinberg, L., & Silk, J. S. (2002). *Parenting adolescents.* In M. H. Bornstein (Ed.), *Handbook of parenting: Children and parenting* (2nd ed., Vol. 1, pp. 103–133). Mahwah, NJ: Lawrence Erlbaum Associates.

Steinberg, L. (2013), *Adolescence* (10th ed), Boston: McGraw Hill.

Taffel, Ron (2005), *Breaking Through to Teens: A New Psychotherapy for the New Adolescence.* New York: The Guilford Press.

Van der Kolk, B. A., MacFarlane, A. C., & Weisaeth, L. (Eds.). (1996). *Traumatic stress: The effects of overwhelming experience on mind, body, and society.* New York: Guilford Press.

Zerbe Kathryn J. (2008). *Integrated Treatment of Eating Disorders: Beyond the Body Betrayed.* New York: W.W. Norton & Company, Inc.

Index of stories and subtitles

Subject Index

"Using a combination of pointed anecdotes about relations between parents and their teenagers and sound advice on better parenting, this is an engaging and useful guide to understanding your adolescent, and yourself as a parent"

– Dr **James Charney**, Child Psychiatrist, *Yale Medical School*

"This book is a rich resource for parents and teenagers as together they navigate the sometimes turbulent waters of adolescence. The authors' many years experience running workshops for parents as well as teaching professionals led to their best selling book in their native Slovenian: Out of Touch Teens and in Touch Parents. *This new book written for a wider English speaking audience builds on the first book but includes new ideas, stories and many suggestions for 'what to do when..'*

Successfully avoiding of the use of jargon the authors invite parents to notice which of the many ideas, reflections, stories, vignettes and tips they share resonate and make sense with the reader's own experiences, both when growing up and as parents. In this way the authors skillfully normalise what many parents can feel are uniquely isolating experiences with their adolescent children and this in turn engages the reader's interest in exploring new ways to be in relationship with their teenagers. There is probably something in these pages that every parent can connect with.

Parents and professionals will find this an invaluable reference book to dip in and out of whether facing one of the many challenges of the teenage years or simply wanting to better understand and respond to the rollercoaster changes of adolescence."

– **Ros Draper**, Family Therapist, Trainer, Facilitator, Supervisor and Systemic Therapist, Texbook Author, Editor at Karnac, London, UK.

Where can you find us?

e-mail:
parenting@vezal.si

Web site:
http://www.parentingteenagerguide.com/

Facebook pages:
https://www.facebook.com/connecteenager/
https://www.facebook.com/lealbertmrgole/

Emotionally focused therapy Slovenia:
http://www.eftvezal.si/en/
https://www.facebook.com/emotionallyfocusedslovenia/

Made in the USA
Coppell, TX
07 March 2020